# RENEGADE GRIEF

## GRIEF

A GUIDE TO THE WILD RIDE OF LIFE AFTER LOSS

CARLA FERNANDEZ

SIMON & SCHUSTER

New York  Amsterdam/Antwerp  London  Toronto  Sydney/Melbourne  New Delhi

Simon & Schuster
1230 Avenue of the Americas
New York, NY 10020

First Simon & Schuster hardcover edition March 2025

SIMON & SCHUSTER and colophon are registered trademarks of
Simon & Schuster, LLC

For information about special discounts for bulk purchases,
please contact Simon & Schuster Special Sales at 1-866-506-1949 or
business@simonandschuster.com.

The Simon & Schuster Speakers Bureau can bring authors to your live event.
For more information or to book an event, contact the Simon & Schuster Speakers Bureau at 1-866-248-3049 or visit our website at www.simonspeakers.com.

*Interior design by Erika Genova*

Manufactured in the United States of America

10   9   8   7   6   5   4   3   2   1

Library of Congress Cataloging-in-Publication Data is available.

ISBN 978-1-6680-0181-3
ISBN 978-1-6680-0183-7 (ebook)

*To my father, José Fernandez III*

*To my friend, cofounder, and beloved dinner companion,
Lennon Flowers*

*To The Dinner Party community, past, present, and future*

*To anyone moving through a loss experience,
wondering if there's another way.*

# TABLE OF CONTENTS

For additional *Renegade Grief* resources, including companion guides to explore the themes of the book on your own and with a group, visit carlafernandez.co/renegade-grief.

To learn more about The Dinner Party, a peer-led grief support community for young-ish adults, visit thedinnerparty.org.

For a curated list of grief and mental health resources for all ages, explore thedinnerparty.org/resources.

# INTRODUCTION

WE BEGIN WITH AN ENDING.

José Fernandez III had green-blue eyes, a crooked smile, and a very low fluency in small talk. He grew up in Brooklyn, the son of a still-water deep father, and a spitfire mother, and the eldest of four kids. Family legend tells of him composing songs as a kid by running a finger over the rim of twenty glasses, filled with water for the perfect pitch, a foreshadow of his time studying orchestral conducting at Julliard. When he later gave up on the conductor dream, those glasses become another hint at his life's work in the wine business, its own form of symphony.

José played the piano with his eyes closed, regardless of whether anyone else was in the room, and his karaoke song was Sinatra's "New York, New York," which he nailed every time. Life with him was full of art and music; full of looking at the world from oblique and expansive angles; full of the paternal perspective and protection I appreciate now for just how precious it was. His three children are all like him, and all completely different. I am in the middle.

When I think of the kind of harmonics my dad could make happen around a table covered in glasses, it reminds me of the conversations that reverberated within his dining room walls. The place where my father definitely held court was around the dinner table; he cooked simple meals, drawn from a repertoire that he learned from his grandparents, whose cuisines were from Ireland and Spain. Mealtimes with him were never rushed; conversation always glinted with threads of philosophy and science; glasses were continually refilled; and kids were never

1

excused from the table before the evening was over, simply because they were kids. The family dining room was our family's church, and mealtimes were my agnostic father's method of prayer.

When I was nineteen and he was fifty-three, José started feeling symptoms of what would turn out to be brain cancer. When I was twenty-one, and he fifty-five, my father died. On that New Year's Day in the coastal California town where we lived, I stood next to his rented hospital bed and newly vacant body, and the initial inquiry of this book was born.

*What do we do now?*

As a young adult with four living grandparents, I had never been to a funeral for a family member or seen people around me grieve. I quickly learned that we're not bad for the first forty days. There's much to do, and people around. In my case, there were fruit baskets to eat, an obituary to write, and lots of calls to make. There was a casket to order, outfits to pick, and condolence text messages in need of response. But then the to-do list dwindled, and the world returned to its routines, and the enormity of it all—and the staggering finality of death—started to settle in.

That's precisely when, at least for me, the twilight zone of shock disappeared, and my father's death became piercingly real. It's also when the lack of social and institutional support for caretakers, families in times of medical crisis, and the bereaved came into sharp focus. As a white woman from a financially stable family living in the Bay Area of California, where feelings are generally welcome and where you can get paid time off to take care of someone who is dying,[1] I comparatively had it good. And yet something felt off.

I came into caretaking for my dying dad as someone active in community organizing, obsessed with the ways in which small circles of people can make unlikely changes happen. I loved looking at how cultural patterns that might appear fixed can, on deeper investigation, be redesigned for the benefit of more people; of how people can come together to create communities that prioritize equity, humanity, and freedom of expression over the cultural norms of efficiency, productivity, and profit.

While my studies and work to date focused on issues of economic justice, I saw similar patterns in the ways the world held grief. What I immediately noticed was that even though we've been grieving as a species for hundreds of thousands of years,[2] the current social and economic infrastructure around loss gets in the way of fully experiencing the major rite of passage that grief inevitably can be. It felt like we, as a culture, had somehow lost the plot.

A death can impact us physically, financially, emotionally, and spiritually, and it can destabilize entire family systems. Even so, there's no federally mandated bereavement leave in America,[3] meaning you're not guaranteed any days off to tend to the major shakeup that is someone's passing. On average, according to the Bureau of Labor Statistics, your employer will grant you three days' leave for an immediate family member, and one day for extended family—which is hardly enough time to plan a funeral, liquidate a home, adjust to life without your partner, parent, or child, and reflect on what it all might mean for *you*.[4] It's not only the lack of time off, but what that lack of time signals—grief is something to tidy up in the margins, while not losing pace in your daily life.

In a country where 65 percent of bankruptcies filed are due to medical expenses,[5] it's not surprising that after someone dies, people feel pressured to keep up the hustle and stuff down the complex dynamics related to their grief. In a country where Surgeon General Vivek Murthy has come to describe loneliness and isolation as a "devastating epidemic"[6]—times of grief can be when that loneliness is felt most acutely, that isolation most stark. And in a country where the rituals and social scaffolding that were once provided by faith institutions are no longer a guarantee—especially for families like mine that had drifted from the regular support of places of worship—we're left without the communities and social safety nets to turn to when facing the spiritual and material emergency that often comes with someone's passing.

There was certainly not a lack of creativity or innovation on Planet Earth around this time; it just wasn't yet focused on reimagining grief. The internet era was booming—we were sending humans to space for leisure; phones were now cameras; and we could, for the most part, get safely into cars with strangers. And yet, the social technology and norms around grief and loss felt stale and stuck. Since we're not culturally literate in supporting people during times of grief, bringing up my dad's death stalled out conversations with coworkers or friends—and it wasn't their fault. Existing grief resources, while led by angelic people, were limited, underfunded, and chronically under fluorescent lighting, reminiscent of the cancer wards I was so ready to be free from. I quickly learned that while grief itself is hard, the culture we live in makes it even harder.

But what I also learned about grief is that it isn't a problem to be solved, or a box to be checked, or something that can be contained in the hours between five and nine. It's an essential process that allows us to, bit by bit, make sense of the impermanence of our time on earth. It's an old and wise and sometimes brutal teacher, but in a world that often feels designed to distract us from depth, it's courageous to give this teacher your hand. You won't regret it. Sometimes, you may not have a choice.

So, back to my question: *What do we do now?* In those moments after my dad died, as we stood by his bedside, I remember knowing the first thing to do was to break out the tequila. A bottle of aged añejo specifically, a gift from my dad's friend, who had insisted they would drink it when the cancer was beat. I padded to the kitchen and pulled it down from a shelf, opening the intact seal with my teeth, and unstopping the cork. It was not time for the decorum of glasses, as beloved as they had been to the man lying before us. I brought it back to the bedroom and took a slug from the bottle, wiping my mouth with the sleeve of the grimy sweatshirt that had become my caretaker uniform. I passed the bottle over my dad's body to my brother standing vigil on his other side. He chugged it and passed it over to my stepmom standing next to him. While the bigger question of what to do now still loomed, in that moment, what felt knee-jerk and natural for us was to toast this man—to cheers to his life, our family, each other, as we braced ourselves for the wild ride ahead.

## SITTING DOWN TO DINNER

In the months following his passing, the place I missed my dad the most was the dinner table. I decided to lean into the reality that dinners were the place I could connect most directly with his memory, refusing to lose the rituals we shared together, in addition to losing him. I wanted a place to continue celebrating his life without being seen as macabre, stuck, or overly sentimental, to be with people who got it, because they had been there, too; a space that was warm and human, with people who felt like friends. A space to complement more traditional mental health support— where we weren't paying out-of-pocket by the hour or being facilitated by an expert in a church basement, seated in a circle of metal folding chairs. I wanted a place where tears could be shared, but so could dating stories and dessert, and where we got to know both the details of our grief and who we were as dynamic people with interests and hobbies far beyond our loss.

Drawing on my instinct as a community organizer, I opened up my dinner table to other people who had recently lost someone and gathered a group of five who I knew from different corners of my life. I invited them over for a potluck to hang out and eat, but also to dig into the life experience we all shared, and that we had also all gotten great at avoiding—the death of someone significant in our lives. The first dinner had the feeling of a social experiment mixed with a blind date, which you'll hear more about in the chapter on Feasting.

By the end of that first dinner something had clicked, and that group of six became a monthly meetup. Over time, what started as a secret supper club evolved into something we were proud to talk about with friends who hadn't experienced a loss. Word started spreading.

One Table became two, became twenty, became two hundred. Over the course of the next decade, it would grow to a nationwide community known as The Dinner Party, thanks to the hard work of an incredible team, led by the beaming, bespectacled eyes I looked into across that first table—my friend, cofounder, and phenomenon Lennon Flowers.

What became clear that first night was that, while the food was the reason for getting us to the table, it was the conversation that made us stay. Around that initial table, and the many more to come, I heard stories that mirrored my own; tales of the reinforced stigmas and outdated, harmful behaviors dictating how we as a culture respond to times of grief and loss; self-doubt and suffering due to the simple lack of social awareness of the wide-ranging impacts of grief; the social anxiety around grief that results in our friends distancing themselves precisely at the moment we need them the most; and more common than we liked to admit, us hiding precisely when friends started reaching out.

But always, alongside the stories of friction and hurt heard around our tables, were stories with another shape to them. These were the stories of how people had made their way through the fire of their loss, as they responded with their own version of *what do we do now*. They were stories of improvisation, ingenuity, and found community. Through them, I learned that there was a way to approach grief that didn't require you to sweep it under the rug. I learned about relating to grief less as a noun, a thing to distance ourselves from, and more as a verb, an active process of metabolization. And I learned that there's a lot more nuance to individual and collective grief than I could have realized, and that it's up to us to resist the culture that would deny a grief experience because of the color of someone's skin, or the nature of their relationship to the deceased, or the way that person may have died, or even the way that person may have lived.

I realized that assuming someone's loss was that of a "loved one," common nomenclature in the grief space, ignores the possibility of complex relationships while someone is living and sometimes even more so when they're dead. I realized that changing the predominant narrative around grief and loss was going to come from shining a light on the real stories of people who were quietly finding another way through; the stories of people who I came to see as practicing "Renegade Grief."

✳ ✳ ✳

When you think about the word "renegade," you might picture a Marlboro man, high on his horse, alone on a hill—needing no one, ready for a shootout or a solo gallop across a desert mesa. But being a renegade— someone who is deserting the status quo—in Western culture looks a lot more like being in community, in resistance to patterns of behavior that have us working against each other for personal gain. Being renegade means we're working to become less independent and alone in our grief, and more interdependent; restitching a social fabric where we're not afraid to ask, "What was their name?"; where we are comfortable sitting with someone's story, knowing that what they're experiencing can't be optimized or solved, knowing that avoiding the discussion because of its inherent discomfort is avoiding life itself.

In this book I invite you to explore your version of Renegade Grief, whatever it looks like to you. You'll find in this book more questions than answers. Only you can decipher whether the way you're relating to your grief is because of cultural pressures to be a certain way, or something truer to you. What does honoring your experience of loss, not as a psychological event to get over but as a doorway into deeper understanding and connection, look like in your world? Is there something that you instinctively feel needs tending in your grief, even if it's not normal or common, as far as you know? Who are the people you can reach for who support the creativity inherent in your grief, and who believe in your ability to show it love, tenderness, and respect, rather than those who would ignore, minimize, or avoid your loss instead? These are some of the questions we begin with, whether our loss was one month, one year, or one decade ago.

# GETTING READY TO RIDE

It's been over a decade since I last sat down to dinner alongside my dad. A lot has changed since then, but there's one thing I continue to cherish. It's an email, fleeting as that might sound. In this email, he responded to some overwhelmed, angsty teenage message I'd sent him about not knowing what to do with my life. He wrote back with a beautiful take on the pursuit of purpose that's become my compass for navigating how I live with his absence.

> I think what you're feeling might have something to do with what is a paradox of life experiences: even as you do everything you can to expand your horizons, the horizon just keeps receding and seems ever more elusive. That's just the nature of life and learning, it's a bottomless well. The universe is expanding, much faster than our ability to keep up. So what can you do about it?
>
> Well, one thing is to just appreciate the vastness of choices and opportunities and paths one can take and come to terms with the fact that you can't take all those paths at once. It also helps to just decide not to be overwhelmed by the infinite array of choices, but to pick a specific path (or at least a manageable number of paths) and explore it (them) with an open mind, and with focused energy and curiosity.

The theory of the expansion of the universe was an obsession of my dad's, a major discovery by Edwin Hubble in 1929 the year my paternal grandfather was born.[7] It was found, and the scientific case since strengthened, that the universe we live in isn't a set and stagnant size; rather, it's continually expanding, uniformly on all sides. Scientists stumbled upon this when they set out to assign an age to the universe; an attempt to see into the past, leading to a major discovery about the nature of our future.

The Hubble Constant, or the rate at which nearby galaxies are receding into space, became a guiding principle of how my dad related to his own time on earth. It's a clue, in a sense that he left behind, as I reoriented to life in the wake of his passing. I remember that it didn't feel like the walls were caving in, but that suddenly, the things that provided containment and protection in my life were farther away, and harder to find. I've returned to this message countless times for instruction on how to face an ever growing unknown. I even printed it out, now framed and hanging on my wall.

I miss getting notes like this from my dad, but I must say as finite as this email's word count is, the meaning it brings to my life has continued to unfold, like the universe he writes about, continually growing. This path that I'm on—one marked by grief and goodbye—is not actually what I would have chosen if I had my pick, but it is the road I am on. And now that I'm here, he reminds me to approach it with an open mind, curiosity, and focused energy for this version of a challenging time.

Chances are, if this is the book you're reading, someone who was once an important pillar in your life is dead, or near to it. It may have happened last week, or last decade; it might feel debilitatingly acute, or numb and far away; it might be looming on the horizon, at the end of a terminal illness. You may be drinking from the grief fire hose or feeling parched, thirsty for ways to tend to your relationship even though, or especially since, they're now gone.

Either way, and all ways, I wish I could reach across the table and hand you the proverbial bottle of tequila—to toast to whatever it is you're going through; to tell you that grief is, and by proxy you are, hard-core; and that even though we've likely never met, we're very much involuntary members of the same team, and I'm proud to be a part of it, especially with you.

So, hi, whoever you are. I think your story is special and deep; your grief is real and shape-shifting; and I think there are ways to relate to it all that we've certainly never learned about in school.

Now, here's the pep talk I wish I had been given, in case it's what you're needing too. For too long, grief has been discussed with cozy pity, something misunderstood as simply sad, to be moved on from and forgotten. But when I close my eyes and think of what it looks like to experience real grief, after spending the last decade in conversation with people in the thick of it, it's much more badass than that.

For me, becoming a griever looks like instant membership in some kind of cosmic motorcycle club, a crew learning how to live with the mind-bending reality that the horizon line is ever expanding; that, despite the heartbreak of certain circumstances and the overwhelmingness of life's hardest chapters, you can find the appreciation, the focus, the curiosity, and the friendship to keep riding the road ahead. This cosmic motorcycle club you're now in is a group of people with a knowing gaze; think less pilly sweater and more weathered leather, less curling up with a tea for a good cry—although that does scratch the itch sometimes—and more clinking glasses with people who get it, in the round.

While likely you wouldn't have wished for this over many lifetimes, you're now part of an underground of people who are familiar with just how precious life is, not in a twee bumper sticker kind of way, but because we can't unsee its opposite.

And now that you're here, it's important to remember that humans have known grief for as long as we've known love; and how to let it move through us is hardwired in our brains. We've just got to trust our balance on the bike, tune in to what feels good to us in our grief as we care for ourselves and for others, even if it requires us to go a little rogue.

Instead of denying grief or resisting it, I invite you to put on the jacket and saddle up. To find the other people out here who get your grief, and get into formation. I found mine around the dinner table that first night; and hopefully, after reading this book, you'll be well on your way to finding yours too.

In the wild ride that is life after loss, we recognize that in this ever more sprawling universe, where the horizon line recedes faster than our pace in pursuit of it, we're less interested in getting to the ever elusive finish line. Instead, we're focused on finding our crew, adjusting our mirrors, and learning how to ride.

## CONNECTING WITH YOUR PEOPLE

If I were able to travel back in time and slip a note to twenty-one-year-old me, I would give myself encouragement to find people who have experienced a loss similar to mine and want to talk about it; a nudge to send that first email that brought five new friends around my dinner table and into my life. The growth from six people at a table to thousands coming together across the country shows that my search for others was not unique. In later years, The Dinner Party conducted research with social scientist Laura Brady[8] that both proved this and helped ground our understanding of why.

The study verified that the feeling that "something is off" when it comes to how our culture relates to grief was widely shared. When asked, participating respondents described a real lack of support and resources before finding The Dinner Party. More than three quarters of respondents felt like their peers couldn't understand what they were going through, which is what sent them looking for a circle of people who could. More than half were clear that what they were experiencing in their grief was not what they would have expected. There's not really a way to prepare for a loss, but the lack of socialization about what grief is really like makes the experience a black box, until you find yourself inside it.

When we asked them to explain the alchemy felt around The Dinner Party Table, the result was surprising. It wasn't that people found their new best friends, although that is the case for some. It was that Dinner Partiers found a place where they had a real sense of belonging; where the part of their story they often hid from the light of day could be heard and acknowledged, where they didn't have to filter what they were sharing or worry that people would shun them for being in their grief. In the words of Brené Brown, they had found a place where they could go beyond fitting in—"assessing a situation and becoming who you need to be in order to be accepted"—and where they could really belong. "Belonging doesn't require us to change who we are; it requires us to be who we are."[9]

In the end, Laura Brady's research found that the big thing happening around the Tables of The Dinner Party is normalization, and that once we can feel seen in our grief, a whole litany of other good things can happen. Being a part of their Table, most respondents expanded their support network, and through these conversations developed greater empathy for themselves and for others. Almost all participants reported enjoying open and honest conversations about their grief, and that the permission to not have to be anything other than exactly how they are is a real source of comfort. It's not always a curriculum or outside advice that we need in grief—it's people whom we can exhale with, who make us feel less alone.

When we were just getting started with The Dinner Party, our work was sometimes met with raised eyebrows. Too often, peer support programs are seen as "nice to have but not necessary" by the medical establishment. We're prescribed pills before people. Some professionals think that if there's not an expert in the room, or someone with a clinical title leading the conversation, then what's happening in that space can't be counted as serious healing. It's renegade to resist such a diminishment, and it's powerful to have a network of people who can be with us in the different shades of our grief.

Instead of groping for a distraction, a way to stop it, or some pathway around, something powerful happens when you instead reach for someone's hand and hold on until the wave has passed. There are people who've been where you are, or are in fact there right now; whose shoulder and warmth and texts can be the lifelines we're longing for. People who can be our companions in grief—not because they have the answer, but because they're asking these questions too.

## EXPERIMENTING WITH CARE PRACTICES

The other thing I would slip into the note to my younger self would be to follow my curiosity around the question *what do we do now*. While there weren't clear grief rituals laid out for me beyond those first thirty days, that didn't mean I couldn't research, experiment, discover, and create my own. A conversation that consistently wows me around The Dinner Party community is about the practices people find helpful—the things grievers do or topics they explore with the intent of inviting their grief out of the shadowy corners of their life and into their focus. Often, these practices are undertaken with disregard to the social norms that might make us seem strange for engaging with our relationship to the dead beyond the first year. Always, they have the courageous air of creativity in motion; showing that, even in the midst of heartbreak, we can approach our healing as its own form of art.

Increasingly, research is proving what we've been hearing anecdotally for years—that rituals and care practices aren't just ways to keep our hands busy while we hope time heals all, but that they are proactive ways to stabilize and make sense of what just happened. Michael Norton, a behavioral scientist at Harvard who studies the impacts of ritual, has found that people with specific actions that honor their past with their person—like continuing to get the car washed every weekend like they used to do—reduce the emotional load of hard grief feelings they were experiencing.[10] In fact, even just talking about these rituals, or remembering that we have access to them, alleviates the stress associated with grief and loss.

Norton's research shows that ignoring our grief doesn't do us any favors. If we instead create intentional moments where we are tending to the memory of our person or people, we can download the lessons grief has to teach us and be steadier within ourselves as we do it.

These care practices can be once-in-a-lifetime actions or daily routines. Some are direct continuations of ancestral grief rituals that contain real rigor around how to care for the bereaved, some of which have been sidelined or disenfranchised over time. In many ways, I've watched people grapple with their grief and stumble upon another way to live, a way that's deeper and truer than the defaults of today, their grief a passageway into a life of meaning, or at least a life of less bullshit or noise.

Other care practices are remixed or created on the fly, and over time, they evolve. These practices become the way we bypass the social stigma that gets placed on top of being a griever—the aspects of grief that make us feel like we're not doing it right, that require us to burn time and energy disguising or masking, pretending everything's fine. These practices become the way of living into Renegade Grief.

While no two stories are the same, there are themes that have emerged, which I'm sharing with you in the form of about two dozen care practice snapshots included in the chapters to come. Many of them—like building altars or telling stories—strive to honor our past, to acknowledge and celebrate the memory of the person who is gone and the acute grief that balloons in moments where we miss them most. These practices have helped grievers be in the present moment—like turning to nature, taking time to rest, or finding people with whom we can explore our relationship to pleasure, as an antidote to our pain. And these care practices also helped grievers create their future, leaning into the lives they want to cultivate, with our loss not as "completed" but in some way integrated, like redefining what home means and finding ways to celebrate. These practices are not linear and look less like a progression from past to present to future, and more like a spiral, as we wind our way through the different eras of our lives.

Every practice here has been a lifeline for people in times of grief, myself included. I'm not giving you instructions or steps to follow, because where is the fun in following someone else's map? My hope is that, by reading through them, you come in closer contact with your inner compass and leave inspired to experiment with a few of your own, now or next time your grief starts knocking. I encourage you to take what is useful and leave the rest. Come back in a year and see how your perspective shifts. Tell me which ones I've missed, and what your suggestion for the next dozen would be.

I find myself shaking my head at how infinite the study of each of these individual care practices could be, and how each chapter here could have been its own book. Our relationship to our grief continues to reveal itself and expand in complexity, even as it recedes into the background of our lives. Five weeks, five years, five decades out from a loss and our grief can continue to surprise, shock, or soften us. Living in the idea of Renegade Grief is a big choose your own adventure, and once you make one choice, you get to keep on choosing.

There's a virtuous cycle between these two pieces of encouragement: connecting with your people and exploring your own care practices. At our original dinner, the care practice that I needed most—sitting down to dinner—also jump-started the friendships I longed for. While some of the practices you'll read about have introverts and the power of solitude in mind, many of them are done in community, and powerfully so. In the same way food brought us around the table, a Trojan Horse into conversations and connections about our grief, these practices serve as entry points into the companionship and collective care we're longing for in loss. I can't wait to hear what places, perspectives, and people your care practices lead you to, whether they're expected or a total surprise.

# UNDERSTANDING WHY

Why does taking the time and space to tend to grief feel countercultural in mainstream America, given that cultures around the world and across time have found ways to honor the presence of the departed in their lives? Whether it's Korea's Chuseok,[11] a three-day festival thanking ancestors for the protection of the harvest; the soulful blare of New Orleans jazz funerals; or Yahrzeit candles burning in Jewish homes, humans have always found ways to honor the dead, not just in the immediate aftermath, but as a part of the fabric of their ongoing life. Being fully alive, and in community, has always involved honoring the people who are no longer here as the shoulders we stand on.

You might not care at all about cultural backstory, and instead want to get as quickly as possible to the parts about what to do now. Permission granted to skip ahead. But if you're wondering why Western culture's societal vibe around grief is off, there are clues from the last century that might make you realize it is not all in your head.

We can track it back, in the Western world at least, to a transition at the turn of the twentieth century. The Victorian era was a gangbusters time for public grief—Queen Victoria herself popularized the wearing of black as a fashion statement after the death of her husband, Albert;[12] death-related paraphernalia like braided tapestries of a dead person's hair were all the rage and elaborate rules around how to navigate the social sphere in times of loss were thorough, albeit stuffy.

But that all changed as war—big, mind-blowing, worldwide, scary global shit shows—ratcheted up grief around the globe to a level that was incomputable and unprecedented. Here's a way to put it into perspective: if the same percentage of the world population that died in World War II died in contemporary times, it would be the equivalent of the entire population of the United States,[13] save for Texas,[14] dying— approximately 300 million people. And if we apply a bereavement multiplier to that—a concept that suggests that for each person who dies, eight people are left grieving—we're left with a quarter of the globe in a state of acute grief.[15]

The shock and scale of this period was a turning point for how Western culture related to grief. Scholars make the case that these wars sped up a shift in mourning practices away from the "flamboyant public to the 'intensely personal,' leading to 'minimal public expressions of private grief.'"[16]

I get it. We all know the overwhelming feeling of scrolling through our feeds when something terrible has happened at such a scale that numbing it out is the only way to not system glitch. But this wasn't a temporary numbing, it became a new cultural protocol, cemented in psychological procedures and a new set of social norms around death. We entered the era of "Keep Calm and Carry On," and it took a lifetime for the tide to change.

But what was behind the discouragement of expressing personal grief? One take from writer Bridget Keown[17] is that in many ways, public displays of grief got in the way of the war effort. Parents were expected to be stoic and fully surrender their sons as soldiers, as were wives their husbands, children their fathers. Expressing extreme sadness at their death—or alternate narratives to the story of their passing other than one of heroism and glory—was in some way disapproving of the state. Censoring grief was a way to keep the military mission positive, the morale high. And when we got demurer in our expressions of loss, some of the social support and cultural rituals that made those times of transition easier also dimmed. When grievers went into hiding, their power dwindled. Their stories quieted.

We see this pattern on repeat. In ignoring or denying grief, the lid gets put on past experiences that are asking for us to reflect and learn, because looking into the pot would stir up questions that are hard and uncomfortable. We see it in the "pandemic amnesia," as we hurry to put the COVID-19 years into the rearview mirror, without fully mourning the more than a million lives lost as a nation. We see it in history textbooks, as we try to minimize the anguish of the slave trade, or the genocide of Indigenous people, refusing a conversation about the roiling grief at the heart of our nation. We've gotten scary good at denying grief. Much too accustomed to turning our backs on it as it transmutes into anger, resentment, sickness, and division. It is renegade to tend to it, despite cultural pressure to hide it away.

Beyond war, the other change was the rise of modern psychology, led by a doctor who had a very specific, and often conjectured, view on it all. Sigmund Freud's grief hot take? Simply "sever" it. In his treatise *Mourning and Melancholia*,[18] maintaining a connection to the deceased is like "clinging through the medium of a hallucinatory wishful psychosis." No wonder people felt shame to continue a relationship with the dead.

According to Freud, maintaining a bond with your person meant you were delusional and needed time on his couch to set you straight. "Normally," he assured readers, "respect for reality gains the day." He was clear that mourning took time, but it did have an end point, which was when all emotional ties to the person had been cleanly cut. And if any ties weren't severed? A griever would be denying their own aliveness. He thought that being in a relationship to the dead was choosing death yourself, and he cast shame on anyone who tried to keep their memory close. In many ways, Freud's perspective became the new gold standard of how to approach our emotional processing of loss in the twenty-first century. And by following the "sever ties" mentality, if we did give ourselves space to grieve, we did it slightly shamefully, and we did it in the privacy of our own homes.

But luckily, as in all stories and all fields of research, new learning builds upon the old, and new perspectives take the lead. It wasn't until early in my lifetime that Dr. Dennis Klass[19] and his research partners released groundbreaking findings that really returned us to some of our prewar—and precolonial—perspectives. That grief, in fact, is not asking to be severed and rejected, but is longing for us to find a new way of connecting.

Klass, at the time a professor teaching a class on Death and Dying, was approached by a group of bereaved parents who wanted to start a support circle, asking if he would lead it. He wasn't a bereaved parent himself, but he accepted the invitation, which would define the rest of his celebrated career.

What he witnessed was that the group's instinct was a strong departure from the psychologically accepted paradigm around grief and loss, which was still grounded in Freud's "breaking bonds" model. These parents wanted very much to talk about their late children and create rituals around celebrating their memory, too—practices like writing letters, lighting candles, and releasing balloons. Klass's time with the group turned into an ethnographic study that lasted years.

The rituals that emerged from this group of American parents reminded Klass of ancestral reverence practices he had witnessed while staying in a Buddhist temple in Japan, a culture that generally prioritizes collective well-being. He realized that the practices at the core of the ancestral reverence festival of Obon were the same human instincts that showed up in his bereavement group. And that human beings are drawn to, as he coined it, "continue bonds."

As he started to share his findings that "ongoing relationships with the deceased are normal and widespread,"[20] he was disturbed by the amount of pushback he received from many of his peers in the field, who disregarded programs run by peers. "We knew that it was a revolt against the Freudian model. We just didn't know it was this revolutionary." Other researchers came out of the woodwork to support him, relieved that someone was speaking out against a misguided model.

A scientific changing of the guard followed, and the research world now celebrates continuing bonds as best practice in grief. But that doesn't mean our social practices have caught up, or that we were raised in households or communities where we learned how to do it. Talking to family members from older generations, their muscle memory is still embedded. So how do we translate Klass's theory into lived reality? We practice.

The more I've been a student of the topic, the more I've learned that grief care practices have survived, even if just in the privacy of homes; supermarket clerks and people next to me on airplanes, as well as friends of friends all have shared the ways in which they have quietly continued bonds. This book showcases those practices, serving as a companion to guide you in discovering, rehydrating, and experimenting with the ones that work best for you. Spoiler alert: this won't be the only time you'll be face-to-face with grief. Whether it's a loss from someone dying, or the end of a relationship with someone living, or the way you'll grapple with changes due to climate change or the next pandemic, we'll need care practices to tend to our grief in those moments too. In these pages, you're building skills not just for times of death, but for all of life.

✳ ✳ ✳

In that parlor game where people ask if you could have dinner with anyone, living or dead, who would it be, my answer is easy: *Sigmund Freud with a table full of other parents who've also lost a child.* In the years after releasing his culture-bending essay, Freud's youngest daughter died of the Spanish Flu of 1918, the largest pandemic the world had known up until 2020. Even though he had set off a series of dominoes that would dominate the field of psychology for decades to come, he wrote in a letter to a friend that perhaps he had been wrong.

"Although we know that after such a loss the acute state of mourning will subside, we also know we shall remain inconsolable and will never find a substitute. No matter what may fill the gap, even if it be filled completely, it nevertheless remains something else. And actually this is how it should be. It is the only way of perpetuating that love which we do not want to relinquish."[21]

At this child-loss table, I would toast to all of the littles who brought people to the table that night, honoring the particular devastation of an out-of-order loss like losing a child. And then I would sit back and listen as Freud shared his story and heard the stories of others, off duty from his psychoanalysis work, participating as a peer. Maybe we would see the guy laugh a little, cry a little, and let the social permission sink in that he didn't have to deny the persistence of his pain, that by opening up about it, the acuteness would lessen and he would realize he wasn't alone, and that he could instead find ways to live with the part of loss that will never let up.

I like to picture him exchanging phone numbers with someone he vibed with, and after helping do some dishes and eating some dessert, he would leave with a new idea that maybe analyzing his grief was only going to get him so far, and that being so critical of himself and others was no way to live. Freud might realize that the other people around the table had a lesson or two for him, that there were care practices he could experiment with to stay connected to the memory of his daughter and still move forward with his life; that he didn't have all the answers, but that the questions he was asking just got a whole lot better. And thanks to the connections he just formed, he's much less alone in asking them.

# ACT 1

# HONORING YOUR PAST

IN MOST CULTURES AND RELIGIONS across human history, there are a set of motions that people move through after a community member dies. For some it's a burial and for others a cremation; for some it's a gathering that's somber, for others a raucous affair. You might come from a culture, a block, a family of people who know exactly what to do in those first thirty days; or you might be left wondering, as the dust settles on the version of your life without them present, whether the status quo of grief support is all we got?

For our purposes, we're focusing on honoring your past and continuing bonds with your person in the season of life after their departure, when the celebration of life is in the rearview mirror and the shock has worn off. Chances are you miss them more than ever. These chapters are inspiration for the fourth (or fourteenth) anniversary of their death; the day you finally decide to tackle the boxes of their belongings slowly moldering in the garage. It's about recognizing your person and their absence in the moments of mundane or unexpected living, when the condolence casseroles are long gone from the freezer.

Even when it might feel excruciatingly vulnerable or a little sappy, it's important to maintain a sense of closeness with their memory. Because in honoring their memory, you're honoring the history you shared. You're resisting the cultural pressure to forget, to just move on, an amnesia our resistance to grief casts over not just their life, but the part of our life that we shared with them.

When someone who mattered a lot to us dies, there's another way to approach life after; an invitation to not wipe them from our memory or eject them from our lives, but to find practices to incorporate our past with them into our present, so that we can carry their legacy into our future.

It's not about clinging or about staying stuck in a story of grief. Paradoxically, by taking the time to consciously recognize your person, you can stay in a relationship with the generations of people who've come before you, never fully having to erase them from your story. And you can find a way to regularly release the grief valve, avoiding the system glitch that can sometimes come from built-up pressure, although in this book you'll find some ideas about what to do when that happens too.

And in consciously, openly honoring your past, you can find the kinds of friends that want to honor their past along with you. You might find companions with whom you can rehydrate traditions native to your people, going through motions that your ancestors went through for centuries, whether it's actively practiced by your family now or you're hearing about it for the first time. In this section, there are examples of care practices that are perfect for solo practitioners as well as for groups of strangers on their way to becoming friends. I've seen devastating losses become an opening for life-long connections—never replacements, but powerful companions nonetheless.

It's through these connections with people who share a story of loss, and the time we spend in conversations that go beyond the platitudes, that has totally reframed my relationship with grief. It's in the moments when we are most gutted, when we are standing amid the rubble of our life, that we have to decide whether we have it in us to make something of what's left, maybe even something beautiful. The realization that's kept me in this work for more than a decade is just this: tending to your grief and honoring your past is an invitation into a creative life; and you can begin your creation by exploring their story, in the past tense.

# FEASTING

BELLIED UP TO THE KITCHEN sink, I scrolled through my phone, trying to make sense of a series of text messages from my dad's younger sister. I had asked her how to make arroz con pollo, a greatest-hits dish in the family recipe book, originating from our ancestral land of Spain. For all the times I had enjoyed this meal—been comforted by its smell wafting from the kitchen as it cooked, lapped up the last grains of rice with a piece of baguette, zapped leftovers for lunch the next day—I had never once made it myself. Over the last few hours, I'd been singularly focused on figuring this thing out. I wanted to make it as close to perfect as I could, because I would be using this dish to introduce my dad to a new set of people, hopefully soon to be friends. And it was important to me that they know him not just as someone who'd died eight months ago, but as the person he'd been when he was alive. I wanted the dish to help them understand, on some deep, visceral level, how life with him, while not without its complications, had tasted good.

When my cancer caretaker duties officially ended, I made a move to Los Angeles and rented a room in an old blue house on a narrow back alley, with a tiled counter and creaking floorboards. On the day I set out to make arroz con pollo, I'd experienced sticker shock in the spice aisle at the grocery store as I registered the price of the small tin of saffron, which is key to the dish's color and taste. I'd bought the prerequisite ingredient of chicken, and despite feeling queasy as slimy cutlets flopped onto the cutting board, I persevered. I had a feeling that if anything could help this evening's conversation, during which we were going to be taking on topics we'd been trained to avoid, it would be the golden aroma of a home-cooked meal. As I pulled out mismatched plates from cupboards and scrounged around for a lighter to spark up candles, the wait until my guests arrived—a table full of half orphans, far from home—became a countdown to something bigger than just one dinner.

A few weeks before attempting this recipe, my therapist had encouraged me to follow the longing I had to talk about loss in an environment that felt like a gathering of friends, rather than a circle of patients. I reached out by email to a handful of people I knew from different corners of my life: Michelle and Maggie, acquaintances from college and high school, respectively; Misty, a woman I'd met at a party; Lennon, a coworker at the magazine where I worked; and Jess, a friend through friends. We were all in our twenties, making our way through early careers, first dates, navigating living on our own—with the presence of a major death never far from our peripheral vision. Each of us had lost a parent at an age that meant we'd become part of a club that most people we knew didn't belong to yet. The email was simple: an invitation to dinner, to talk, to share our experiences with grief. And to bring a dish— because to really get into this, we were going to need some sustenance.

The first knock came, followed by others, and soon we were all in my tiny kitchen with potluck bowls to add to the table. I led everyone through the creaking maze out of the back door and onto the deck, where a fold-up table was flanked by mismatched chairs. On each plate sat a twine-wrapped stack of conversation starter cards, different quotes that I was eager to share, messages that had given me solace in my first eight months of grief. Each card pack included a *milagro*, a small tin figurine, symbolizing the parts of our lives that might need a blessing: a leg, an eye, a heart. Who said a dinner about grief couldn't include party favors?

The downtown Los Angeles skyline sparkled through a curtain of bamboo rustling at the edge of the backyard, and voices and music drifted in from neighboring houses. We all sat down and started the standard small talk of a meal with new people. We made the rounds, chatting about where we worked, lived, liked to go dancing, where we grew up, and our reaction to whatever celebrity gossip was making head-lines that week. When there was silence, someone would rush in with some new bit of small talk. We all knew why we were there, but we had also gotten skilled at steering conversation away from stories of grief. Bringing up our common experience was like playing a game of conver-sational chicken. Who would introduce the topic of dead parents into the din of dinner party conversation?

When I placed the steaming pot of arroz con pollo on the table, I sensed an opening. Food and drink, an unstoppable social lubricant. I had mostly pulled off my first attempt at this family recipe thanks to my aunt's guidance over text, and I felt proud of what I had accomplished. After passing and plating, participating in the tender act of sharing food, I raised my cup to toast to my dad, José, whom I had spent some of my most cherished evenings with around the family dinner table. I re-alized then the quiet power of simple rituals like clinking glasses, one of the ways humans honor lives, living or late, the kind of secular ritual that can get a room of strangers ready to talk about something bigger than themselves. The six of us then toasted to the other people who, in their absence, had brought us together that night—Lennon's and Misty's moms, Michelle's, Maggie's, and Jess's dads.

The things we had all been avoiding came tumbling out. Stories of the accident, the diagnosis, the death—but also of navigating life after. We were able to share our own grief deep-cuts, the nuanced elements of the experience that you really can only relate to if you've been there too: been on the date when someone asks what your parents do, and you worrying how to be honest but not ruin the mood; gone home for the holidays and realized that the time of year that once felt like everything in the word was right is now really, incurably wrong; been in the grocery store having a meltdown, when you realize you're the only person who can parent you. There were big bursts of laughter, with tears welling, all of us overcome by the feeling of something in us flipping from silence to resonance. Six voices finding a harmony we had all been longing for.

In the discomfort of grief, I had fidgeted through libraries and different forms of therapy. I had discovered Elisabeth Kübler-Ross's "five stages of grieving,"[1] but then uncovered that it was a theory that emerged from her study of the dying, not the grieving. And while she is forever a legend in the field, she never meant for her phases of grief—denial, anger, bargaining, depression, and acceptance—to be seen as a linear set of boxes to check, but rather as an expression of just how wide a spectrum of emotion we're capable of feeling after a loss. I found it to be more a source of confusion than help.[2]

But around a wobbly table in the dimming light of a setting sun, I finally found it. What I had been looking for in the prescriptive framework of five steps, I discovered in the smiles and tears of five strangers. The place where I could begin to unpack what had happened without worrying about how many more minutes were left in the therapy session, or if I was the only person in all of Los Angeles who felt this way. It had the ease and flow of being in a group of friends. And we could all talk about the thing that we were longing to talk about, without feeling like we were a burden, or dampening the mood. Around this table, we were not alone. We were refilling each other's glasses and settling in to listen, to each other and ourselves.

Back in 2010, the idea of a dinner to talk about the unspoken aspects of grief felt like a grand social experiment, and I'd been nervous the whole time I'd been prepping the arroz con pollo. I'd comforted myself that even if it was a disaster, experimental grief dinners—like bad first dates and drug trips—always come to an end, right? But I was desperate, hopeful, and hungry for something that the existing grief infrastructure wasn't serving up.

The idea of inviting people over to talk about grief in an informal environment, without a therapist playing the role of Victorian-era governess accompanying our grief promenade, felt quite wild. I've learned over the years that sometimes the instinctual desires we have after a loss are worth heeding, even if they seem far-out. If they're not going to hurt us or others, why not try them out? Sometimes, because of our avoid-ant and individualistic society's view that death isn't to be talked about over dinner (or anywhere), trusting our instincts toward collective care requires a little rebellion. For me, this work has been about trusting the part of myself that attended grief groups and therapy and was still left with a craving I couldn't help but satisfy.

And what was making this feeling of closeness and ease while dis-cussing a topic that normally felt cold and alien come alive? Bowls of food. Looking back, meeting up to eat had been a crucial, emboldening element of the evening. We could have met up for a hike, or in a circle of metal folding chairs in a traditional support group formation—but I doubt the same depth of connection would have happened. Food, this quiet ally, got us all to quiet down and listen up. Food is a timeless tool for humans in grief, a direct line to honoring our past. In fact, as people began to ask us how these grief dinners worked, our simple response was, "It's just a potluck!" But for too long we've discredited the power of a feast and what food can unlock for people around a table. When I look back at that night, I understand food as a crucial gateway to other care practices.

All in all, that first meetup ended up being quite a tame evening (although Michelle did spend the night, having had too much wine to drive). Even so, the evening was marked by a quietly rebellious spirit. During this dinner, with its secret society air, a feeling of power started to emerge. It made me realize that the loneliness I had been feeling, the hole in my chest, wasn't exclusively in the shape of a pill or a book, an online forum, or a bag of bath salts. It was other humans—being with people who had been through what I had been through, people who felt like friends, in a setting that felt like some new version of home.

I didn't know that first night that the social experiment I'd set in motion would become my focus for the next decade and beyond. And rather than being a one-off, it was answering a call that many of us in the club were feeling. In 2021, the surgeon general issued a report emphasizing the importance of regular mealtimes as a key component of mental health and stability for young people.[3] But what about those of us who, in times of grief, didn't have a family table to return to, or never had one to begin with? Or if what we needed might be a space to unpack a loss experience away from complicated family dynamics? What if we no longer lived in the city or town where we grew up, but still craved the feeling of sitting around a table with people who understood our context? Now we had something to do with all those different circumstances. We could create a table.

At the time, I didn't know that this group of strangers on my back deck would continue meeting monthly and would become my chosen family. I didn't know that the spirit of this first meal would be re-created around hundreds of tables, where thousands of stories of people who, like me, had fumbled their way through the unimaginable would be shared. Who, like me, had tried to keep their stories of loss buttoned up within the confines of current relationships and cultural norms, but found that those buttons had a way of shooting off when life's pressures mounted.

Nor did I know that Lennon, who had nervously knocked on my front door and sat across the table from me that night as she introduced us to her mother, would become a life-long collaborator, a fierce friend, and the courageous leader of our community. I definitely didn't think that in the coming years she would quit her day job to turn whatever alchemy was happening in this moment into not just a conversation around one table, but around a nation.

It all started for me with that simple pot of arroz con pollo, a humble meal of countless intergenerational gatherings in my own family. Perhaps my immigrant great-grandparents, when they prepared their own cauldron of yellow rice in their Brooklyn kitchen, were conjuring up the relatives that they had lost forever when they boarded a steamship in

Spain bound for a new world. My grandparents and parents, my uncles and aunt, were certainly honoring the past through tastes and smells and rituals every time they served arroz con pollo at a family gathering. That night, at the first dinner party, perhaps I was simply broadening the concept of family to include a group of peers bound not by blood, but by tears.

I laugh now that it felt so novel at the time, gathering around a meal to talk explicitly about death and the way our lives were informed by someone else's departure. Making death a main course and not a forbidden topic, at the time, felt radical. Yet what we were tapping into was one of the oldest grief care practices known to humankind, one of the most ancient ways of tending to loss. We see it alive and well the first week of November in Mexico, when families gather for Day of the Dead feasts or at Chinese Hungry Ghost festivals, where families build shrines to honor the dead, setting tables with empty seats and serving up elaborate meals. We see it in the catacombs deep underground in ancient Egypt, where burial places had adjacent rooms for family feasts, or in the cookbooks of Southern funeral feast traditions. We see it even in contexts where death and grief are not immediately present or visible: for what is preparing and eating a dish enjoyed by our long-gone forebears if not a way to celebrate and even ingest the presence of the past?

I'm not surprised that bringing our conversation about grief to the dinner table felt both revelatory and right. Humans, across dimensions of space and time, have always found a way of feeding one another in times of loss. Study the foodways of any culture and you'll find a dish meant specifically for the meals after someone has departed. If there is any kind of breadcrumb trail connecting our ancestors to us, guiding us in times of loss, then the path leads right into the kitchen.

Often when we think of food cultures and care practices around grief, we think of the first stretch. The funerary foods. The drop-offs on front porches. I'll never forget the exact contents of the food deliveries we received in the weeks surrounding my dad's death: A Tupperware of homemade minestrone with pesto on the side from Deborah, my step-mother's best friend. A freezer of ice cream pints; many spoonfuls of relief gifted to us by our family friends, the Benjamins. A greasy paper bag of Brazilian cheese breads and a cardboard carrier of large black coffees sent by my dad's coworker Norah got us through writing the obituary. Eating after a loss reminds our bodies that we're still here, even in the wobbly liminal space of someone we love being gone. Being close to death can be disorienting, but food returns us to the land of the living. Whether our grief makes us ravenous, or without appetite, there are menus we can turn to as we move through those first few weeks. If we're eating, we're still alive, even if we feel like the lights just got knocked out of all of us.

I'm always delighted to learn about other people's creative care practices involving food and gathering. Maggie, who attended the original Table, started her own annual pasta-from-scratch party, honoring her favorite pastime with her late dad on his birthday every year. A friend, Eve Brad-ford, hosts dinners called Feasting the Enemy, where participants are instructed to research and prepare a meal from a culture that someone in their ancestry was in conflict with—a grave enemy, a colonizing force, a not-so-nice neighboring community—knowing that finding forgiveness for old hurts and clearing ancestral grief comes faster when you can stop the loop of grudge-filled stories and instead taste the delicate flavors of your enemy's cuisine. And yet, for some of us, hosting a party during times of grief is more of a nightmare than an exhale. Sometimes what's called for isn't a crowd but a solo endeavor. Sometimes the kind of food that can help us metabolize our grief doesn't even require us to cook.

Mary Pauline Diaz-Frasene has fond memories of her older sister Paz coming home from her shift waitressing at the burger chain Red Robin with bags of chicken strips, fries, and chilled plastic cups of what they call freckled lemonade, glittery with ice and flecks of frozen strawberry. When Paz died of cancer in Mary Pauline's early twenties, she knew she wanted to find a way to commemorate the anniversary of her sister's death. But she also knew she didn't have to be too precious, or take on something that felt like too much work. Growing up of Filipinx descent, Mary Pauline has memories of visiting family in Manila and heading straight to the mausoleum for a picnic with her ancestors; there was always deliberating over who was bringing the 7UP, and she'll never forget the sight of a bucket of fried chicken balancing on a gravestone. Where her family's from, they're not so tense about dead people. When a gust of wind throws a door open, her parents would quickly try to remember which ancestor's birthday it was and deduce from there who might be visiting. There was an active relationship to the dead as ongoing presences in their lives.

So on that first anniversary of Paz's death, she invited a group of friends to Red Robin to honor Paz, sending out her own version of a vulnerable "come eat dinner and honor someone who died" email. Yet Paz never came up in conversation. No one, in this instance, went first. She remembers friends talking about dating and what grades they were getting in school. And Mary Pauline, tender and raw in her grief, didn't feel like she had the capacity to bring her sister up herself. She went home that night, having eaten her Red Robin burger, feeling even more isolated and disconnected. What ends up being one person's grief care practice epiphany can be the opposite for someone else. That's why we approach all these care practices through an experimental lens.

Mary Pauline has returned to Red Robin every single year since then, but now with a smaller group—just her husband and one close friend. Because she shared her disappointment in year one, her companions knew to break their own awkwardness around death and ask her to tell a story about Paz at the table. This has created a moment every year during which Mary Pauline gets to reflect on her relationship with her sister, out loud and with people dear to her. Even the years where she's not fully in the mood, there's something about grabbing a seat at the bar where they won't be rushed out, indulging in an order of a boozy shake, gathering all the dipping sauces, and taking an evening to recognize the fact that she had a sister. Sometimes her husband and friend will ask a question, and she'll get to share stories from growing up. Sometimes she doesn't know the answer to the question, and she's honest about the limitations of her relationship with Paz. With a fourteen-year age difference, they didn't overlap much growing up, and by the time they had started to develop their own relationship as independent adults, Paz's cancer was the main event.

When I ask Mary Pauline what counsel she has for other people wanting to create a food-based ritual for themselves around a death loss, she's quick to reply to not be a perfectionist about it. Keep the stakes low. She's committed to taking the day off every year to do something that gives her the space to reflect on the time that's passed since Paz's death, and she saves one of her vacation days for the occasion. Sometimes the days have included long walks or visits with friends. But sometimes the only thing of note is a gloriously greasy burger and freckled lemonade— and that does the trick.

Even when we're not interested in being social, we can turn to food care practices to give ourselves accessible, nourishing, enjoyable ways of staying connected. I have a friend who orders two cups of coffee every year on his mom's death anniversary. He sets one across the table from him and savors the other, reflecting on the year before. When he has drained the last drop from his mug, he gets up and walks out, leaving the second one standing vigil, as if waiting for her.

Another friend has become really dedicated to the sourdough starter she concocted in the weeks after her mom, a person who transmitted love through baked goods, died. After years of practice, she has become a baker who could rival her mom and has found in bread the perfect metaphor to mirror her own grieving. The fact that simple ingredients like flour and water, set together and given some alone time in a kitchen cabinet, can turn into a bubbling, rising form of life whispers to her in a profound way. She just had to be patient, to keep working the dough, to keep feeding the starter. To let the part of her that was heartbroken from her mom's death do its own form of rising.

Nevertheless, one person's care practice can feel like another person's curse, and for some of us, feasting is far from comfort. Our appetite is one of the things that grief can mess with, lurching us between being repulsed by eating or being driven by a bottomless hunger. In grief, we might not be up for the logistics of a coordinated potluck sign-up spreadsheet, and eating foods that remind us of them might feel too heavy. During these times, we might practice caring for ourselves through food by simply remembering that even in times of grief, we cannot photosynthesize. The foods we eat impact our mood. It's okay if all we have the energy for is an unsentimental bowl of cereal in bed. It might also be useful to remember how, if we already had a complicated relationship to food, there are a myriad of ways that grief can compound that.

I remember when Hannah, who'd later become one of our earliest hosts in New York City, lost their dad when we were in college. The stress of the death piled stress onto their life in a way that exacerbated an existing eating disorder. Eating was something they could control, in a life that felt like it was spiraling into chaos. Not eating was a way they could dissociate from a body that felt sad, heavy, and hard. Their grief was a socially sanctioned reason for a lack of appetite. The gym was a place where they could go to regain a feeling of agency. While their eating disorder was never diagnosed, and they were able to maintain the trappings of a normal twentysomething's life, Hannah's wrestling with food was a loop in which they felt ensnared for years.

Hannah's friends showed up in ways we all hope our friends would— with regular phone calls and invitations to grab lunch—but Hannah's friends didn't fully see the depth of their struggle. Hannah's mom was spinning from the unexpected loss of her husband, the sole breadwinner in the family, who died as the markets nose-dived harder than they had since the Great Depression. So Hannah had to navigate their twenties, grief, and disordered eating mostly on their own.

Fast-forward through a few brutal and defining years, and Hannah has made it their life's work to be the kind of adult they wish had stepped in when they were freshly grieving. Their path wasn't always easy. It included walking out on a job in public health, and a three-month hiatus at a Buddhist monastery that turned into over a year. Now a professional nutritionist, Hannah's focus is on being a resource to people who fall outside the stereotypes of the types of people who get eating disorders—normally people who are thin and white. Grief is often deeply interwoven with the stories that bring clients into their office. In Hannah's case, confronting their disordered eating wasn't a one-off care practice, but a paradigm shift. It was a brave reframing that helped them step more fully into their life.

Hannah's advice is to ask yourself, "How much real estate is this taking up in my life?" as a way of understanding whether your relationship to food is a dynamic to seek out support around, whether that support is through peers who get it, or a professional. In Hannah's experience, grappling with disordered eating in addition to a major loss is a double whammy that no one should have to deal with in isolation, no matter the size of your struggle.

Little did I know as I stirred saffron-stained rice in the pot of my tiny kitchen that over the course of the next decade I would sit down around similar tables and get my mind blown by the stories of other people who had similarly fumbled their way into their own creative care practices involving food.

What I did know in that moment around our inaugural candlelit table was that my arroz con pollo recipe had turned out pretty good, and that after we all settled in and made our way through the small talk, it was toasting to whoever brought us there that night that dropped the conversation into the place I had been longing for. Between friends and family and roommates, I had hardly been alone since my dad died, but in this moment, I knew that I had finally found a place where I didn't have to feel like I was all on my own. Whatever had happened here, we all wanted seconds.

As the participants in that first Table continued to get together, we didn't always come with sentimental dishes from family recipe books. Life got busy. Takeout was ordered. One night we all chaos-theory-style brought a pint of ice cream, which meant "setting the table" was passing out spoons and starting a clockwise rotation, eating straight from the carton. But the deeper we got with one another, the less the actual food on the plates mattered. The meals had done their great service of giving us a reason to gather, a way into each other's hearts. We were practicing a way of grieving that didn't have a rule book—not just accepting the status quo, but asking: *How are you feeding yourself in your grief? Want to try the dish that helps me honor my past? Because maybe it'll inspire a way to honor yours too.*

# FINDING YOUR ALTAR

PICTURE A GRASS-COVERED MOUND EMERGING from emerald hills, a temple built into the earth. You spot a doorway in the white stone facade that takes you into a narrow tunnel, eventually pooling into a cross-shaped ceremony space. It's a place penetrated by a single beam of sun, only at dawn on the winter solstice. Newgrange, north of Dublin, is both an architectural wonder and a burial ground, and has been reminding inhabitants and visitors for millennia to celebrate the presence of light even on our darkest day.

Next, imagine you're in a room of terra-cotta soldiers, protecting the grave of a former emperor, standing vigil for over two thousand years. Or you're standing at the edge of an ocean inlet in western Patagonia at a canoe burial launch site, where dead relatives were sent off in hand-hewn boats to Nomelafken, the Mapuche word for the "Land of the Dead,"[4] residing on the other side of the sea.

Or you might visit in your mind's eye the Virginia estate of America's first president, taking in the brick archway leading to the burial grounds for the people he enslaved. Once covered by a thicket of vegetation, historians have revealed over 150 unmarked graves in what is now the Mount Vernon Slave Memorial. According to oral tradition, enslaved people buried their kin with feet pointing toward the Potomac River, symbolizing a desire for their souls to return to the homelands from where they were stolen.[5]

Across the globe, human beings have consecrated physical places to put our dead, which turn into the places we also get to go with our grief.

It's an instinct we can't ignore. We decorate altars. We erect shrines. We design buildings or find places in nature that make us feel the bigness, and the awe, that their life, and their death, has left us with. It's renegade in grief to resist the urge to wipe them from the map; and instead, follow the timeless human urge to make a place where you can find them, even in their absence.

There are many reasons why humans have always wanted a place to orient themselves after a loss: secular and religious reasons, personal and collective. But neuroscientist Mary-Frances O'Connor, who leads pioneering research on how the brain processes grief, has a reason that rings true to me.[6]

Times of loss can be wildly disorienting, and O'Connor's research explains why. She's discovered that our brains make a mental map of the people we are closest to: where they are, when we'll see them, how close we feel to them on any given day. When someone dies, our brain continues to run the program of trying to locate our person, refreshing the map until we know exactly where they are. When we feel like someone is about to walk through the door, it's because our brain is activating the program, cuing up our anticipation of their physical presence.

Even though you were the one to identify their body, you still might cock your head to listen for the sound of the garage door opening at the time of day they usually arrived home. You might look up from your laptop expecting to see them in the doorway. Death, to our brains, is experienced first as a system glitch before it's accepted. In grief, we are rewiring.

Compound that with the realities of living in an American over-culture that really doesn't like talking about death with sincerity. When most people think of the word "memorial" in present-day America, it has more to do with the start of barbecue season and wearing white pants than it does with tending to the memories of fallen soldiers. We live in a culture that would have us not talk about our loss, to move on. We're left holding someone's memory inside us, a weight that over time can be hard to manage, a weight that we very much might want to externalize, to place down, to visit when we want to, but not always carry on our backs.

Here, O'Connor has some good news. In the same way our brains can learn to do all kinds of things that once felt impossible—like tying our shoes, or texting at top speed—our brain also learns how to grieve, and how to adjust to life without our person. And that's where altars, shrines, or other memorials come in. According to O'Connor, when we create an altar, we are making a place where we can locate our person on the map—whether it's their photograph on an entryway table or a candle we light for them on the kitchen counter—in an altar, we give them physical coordinates. Instead of looking to the garage door or waiting for their car to pull in like they did every day at five, over time, the altar can become a place for our brain to rest, to stop the system glitch of not knowing where they are. It'll never be as good as looking up to see them in the doorway, but it can let our mind stop the restless search.

O'Connor explained to me that the problem that altars can help us solve is clear. "The basis of relationships is all about returning to each other. The whole point is that we can go out and explore the world and know that we can reunite and have security and love and support and fun. And that function of relationship makes us have healthy, productive, flourishing lives." In their absence, altars give us a place to return to. As O'Connor puts it, just because "that person is no longer on the map of the external world, it doesn't mean that they're off the map of our internal world. We need that feeling of returning to them."

At altars—whether they're cloth-covered tables where we refresh flowers and lay their favorite objects, or the park bench that reminds us of them—we can enact what she calls "that ongoing continuing bond—that reunion—in the real world." The drive to seek out this person, when thwarted or unfulfilled, can be incredibly painful. Altars,

O'Connor points out, "can offer an off-ramp to that round-and-round thought pattern that asks: 'How are they? Where are they?'" and the equally disorienting thought that they aren't looking out for our where-abouts or well-being, that one less person has our back. "Its function can be very soothing by giving us a place to interrupt that."

When we first learn how to find our balance as kids, we discover that finding a single place to anchor our gaze, such as a static knot on the wooden floor in front of us or the edge of a picture frame on the wall ahead, is what allows us to find stability. Even while standing on one leg, we can still find a sense of balance. Spinning in circles, we can still orient ourselves by keeping track of where our circle began. So long as we have something our eyes can focus on, we can defy wobbliness in the shakiest of times.

This is how I've come to understand altars. In times of grief, finding a place to focus our attention can be the thing that allows us to maintain our balance, or at least locate ourselves in space and time when we've been knocked off-kilter. Altars can be the places where, when we can't tell what's up and what's down, we can sit it out as we make it through a kind of grief-induced vertigo, until we're right side up again.

So, where are the places you go to honor your person? To find your balance in times of grief? To tie into this timeworn tradition of honoring places where we can honor our past, by locating them in our present?

What I love the most about altars is that they can take so many forms that finding your altar is inherently an agency-filled and creative act. They can be as simple as a single stone, or as complex as a cathedral. They can live in different spaces, in different forms, on mantels or in classrooms or at the corner of our desks. They can be etched into skin with permanent ink or be the vistas we like to visit where we feel close to our person. They can live in the corners of our private life on bedside tables and bathroom shelves, or in public spaces like parks and school-yards, or even the digital sphere on websites and WhatsApp groups.

Yours might be a newly laid tombstone, standing out among the mossy ones with the sharp edges of a fresh haircut. Or it might be the place where you decide to spread ashes. Or a public memorial dedicated to deaths like theirs, such as a white ghost bike at an intersection where a friend last rode.

In a collection of rituals The Dinner Party released,[7] a young rabbi named Elan Babchuck explained how he found a way to forge a meaningful connection to his late father's grave by continuing a centuries-old Jewish tradition called Kavod HaMet—or "respect for the deceased." The practice has guided him to collect stones from his travels to leave on his dad's tombstone. It's a two-part process consisting of mindfully finding the stone while visiting a place that reminds him of his dad in some way and then leaving it at the graveyard like a souvenir, sharing the story of the trip while he's there. Elan encourages fellow grievers to not just complete the process in quiet, but to find a friend to talk to about the stone and its significance, before leaving the stone on their headstone, or even just their own windowsill.

One Dinner Partier—when preparing to give birth to her first child—packed an altar in honor of her dead mom to break out in the delivery room, knowing that in the throes of labor, she would probably want to conjure her mom's memory in the room. The altar, consisting of a few electric candles, a vial of her mom's ashes, and her parents' wedding rings, helped ground her during the waves of contractions. And her doula, a friend she made through her Dinner Party Table, was there to support her with the grief she knew would be present at the birth.

There's no such thing as too small or too elaborate, too cheesy or too weird. I've helped build altars for our community with cartons of Marlboros (an ode to someone's favorite vice), right next to a toddler's psychedelic stuffed animal and unicorn horn. Others that I've put up include photos and letters and seashells and food, with candles and jewelry and CDs that haven't been played since pre-iPod days. Your altar might be portable, a few special items kept in an Altoid tin in your backpack pocket. It might be an altar in disguise, a necklace of theirs swinging from the rearview mirror of your beat-up car.

So the question is not whether an altar does anything—we can thank Mary-Frances for that. Instead, we ask how you can create an altar that best represents what is important to you, with wherever it is that you're at with your grief. What matters most is that when you turn to it, it becomes a place that reminds you of your person. That it isn't performative, with an audience in mind who is anyone other than you, not for the feedback from others but because it does something for you. That it can change, like you will, countless times. And that it in some way helps you find your balance when the world is spinning.

I've bonded with other Dinner Partiers about how graveyards are places of significance for older generations, but for us they don't pack the same punch. With more than half of Americans getting cremated, the commonality of a burial place isn't what it used to be.[8] I remember visiting my dad's grave, primed for some feeling of transcendent connection, and leaving disappointed because, as I stood there, I felt next to nothing. Sort of neutral. A little annoyed, if anything, because it reminded me of just how gone he was—worm food. I knew I would have to find my own place to remember him.

While it was initially frustrating that one of the only culturally accepted grief care practices—a visit to a graveyard—didn't scratch an itch for me, I've realized since then how it was a form of liberation. It was up to me to find my own place of connection, an initiation into my own active participation in my grief.

In my grief, I didn't seek out to build an altar, but found myself drawn to a place that over time became that for me. Mine began taking root even before my dad died, in the months preceding his passing. During that time, I would take the stairs three floors up to the roof of our apartment building after he went to bed, bringing along a tote bag of books and journals, colored pencils and watercolors. It was my Mary Poppins sack full of tools that I thought might help tend to the wild array of emotions inside me—sadness and fatigue, adrenaline and anger, sentimentality and the slapstick humor of how shitty this year had become.

Sitting in a folding chair on his roof, I would always orient myself toward the lights of Coit Tower, the memorial for San Francisco's firefighters, a glowing white cylinder on one of the city's tallest hills. To me, as it does to many others, it resembles the nozzle of a fire hose, although that wasn't the architects' intent. Over the months of caring for my dad, Coit Tower became my Newgrange, my room of terra-cotta soldiers, or in other words, the physical place where I could deeply honor his life, in the context of his death.

Sitting on the roof, I felt relief when I set my eyes on Coit Tower, unflinching and solid in the midst of so much change. I wished that the fire-hose-looking tower would rain down on my family, to lessen the burning feeling of being with someone as they're dying. Somehow, sitting under the glow of its presence, it did. Under its glow I would unpack my supplies and spend an hour decompressing. Painting or writing bad poems; texting with friends or reading a book; soft gazing at the tower on the hill while my brain caught up with what was happening downstairs in my dad's rented hospital bed.

Those times on the roof, the tower acted as my altar. It was a fixed point, a lighthouse in the distance, from which I could orient and steady myself, exhale and unpack what had happened. I returned to the roof in the weeks after my dad's death, and there I found my center of gravity in the foggy breeze of the city, under a reminder that even in the face of fire we can still find a way to rebuild; and that even in the dark of night, there might still be something bright to lock eyes with on the horizon line.

I'm one of three kids, with an older brother José and a younger sibling Claire. Leading up to the ten-year anniversary of our dad's death, my siblings and I met up at Coit Tower. We knew that we couldn't let the decade marker pass by without some kind of recognition. We had learned that being in a relationship with our grief meant taking time out to tend to it, and the ten-year anniversary felt like a moment that called for some focused attention. It made sense to go back to the neighborhood where our nuclear family spent its final months, a kind of pilgrimage to the place that was so deeply etched into our memory as a time of heartbreaking beauty and a big bomb going off.

We pulled into the parking lot that encircles the base of the tower and looked down upon the neighborhood where we used to live. Some other family was living in the apartment, sleeping in the carpeted bedroom where our dad had died, but I could still make out the roof that had supported me. For all the times I had spent staring up at this tower on the hill, I had never actually seen it up close. On those days that I'd sit on my dad's apartment building roof, I'd never once thought about the people in the tower, visiting from around the world with their selfie sticks and San Francisco sweatshirts, looking down on my neighborhood as I looked up.

My down-for-witchy-shit siblings had agreed to mark the night together with a ritual of our own making. I brought journals and pens, flowers and candles, supplies that echoed my Mary Poppins bag from a decade before—my own emergency altar go-bag.

Sitting on the stairs leading up to the tower, I gave the three of us our assignment. Each of us was to write a note to our dad, catching him up on the last decade. In this case, honoring our past wasn't just about the time when he was alive, but the decade we'd spent without him in the flesh. It could be about anything. New relationships and epiphanies. National shit shows that have been stranger than fiction, and personal accomplishments. New homes and jobs. Old friendships, and other deaths. After writing it all down, we went around and shared back with each other, year by year. Even though we knew the ins and outs of each other's lives, there was something powerful about zooming out at our first collective decade, fatherless. We cried and laughed, memories jogging, speechless about the way ten years of time can accordion into eighty-seven-thousand hours of life, but also which, somehow, have gone by in an instant.

We shared the insights we would have wanted him to know. The surprising interpretation of events that he would especially appreciate. When we wrapped up, we headed to the diner he loved and ordered his usual, a French dip with fries, appreciating the things that never change in the face of so much transition. In spending time at our altar, the whole evening was imbued with his presence. Like one of those Magic Eye images, by taking a look up close, then slowly drawing the image away, we couldn't unsee what had brought us together that night. That tower, but really the broader neighborhood where we'd lived. Our father, but also the next generation. His death, but really a whole decade of living that had unfolded since.

I no longer live in San Francisco, but whenever I drive into the city on one of its iconic bridges—the amber art deco masterpiece of the Golden Gate, or the twinkly light Bay Bridge—I see the white tower poking up from Telegraph Hill. It always feels like a pang of sadness, but never just that. It also feels like a wink from the version of myself who found in it her altar, and also from my dad, a moment to remember that he is, in this way, still on the map.

Over time, we grow to accept that the one constant of being in a relationship with our grief is that it'll evolve and change. Our altars can reflect those shifts inside us. They can grow bigger during times of the year when we need to see our grief taking up more space. They can shrink down, or be put away, when we want to change the channel. We can take items off our altar and tidy them up, giving ourselves the satisfaction of organizing ourselves. And conversely, we can choose to add things as our life unfolds and we find ourselves with new things we want to place in the growing headquarters of our hearts. Our altars can help us track the changing landscape inside us.

To make something your altar, all you really need is a little time and an intention to make a space where you can center yourself and find your balance. The rest is up to you. What place you choose and the materials you use and who you invite there is all your own choosing.

Pick a place and spend time there, even if you're just walking by. See how it changes over days or months. See how it can become a landscape that holds both what's visible—photos you display or mountain ridges you face—but also the unseen: your memories, the full breadth of your feelings, and your growing capacity to hold them close and let them go, all in the same visit.

# EXPRESSING YOUR STORY

IT CAN FEEL DAUNTING WHEN you're back at work after bereavement leave and your clueless coworker asks what you got up to over your vacation. "Not a vacation!" you might answer, and scuttle back to your desk, fighting off tears. You might be at the family dentist, who has a gloved hand in your mouth when they ask you how your siblings are doing. "My sister's good," you might mumble, through the taste of latex, without mentioning the brother who's no longer here. For my friend Sol Guy, telling his housemates that the call he just got was news that his dad was not going to make it was the first time he had to put words to what was happening. He raced outside of his shared apartment to get some fresh air. The friend who followed him to the street and sat with him on the curb was the only other friend in their early-twenties crew who knew all too well what a call like that felt like, because he'd once gotten one too.

Often when we do manage to share the unpopular news of someone's passing, we're confronted by our social conditioning to not talk about the dead. I found that when the topic of family came up, I rarely had the chance to go beyond the very simplest version of the story—"Oh, actually, my dad died"—before the conversation would veer in a dramatically different direction. Oftentimes the one ripping the conversational steering wheel in a ninety-degree direction was me. I found myself so concerned that I might be making someone else feel uncomfortable that I'd shift to topics that seemed less disturbing to talk about. "How was your day? Any plans this weekend?" Anything to skip over the existential void that sat at the center of any question that included my dad.

After many hours around dinner tables with other grievers, I've learned that for lots of us, talking through our loss, or finding some other way to express ourselves around the loss, is a tried-and-true tool to bring ourselves into alignment with what has happened. It's not as if by sharing our story the sadness or trauma or tragedy will be gone. But by expressing our experiences, we get a chance to examine more fully what happened, to consider the variety of ways we can narrate our own story to others and also to ourselves. *Was that cancer battle a complete shit show, or were there some hints of grace in the moments of chaos? How do I feel about what happened, deep down in my bones, away from the reactions of my friends, family, or culture at large? Is this loss something that broke me down, or something that, in a quiet and strong kind of way, broke me open?*

What was alarmingly satisfying about those first few gatherings of The Dinner Party was that we had created a space where we could go deep into the nuances of our grief, but not get stuck there. We could talk about our stories of loss, but also about our work, relationships, and creative projects. While grief was a part of each of our narratives, it wasn't its totality. And because we had a whole evening and dessert in front of us, and a group chat to keep us in touch in-between our monthly meals, we could take our time. By talking about our loss, we were clearing space to be more open about the people we were evolving into. And by forming friendships with people who had witnessed us in our stories, as we had in theirs, we could exhale, regroup, and ask ourselves, *What now?*

If I were to exit from the imaginary grief gift shop, I would consider a baseball cap with *Dead Daddy Issues*, or flirt with the idea of an *I Talk to Dead People* coffee carafe. I would likely skip the more macabre merchandise for a ginormous hooded sweatshirt with the phrase that feels even more true to me now that I've gotten more comfortable riding through the curves and valleys of my grief. *VERBAL PROCESSOR*, it would say, loud and proud.

The science stacks up as to why it's helpful to speak our grief. It's widely studied that in sharing stories, humans experience surges of oxytocin, a chemical that modulates our stress response and is the glue that connects us with others.[9] Verbalizing our feelings can make sadness, grief, and anger less painful. Sharing an emotional experience with someone can activate the reward circuitry in the brain, where we can transmute our grief into pleasure just by talking about it.[10]

By not talking about it, we're suppressing emotions that can increase levels of the stress hormone cortisol in our bodies, which can have cascading health effects, including elevated blood pressure and changes in mood like increased aggression.[11] It can also increase your mortality risk,[12] even if you're still young. It's no longer just conjecture that by opening up about our loss story, we can improve not just our mental health but our physical well-being, as well.

And there are different ways to express your grief—whether it's in a circle of fellow grievers, or on the phone with a friend one-on-one; whether it's in the privacy of your journal, or in brightly layered streaks of watercolors, part of exploring the care practice that expression can be is finding the form that feels right for you.

And we have, now more than ever, an abundance of places to go to share where we're at and get the immediate validation of likes and shares. It's relatively recent in the span of human history that you can tap an icon on the screen of your phone and through some internet wormhole infinitely swipe through grief confessionals of people you'll never meet. It is a radical sea change from stories I've heard from even just twenty years ago, when grief support centers were few and far between, and when the hospice movement was just gaining steam. We're living in a rapidly evolving culture when it comes to permissions and pathways to talk about our most vulnerable and tender stories. I'm both thankful for the proliferation of spaces to be heard and lightly skeptical that connections that start and stop with online interaction are all we need. I'm biased, because what I needed, I found through The Dinner Party, connections aided by the internet, but that evolved far beyond text on screen.

✳ ✳ ✳

I love a cold plunge in a natural body of water, and on a trip to the Scottish Highlands, I spent the day with a "wild swimmer," someone who's made it their life to find little lakes in fields that look like fairy country, and hard-to-access beaches, and swims, well, in the wild. He told me that people who swim with him will usually dive straight into the deep end of freezing cold waters, tough and ready to show off. But as fast as they jumped in, they will come rushing out, shivering for the rest of the day. Cannonballing into cold waters, while exhilarating, can leave our bodies more shocked than secure. The other folks, who heed his advice of gradually entering the water, work on getting their feet acclimated, then their ankles, then their knees and groin, their chest, and finally their head, can eventually backstroke through frigid water with no urgency to get out.

I think this applies to how we handle storytelling about grief too. There are ways that we can ease into telling our story. We might begin with writing prompts that feel a little less heated, talking with people who we can really trust, knowing that even just mentioning a late person at a brunch with friends can be a big step toward expressing our story of loss.

This professional cold-water swimmer also told me how some people get themselves so worked up in anticipation of how the cold water is going to feel that they end up hyperventilating on the sidelines without ever getting in. There's an interesting line between tending to the parts of ourselves that say "not yet," and the parts of ourselves that may be psyched out and standing on the edge, telling us we're frozen before we even get in the water. When do you need a little encouragement, and when are you happy watching other people dive in?

One of the tenets of our gatherings, which started over dinner

tables, and more and more happen over video calls, is that no sharing is mandatory, and that silence is heard just as much as speech. For many people, it wasn't until years after their loss experience that they felt stable enough to really unpack what had happened. Maybe it's the year they turned the age their parent was when they died, or the year they left an unhealthy relationship, or the year they finally figured out their health insurance and found a therapist they could let in. There's deep value in just observing, of hearing other people open up about their stories. We don't have to pile on with our own take on things to get value out of a conversation. Sometimes, deep listening is the deepest healing we can get.

I've also heard people introduce their story of grief but reveal different elements of their history, depending on who they're opening up to and what they want to share. A friend talks about her sister dying when she was young, sometimes explaining that it was a car crash that ended her sister's life. Only on rare occasions, when she's among people with whom she feels safe, have I heard her share that she was in the car, too, but walked away from the crash.

Dinner parties worked for me—but for other people, that's not the place where they want to open up. Thousands of people in our community have opted for a one-on-one connection through our Buddy System, more interested in being matched with one person with whom they can go deep, rather than coordinating with a gaggle of others. Research has said that for men, sitting side by side is the orientation that helps them get vulnerable—think, sitting next to each other on a road trip, or saddled up next to each other at a bar. It's important for us to find the ways that help us feel comfortable opening up.

Some stories related to our loss, when rehashed, can be harmful if not held well. Co-rumination—repeatedly discussing problems without arriving at a solution or sense of release or forward motion—is something to be careful of, and what might feel like a satisfying exchange can really be two people reinforcing each other's negative beliefs about a

situation. There's the talking about our grief that is hard but ultimately feels healthy and good, and then there's the talking about our grief that feels like tires spinning and getting even more stuck in the mud. Learning how to distinguish between them—when are we processing and when are we ruminating—can take some time, but it's something we can all learn how to do.

Being renegade in our grief is not about being swayed by the peer pressure of a moment to share before you're ready, it's knowing when the best thing for you is wading into the waters of your loss story, bit by bit, even if it feels uncomfortable at first. It might be a year or a decade until you're ready to go there, but at some point, the water will feel better, if not refreshing beyond compare.

When I asked Sol Guy, the person who ran to the curb outside his apartment when he got the news of his dad's impending death, what his grief gift shop impulse purchase would be, he didn't miss a beat. A flat-brim hat emblazoned with the words *Healing through Creative Practice*. For him, tending to the grief of his father's death wasn't just about talking, although that helped too. Sol found his own way through telling his family's story in the form of making a documentary, twenty years after the fact.

Sol came from hippie parents, his mom white and his dad Black, who defected to Canada during the Vietnam War. He grew up on a commune but couldn't resist the pull of life outside the British Columbia woods, and left home as a teenager to pursue a career in music.

When his dad was diagnosed with cancer, Sol was part of a rising Canadian rap group called Rascalz, touring and recording. He remembers being home and hugging his dad before leaving on tour, and feeling the tumors in his back. Instead of getting off the fast-paced trajectory of his musical career and caring for his father, he chose the opposite direction. He ran.

While Sol was still working through his denial about what was happening, his dad was making his own preparations. He left a case of eight hours of tapes, speaking directly into his camcorder about the peaks and trenches of his life. What he wanted his kids (and not-yet-born grandkids) to know about him. While other people in his family were grappling with the imminence of his passing, Sol's dad was doing his own, coming to terms by looking straight into the camera's lens.

Sol remembers throwing dirt on his dad's grave, feeling pulled between acceptance at the finality of what had happened and a sort of surreal disbelief. While not yet ready to watch the tapes, it was around this time that he started using the memory of his dad as an active part of his decision-making. He'd ask himself whether his response to an impending choice would make his dad proud, and if it was good for the world. If the answer was no, he'd decline. If it was yes, he'd move forward. In that way, his dad remained a force that was helping Sol to navigate his way true north.

Meanwhile, as the years passed, he lugged the tapes from apartment to house to tour bus to apartment, transferring them from the original eight-millimeter tapes, to a video cassette, to a DVD. And that DVD, he remembers, traveled around the world with him, riding in the front pocket of his backpack, along with the gum wrappers and ticket stubs and foreign coins collecting lint. It didn't physically weigh much, but the disc had a psychological density to it, carrying both the burden—and the possibilities—of his dad's stories.

In a recent conversation, Sol shared that as a young Black man, there weren't many places to go with his grief. "Because of stereotypes and tropes, Blackness, especially male Blackness, is looked at as a monolith. You can be a deeply feeling, emotionally aware, sensitive Black man, but the spaces that you're given and the frame of masculinity that you're culturally expected to fit within are painfully narrow." Because of that, Sol took note of how his grief came out in different ways: "Sometimes beautiful expression, but also anger, protection of emotion rather than communication, which is what grief requires." Sol didn't feel like he had a "safe space to say, *hey, I really miss this person*, or *I don't know what to do.*" He thought that by talking about it, it might seem like a limitation or a crutch. He also didn't want his dad's death to become the dominant narrative of his life, walking around with the story of loss like a scarlet letter, limiting what he could achieve or who he could be or where he might go with his life. So he pushed forward into the future of his life, becoming a father himself to two beautiful children and assuming he had done what he needed to do to let his dad go.

Sometimes people come to The Dinner Party Table asking if they belong there because of the length of time that's elapsed since their loss. For many of us, the life experiences that really call us into telling our grief story come way after the shock has worn off. For Sol, the question of what to make of his loss arrived on a walk with a friend, two decades after his dad's passing.

Sol and his friend, strolling through downtown Los Angeles one weekend afternoon, started throwing ideas around for a possible film project. Sol's friend nudged him to dive deeper than the surface-level ideas and make something about the thing he found most frightening. It was in that moment that Sol realized he had to face the shadowy corners of his own heart—the one that had been avoiding watching his dad's videotapes, and the part of himself that had never taken the time to get to know his paternal family, who his dad had drifted from over his lifetime, but who were alive and well in Ohio. As a mixed-race person, Sol's experience losing the parent who was tied to his Black lineage brought up big questions about grief that accordioned—as they often do—into even bigger questions about identity, belonging, and where he called home.

It was the spark of an idea that evolved over the coming months, but by the time Sol sat down to begin the project, the starting point was clear: he would finally watch those tapes and see what his dad was so eager to talk about as he was dying all those years ago. Eight hours later, Sol was inches from the screen, spending time with his dad. He realized that the story he wanted to tell was the story of the man who had left these tapes behind, and how knowing more about him would inform the kind of father Sol could be to his own children. He would start by making a film that was a letter to his children and see what wanted to unfold.

Sol embarked on a journey of retracing his dad's family legacy, reconnecting with distant family members, all in the format of a letter to his own kids. Halfway through filming, Sol's stepdad was diagnosed with ALS—and he knew the film he was creating was not just about the death of one father, but about how he could show up differently for the death of a second as a more mature person, trying something different this time. Not running, but caretaking. Not looking away, but sitting down and really listening to what his stepdad had to say about life from his deathbed.

Sol's film, *The Death of My Two Fathers*, was a major success in the traditional sense of the word. It premiered at the Tribeca Film Festival and now can be watched on PBS. But for Sol, one of the most profound moments of introducing his film to the world wasn't in the glitzy limelight of a festival. It was in the walls of a prison in Southern California, where *The Death of My Two Fathers* screened for a group of incarcerated men, followed by discussions around how to manage grief, memory, and loss. At one of these screenings, looking out across the sea of faces taking in his father's lessons, Sol recalled that in one of his dad's many professional reinventions, he had declared to the family that he wanted to be a motivational speaker. Sol remembered thinking this was kind of corny, but nevertheless endearing.

Standing in the back of a prison cafeteria, Sol watched his dad post-humously speaking out to the crowd about the lessons of his life—lessons about appreciation, gratitude, and perseverance—and Sol realized that his dad's dream had come true. That in some kind of bizarre, delayed ful-fillment of destiny, his dad had become a motivational speaker through Sol's film. And in front of exactly the types of people that his dad would have most wanted to connect with—other Black men who had landed in one of the most ignored corners of American society. Sol never could have predicted that this was where his story would take him, but he couldn't be more proud.

* * *

There's a word that Sol had been sitting with a lot on the day that we talked. *Sonder.* The word was coined in 2012 for a project called *The Dictionary of Obscure Sorrows,*[13] in which the poet John Koenig coined words for emotions that didn't yet have a name. *Sonder* was the word he created to express the awareness felt when you realize that each in-dividual is a universe unto themselves. That the strangers you pass on the streets have their own version of big stories coursing between their temples and rising from their hearts.

For Sol, in deciding to tell this story about his two fathers, he had to overcome the part of him that said, *Why me? Who cares?* It was while contemplating the phenomenon of sonder that Sol realized, *Why not me?* It occurred to him that he wasn't the only person grappling with these big questions about fathers and legacies, and that other people who were the main characters in their own lives might benefit from him opening up. So he made his film and it led him to that day in the prison and a feeling of healing that felt like it encompassed not just himself, but his father as well. Externalizing what's happening on the inside through stories—or expression of any kind—allows for points of connection that can transcend our individual bubbles.

When I asked him what advice he'd share with other people

grappling with how to tell their story, he said "to document." And not just film the concert you're at where ten thousand other people are getting recordings of the same thing, but to turn your camera on yourself. To take inventory of what's coming up in your own heart and life and then put it to paper. Or if that's not your medium, to sing it, to plant it in a garden, to sketch on a pad, to find some way to externalize what you're feeling through creative practice, regardless of how amateur it might be, regardless of whether you ever share it.

Making this documentary led Sol to see exploring grief as a mechanism to transform. For him, entering into the heart of his feelings, by not ignoring the story he was carrying in his actual and metaphorical backpack, meant he was able to turn previously shadowy corners into sources of direction. Now, with a film that exists outside himself, his relationship to those questions of fatherhood has evolved. His film is out there, providing a feedback loop between his story and the stories of others.

The ever-fascinating thing about stories of our past is that they're constantly evolving. New information is revealed by the uncovering winds of time. Our perspective changes as we become the age our parents were when they died, or when we fall in love again as a widow, or when we realize that, maybe there will be another person who we can call "best friend." Sometimes we reach a summit in our lives and look down and realize that it all looks a little different from up here.

Part of being a renegade griever is knowing that the version of what feels true today might remain that way, or it might dramatically change. We learn more about our people, and the plot thickens. The story we've gotten good at telling sits stale in our mouths. I think of the ways in which our own growth and change shifts our relationship to our people. Even if there have been no new inputs from their side of the relationship, there's something uncanny about how we can still learn so much about them as time progresses. In our own lives, their stories activate. In our eyes, we come to understand them anew, even if nothing has changed.

When I talked to Sol, he shared that his mom had been diagnosed with cancer, and that it is now becoming her time to go. This time, he's a little more familiar with this kind of sadness. This time, he'll go through it with her, eyes a little more open. Heart a little more tender. Certain that, however her final chapter unfolds, he'll be able to turn to expression, and in the wake of her departure, heal through creative practice.

# ANIMATING THE INANIMATE

I RESIST THE NARRATIVE THAT grief gives us baggage. That our grief is something to be seen as a negative weight we're carrying. I reject the idea that somehow, in the exquisite design of the universe, the inevitable thing that happens to every person, one of our most poignant rites of passage as a species, would leave us ill-equipped to participate fully in the world.

Instead, I see it as the ultimate initiation. I see grief as a sharpener of our senses and an enhancer of our ability to connect. I see it as an expander of our empathy, and as an express elevator that brings us closer to the burning core of the human condition. Sure, we'll need to heal and process what's happened, and at times it will be excruciating, numbing, and disorienting. No, it isn't going to be resolved in a year. I bet it might make the way we view the world more nuanced, which you can argue is really witnessing the true nature of things. But baggage? That makes grief itself sound toxic.

While I refute that grief gives us baggage, it is unignorable that it sometimes gives us boxes. Or storage units. Or households full of things to figure out what to do with. Quite often, after a loss, we are left to deal with lots of stuff.

And that stuff can be the impetus for some intense relational struggles after a death, not with the dead but with the living. It can leave us with disagreements between family members on what to do with someone's belongings, or regrets that we didn't hold on to those items in the times we didn't know just how precious they would become. In those literal ways, loss can give us a lot of baggage.

There's the proverbial question: Your house is burning, and you only have a few moments to grab the things that matter most to you. What do you reach for? In the wake of a death, we're left asking this question in a non-hypothetical manner. What are the objects of theirs that matter to us the most? What are the things of this person that we want to carry with us, and what do we do with the things once they're in our care?

But for me, the most thrilling question isn't just what I will hold on to, but how will I use it in a way that helps me metabolize my loss and honor my person? How will I put the objects to work in honoring my past?

Through conversations with other people in the club, I came to notice that objects weren't just things to shuffle around or baggage to handle, but actually some of our most powerful tools in tending to our past and practicing Renegade Grief. These objects can transform, mightily and mystically, in so many ways. Suddenly, some things that felt most mundane can take on a sacred feeling, a talisman-like quality; the last thing they touched, the last toothbrush they used, their watch, never before a special watch, suddenly a touchstone brimming with significance. Through the kaleidoscopic lens of grief, straightforward things can take on multiple meanings.

When we start looking through a renegade lens, objects can shift from being just a random assortment of stuff with quotidian purposes to tools that aid in our own processing. And as this happens, a whole world of care practices opens up to us.

We had a reporter who was writing a profile on the organization attend a Dinner Party one night. One of the attendees gave an update on her life, with the context that the losses that brought her to the Table were both of her parents. None of the participants gasped, or stared at her wide-eyed—being a part of The Dinner Party means that you learn to sit with stories that make some people uncomfortable, and instead of reacting or behaving in a way that would force the person who is sharing their story to comfort you for their loss, we lean in. But this was the reporter's first rodeo.

"So," the reporter butted in, clearing her throat, pencil in hand and ready to scribble, seemingly looking for some language to emphasize the drama of her article. "That doesn't make you an orphan though, does it?" Her voice was full of pity, invoking an image of a pauper child from some Dickensian scene. Those around the table sent eyebrows straight up.

"Yes. Yes, it actually does," the Dinner Partier confirmed. Orphans aren't a mythical species stuck only in redheaded wigs on Broadway, or in Grimm's fairy tales. "Orphan" is not a dirty word. It's a reality for many people I hold dear, and the interaction with the reporter made me realize just how uncomfortable people are at what is for many of us a lived reality we have no way out of, and how badly we need spaces to share our stories without sensationalizing or exoticizing what for us is just life.

I've learned a lot about the experience of losing both parents from my friend Amelia. After both of her parents and her older sister died in the same harrowing three years, Amelia's dubious prize was the inheritance of nine storage lockers chock-full of family archives. The lockers, which were in a sprawl of suburbia outside LA, were packed full of everything from clothing to historic heirlooms to furniture sets. The annual fee to pay for the lockers was far beyond her means, and in the midst of overwhelming grief, Amelia also had to downsize quickly.

Amelia's dad was an early internet pioneer, a rock-and-roll icon, and a descendant of Wyoming's earliest cowboys—a man too brilliant to be bothered by minutiae like organizing the multiple generations of belongings in his care. So he left it to Amelia to sort through after his death. She realized quickly that she could manage the storage of things that were pocket-sized, but other items would have to be purged.

Now, before we enter too far into the story of someone "dealing with stuff" and the ways it can feel like a burden, it's important to acknowledge that having anything related to your person is in itself a privilege. That in all the labor we may undergo to tend to belongings, there are plenty of people who've gathered around the proverbial Dinner Party Table who don't have physical objects in the first place. Perhaps you were too young when your person died to have the foresight or the agency to squirrel something special away; or maybe the nature of the relationship, estranged or long-distance, meant that there was no physical evidence of their presence in your life, even when they were living. The encouragement I've heard from others around the table is to pick an object that reminds you of them and imbue it with meaning as best you can. Find a smooth stone with a weight that satisfies your palm and write a word on it that reminds you of them. Find a replica of the thing that got chucked all those years ago, the thing you most regret losing, but might be found on the shelf of a thrift store. While it may be unsatisfying to say, I dare you to find creative ways to connect to your person through the material world, with objects that they never touched, and see what might unfold.

Back to Amelia and her lockers full of things. She wasn't the first person left behind to clean up someone else's mess, or to have to contend with the overwhelming expense of storage bills. There are 23 million storage units in America alone; "in other words, every one of the 340 million Americans could simultaneously find a place to stand inside one of the nation's storage facilities."[14] I wonder how many of those square feet house the belongings of people who are no longer here, caught in the limbo of family members deciding how to make sense of all the stuff packed in the unit.

Expecting to get rid of most of the belongings, there was one set of boxes that Amelia couldn't bear to part with. It led her to rip into my driveway on a Sunday afternoon in spring, with a cloud of dust billowing behind her black hatchback, her back window blocked by brown cardboard. I'd insisted she stash them in a closet at my place, and one by one, we unloaded boxes with big fragile stickers on the sides. Inside? Her grandmother's china set, a black rose pattern.

Instead of just putting the boxes directly into the shed behind my house, we decided to take them for a spin. We asked whether using the dishes, which hadn't been out of their boxes for decades, would make the process of clearing out a bunch of stuff feel like a moment of honoring the lives that she was unpacking rather than just a storage unit nightmare. Instead of transferring the boxes from the trunk of her car and into the closet, we loaded them onto my kitchen counter and got to work.

My husband and our friend, Jonathan Harris, joined us as we filled the sink with soapy water and pulled out the newspaper-wrapped treasures one by one. Aperitif glasses and water glasses, with crystal vessels balancing on black stems. Stacks and stacks of teacups and saucers, a gravy boat and great plates, and a teapot and serving bowls. We washed and hand-dried, with a soundtrack from her grandmother's prime— midcentury country—piping in the background.

As we took inventory, we got to hear about the history of this set of plates, a white bone china edged with a swirling pattern of black roses and sharp thorns, and why it was so important for Amelia to save it. Her grandmother had been a woman of many complexities. Of the different parts of her grandmother's story, Amelia felt most connected to the part about her grandmother as a two-time widow and a tough-as-nails rancher who was *also* sensitive enough to pick up the change in mood of a room. While Amelia's late sister would have likely kept one of the softer and more femme sets in their grandmother's collection, pink roses or white swans, a talisman for their grandmother's warm and sweet side, Amelia felt drawn to the thorn-covered version. The set reminded her of the cutthroat aspect of her grandmother's personality that had earned her the nickname of "The Dragon Lady"; someone who could castrate a bull in the morning and host a dinner party to sway Wyoming state politics using these very plates that very same night.

The china wasn't so much about conjuring that side of her grandmother as much as it was about reminding herself that she also had that ability inside her. That, landing in her early thirties with most of her immediate family underground, she was going to have to channel the frontierswoman laced inside her DNA.

As we dried plates and stacked them, Jonathan, my husband, and I also got to check in on how our friend was doing. *Not great,* Amelia confessed. She shared how the process of cleaning out the storage spaces was just hellacious. That this wasn't about love and life and cozy collectibles. Moving through the storage units, she felt how these objects held the energetic signature of her family. This history could be brutally heavy—with the literal weight of old oak furniture sets—but also energetically, as she looked through complicated family paperwork, old firearms, and taxidermied animals. As the days went on, she found herself disassociating as she dropped load after load at the Goodwill. Even though it was brutal, she also discovered that if she couldn't care for something, she wanted to let it go. If she couldn't be a thoughtful steward of it, she would give it away. She was learning how to find togetherness with her family in a handful of things and liberating herself from all the rest.

While our dinner later that evening wouldn't take away any of the complicated feelings, it would give us a chance to toast her and all she was going through. In this case, spending time with objects was providing a reason for us to gather and talk. Oftentimes our care practices, when practiced collectively, give us a reason to slow down, connect with other people, and remember we aren't as isolated as we may feel.

As heavy as it was, when we finally sat down to eat, it felt a little like we were playing some kind of dress-up, kids pretending to be the kinds of adults that didn't seem to exist anymore, like clomping around in her grandmother's much-too-big cowgirl boots. Sometimes, when sitting with community members in their care practices, there's a feeling of play that's afoot, like the realization that our dinner on fancy china felt a little bit like having a mixture of a séance and a tea party. We realized that to shift gears from the productive, efficient storage wars of liquidating her family's estate, into creative ritualists taking a moment to reflect on the past and honor the people whose stuff this once was, was going to require a childlike sense of wonder and curiosity. And that felt a little bit like an act of rebellion. We took a beat from the very adult task of organizing belongings to reflect on what the bigger job was we were doing. This was more than just "dealing with stuff." This was honoring a life, many lives, and the ancestors of a friend. We were many months past any memorial service, but something told us that by slowing down and bringing in a little imagination, we were going to be able to do some very important remembering.

The part of tending to our grief that might make us feel like we're playing pretend is important to consider because learning how to deal with the impermanence around us is something we first begin learning how to do as kids, through the act of play. Richard Goldstein,[15] a researcher at Boston Children's Hospital, led a pioneering study on how a term that derives from adolescent development—*transitional objects*—can play an important role in grief for adults. "Transitional objects" is a phrase coined to describe the types of toys or comforting belongings that kids use to separate from their parents as they get older. For example, carrying around a teddy bear helps us feel a little safer in the world without sleeping in bed with our parents. These objects can be tools for both the imagination and our independence.

Goldstein's research demonstrates that, in many ways, grievers use this kind of tool, too—it's just that they rarely talk about it, because they aren't often asked about it. Goldstein's team conducted a broad study of mothers who had lost a child to sudden infant death syndrome, "the leading cause of death for infants between one month and one year." Regardless of whether the mothers were from the Pine Ridge Reservation of South Dakota, or the slums of South Africa, or suburban moms near his lab at Harvard, they all shared what was essentially some sort of transitional object—a baby blanket or toy, a piece of clothing or other memorabilia—that they had kept and might take out one or more times a week. When they brought out the object, they would have some kind of tactile moment with it by either touching or smelling it. The visits weren't always easy—a quarter of the mothers reported that it was sometimes distressing to visit the objects, but that overall, these times of communion helped the mothers continue bonds with the memory of their children.

Interestingly, the women in the study described the conversations they had with researchers as "positive" and "liberating." The objects helped, but so did being able to talk about them. Almost all the mothers were surprised at being asked about their objects—and a quarter of them had previously only interacted with their objects in complete privacy. Goldstein's report mentions that the moms felt the impacts of "social constraint theory" when talking about their objects—the sense that the people around them would be intolerant of the behavior if shared publicly.

In reality, and what I take from Goldstein's study, is that if teddy bears once worked for us in separating from our family members, their mature equivalents—be they a rocking chair, precious book, or china set—could also step in and help us during this time of separation too. And that we shouldn't feel shame or hide if we turn to objects for comfort. According to Goldstein, we can instead "cherish the enduring qualities they evoke for their presence in our lives."

That day we unboxed the dishes, the four of us sat around my dining room table and daydreamed about what conversations would have been had over these plates in their heyday. We wondered what our parents, as kids, and their parents would have been talking about around the dinner table. For Amelia, we decided it would probably be a discussion on the prices of cattle, repairing broken fences, and the future of the West. For my husband and me, the running of our respective family grocery stores, in Brooklyn and Detroit. For Jonathan, the ups and downs of life in rural Vermont. Spending time with these objects allowed for a conversation to happen that wouldn't have come up otherwise, and an evening where the lineages from which we'd each descended were invited to sit with us at the table, reminding us that we are a part of a longer line of losses, yes, but also of lives. And that as we say goodbye to the generations that came before us, we can continue telling their stories, using their objects to prop up their memories, and as a mirror to reflect on the lives we're living.

For many of us, we're grieving more than just the person we lost. We're also grieving the relationship we never got to have in the first place. I've been moved by how grievers have used objects to help process and release stories that were already full of heartbreak, even before a death occurred. In fact, the Jonathan who joined us for dinner on the black rose china had just completed his own exploration of how to tend to the belongings of the dead. Jonathan Harris is an artist, and one of those exquisitely creative souls who I wish had an auxiliary jack behind his ear so that I could plug headphones into his brain just for one day and hear how he interprets the world. Luckily, he let us into his inner world through a series of films he made, called *In Fragments*.[16]

When his mother died after a struggle with depression and drinking on the Vermont land that's been in his family for five generations, Jonathan became obsessed with exploring the role that ritual can play in moving energy and creating change in the physical world. He explained to me, "I think there are three types of rituals. There are the daily things we do—like swimming, or journaling over a cup of coffee—which can really be described more as routines. There are rituals that bring groups of people together, like Christmas dinner or Burning Man. And then there are rituals we conduct that feel more like magic spells—helping us move from one state to another, and cross over some kind of threshold."

His work focused around this third kind, although he knew that the first two types would help him seal and cement the latter.

His rituals helped him realize that the same habits and shadows inside his mother and her father before her were swirling somewhere within him too. That the illness that plagued his mom had impacted him. So he dug into creative care practices not just to close the chapter on her life but also to set himself up for a positive future.

What emerged was a real question of what it would take to, in a sense, reboot his life. To officially change the guard, not just by throwing a new coat of paint on the walls (which he certainly did), but to usher in a new era on his family's farm. No more closeted pain. No more self-destructive behavior. No more uptight, unexpressed feelings. Instead there would be more community, more openness, more connection to the people who lived on the land before his family had arrived, and the people who lived nearby. More laughter. More lightness. For himself as well as for the people who worked on the farm, and for his sister's daughters, who were growing up nearby.

The piece he ended up releasing, *In Fragments*, took the form of twenty-one videos, with twenty-one accompanying essays, capturing Jonathan's seven-year-long process as he designed and conducted various rituals on his family's farm on the shores of Lake Champlain, in the heart of Vermont. The rituals were exquisitely executed and deeply thoughtful, a master class in creative care practices following a loss.

One video, for example, looked at his mother's long history of scary dreams. She had been haunted her whole life with night terrors, which a therapist suggested she write down whenever they occurred. In cleaning out his mother's home, Jonathan found a hidden stack of a dozen spiral-bound notebooks, filled with her detailed depictions of spooky scenes. He wondered if, instead of throwing them out or leaving them in a box, there could be a way to turn those journals into something that held light and buoyancy.

The exploration of that question turned into one of the twenty-one rituals he undertook. Jonathan started by taking an old wooden bed that belonged to his mother's grandparents and placing it in the woods outside his house to bathe in the fresh air. In the bed, he set his mother's 1950s childhood doll, sitting upright against the pillows and amid the trees, a scene that in and of itself looked like a dream. Next, he took hundreds of pages from her dream journals and hung them with clothespins from a network of blue strings running from tree to tree throughout the forest surrounding the bed. By tearing each page from its journal, he felt like he was airing out memories, letting them breathe, creating a place where his mother's secrets didn't have to be secret anymore. He left the pages hanging overnight in the woods, and the following morning, with the help of his sister and her two little daughters, he collected the papers, and brought them to a nearby hillside, where they worked together to transform the pages into papier-mâché kites, which they then flew in the bright spring sky that Easter Sunday morning. He was able to recognize his mother's suffering, while also reshaping her pain into something joyful for her granddaughters to experience—seeding playful memories into the next generation in the family line.

He didn't stop at that. Other rituals included creating an urn for his mother's ashes from scratch, repairing a boat he found in an old shed and taking it out on the lake, and systematically destroying the liquor bottles he collected from around the house, while wearing his grandfather's military uniform, a way of exploring how to evict the history of addiction from his home, given its direct tie to the trauma his grandfather suffered while deployed.

Jonathan had shared with me that grief rituals were the focus of his art practice since his mother had died, but it wasn't until I attended the premiere of the twenty-one films, in the hayloft of a large red barn on his family's property, that I fully took in what a feat it all had been. I was moved by what it looks like when a creative spirit pours themselves into tending to their grief, turning someone's inanimate objects into material inspiration. In Jonathan's work, I saw a maximalist exhibition of Renegade Grief, and walked away buzzing with ideas of how threads from his seven-year exploration might inspire others to go big or go home, or to take little pieces of how he approached tending to his family's stuff and get inspired to right-size the assignment for their own process.

Jonathan's advice for embarking on this kind of work, at whatever scale, starts from a simple place. "I might suggest [you] begin by becoming conscious of what's blocked. What's preventing the life force from flowing in a particular life situation? Perhaps a certain behavior pattern, a certain relationship, a certain place, a certain set of objects?"

Sure, the broader answer might be, someone big in your life just died. But when you zoom in to the details of how that experience is actually hitting you, you might find certain places that are in need of tending—the unfinished plans, the now unaccompanied traditions, the shifting relationships with the living. "Start by identifying those places, along with the objects that embody those blockages. Then ask if there's some kind of judo flip that you can do, using the energy stored in those objects to help you break through the impasse they embody. You can think of ritual as an elaborate choreography built around a symbolic gesture, a kind of technology for bending belief." For Jonathan, he created an inventory of the materials he had to work with, relating to them as practical tools in his own healing, and then started designing his twenty-one rituals. Start by taking stock of the inanimate objects that you have access to, and then dream up ways they can help you bring a certain feeling or release to life.

Thinking back to our Black Rose China night, I was reminded how washing the dishes for the second time, the mood felt entirely different. How these objects forced us to pause the frenetic energy and busyness of death and sit down together. There was something in those plates that had invited us to slow down and breathe a bit, to look across at each other, to be lit by candles and not the fluorescent glow of storage lighting, and take in the moment. There was some kind of enlivening happening here. Some kind of digestion, served up on plates that introduced some kind of alchemy.

The next day, Amelia laid the china out in heavy tubs. We found a corner of my closet where four bins fit perfectly. Until the next time life allows us to have another night like that one, we both love knowing they're there. In this way, we can help each other hold the things we've inherited, and be stewards of them, to aid in our own healing. How we relate to it not as a burden, but as material to work with. An invitation into a renegade act, a creative exchange where we keep some things alive while letting other things go.

What else did Amelia decide to carry with her? A braid of her mother's hair, tied with a bow; a Buddha figurine; two vials of ashes; a small doll that was a gift from her sister to her mother the year their family battled cancer, all neatly tucked and tied into the pocket of a carry-on bag.

# DESTROYING

AND YET, RELATING WITH SENTIMENTALITY to the objects of our people is not always what our grief is calling for. We're not always in the mood to tie a golden bow around an experience, to unpack the learnings, to lean into new friendships. There are times when it can feel better to replace heirloom plates with ten-cent dishes from the thrift store; to swap napkins and serving spoons for safety gloves and goggles. Instead of cooking a family recipe and placing it on a platter to bring to your new friend's table, the thing you might want to pick up is a hammer, smashing it through something fragile, feeling porcelain yield to the pressure of your might. Sometimes, when someone dies, and it feels like your world is shattered, the only thing that can feel like comfort is to break something right back.

Kim Strouse taught me this when she invited me to take the brute force of my grief and unleash it at her studio space on Sunset Boulevard in Echo Park, Los Angeles. In the months after her sister Kristin Rita died by suicide, Kim found that talk therapy groups weren't scratching the itch. She didn't want to discuss how Kristin took her own life. She didn't want to chat about the way everything felt blown apart. The kind of therapeutic care she needed was less discussion and more destruction.

There's now a whole industry of Rage Rooms, places where you can pay a one-time fee for access to a private stall, a baseball bat, and an old VCR. But at the time, such places didn't exist, so Kim made her own. She called it Rita Project, an open studio where people struggling with grief or suicidal ideation could come and make art in a beautifully messy way. It felt like the perfect testament to Rita, who had had a fierce creative spirit and had been a freshman at Parson's School of Design before she died. My first time at her pop-up studio in an old glass-windowed storefront on a busy street, I was thrilled. For all the books I'd been given with pastel-colored covers, or support groups I had sat in with hushed tones, this was an invitation to be loud and messy.

Anger, while one of thanatologist Elisabeth Kübler-Ross's stages of grief, doesn't have many socially approved outlets, especially for people who are expected to never show anger or who are socially punished when they do, either because of their gender or the color of their skin. Without healthy places to let it rip, our anger usually stays bottled up until a point of combustion. I look back to times I've pushed people I care about away or said something hurtful because of the way I hurt inside. I look across headlines recounting acts of violence, and I wonder how many of those violations can be traced back to a story of loss as the first domino falling, never tended to, never released. Invitations like the one from Kim helped me recognize that, oh yes, it sure did feel good to do some destroying. That, yes indeed, I did have some rage that needed releasing, and that I could do it in a way that was encouraged and contained.

Recently, Kim and I emailed about her work, discussing how Rita Project gave her a way to observe how her feelings of sadness and grief could "come and go like clouds." For her, sadness and grief weren't a constant state, but something that would shift and morph and change. Through the container of the project she discovered: "It's me who holds on to my feelings of grief so tightly sometimes. It's me who stays in it because of comfort or fear or attachment or resistance to moving on and through to the next thing, so for me, the release within the smashing was helpful."

I can still remember placing old plates, the corner of a mirror, and the ceramic chunks from the last guest's smashed remains onto a crate, then picking up a hammer and going at it. The first strike sent cobweb-shaped cracks from center to edge. The second one sent the pieces flying to opposite sides of the crate. After spending so much energy acting as a glue for my family and being part of the connective tissue for this nascent community of grievers, it felt unforeseeably pleasurable to make something, in a very low-stakes setting, release into pieces. I was tired of holding on so tight to my grief, and in that moment, I recognized that an important step on the path to repair it is its opposite.

Over the course of its fifteen-year run, Rita Project was exhibited in museums and universities across the country. Nearly five thousand people came in and out of the studios, popped up at the National College of Art and Design in Dublin; Bergamot Station, Santa Monica; and the American Visionary Art Museum in Baltimore. While Kim always provided other materials for creation—sewing machines and fabric, paints and papers, she recalls that participants usually gravitated toward the part of the room that was set up to break things. I found resonance in Kim's story—the thing she longed for didn't exist, so she created it for herself, and brought other people in with her. She wasn't a grief counselor or a therapist, although she consulted professionals to make sure that what she was building was psychologically safe. She was a griever, reaching out to other grievers, wondering if they too felt a certain kind of ache inside. And it turned out, they did.

There are other ways that we can release this destructive feeling, even without being in the container of a place like Kim's art studio. My Dinner Party cofounder, Lennon, tells the story of an aunt who brought a carton of eggs to her mom's house during the week of her funeral, and that they chucked a dozen little yolky bombs at the fence and screamed into the night of North Carolina suburbia while doing it. I helped another friend build a simple structure in her backyard that we covered in messages to her late mom, and then burned to the ground after waiting for high desert wind conditions to settle, building on the tradition of funeral pyres from around the world, in Hindu, Viking, Roman, and Sikh communities. Of course, it's up to us to seek professional help when our anger scares us or other people, and it's important to remember that we don't have to do it alone.

If you've already thought to look up Rita Project, jonesing for your own chance to partake in some facilitated destruction, chances are you won't find it. Not, at least, in the present tense. A decade after her sister's death, Kim felt, in some kind of way, complete. The pursuit to quench the thirst she felt to make messy things with her grief and find a way to relate to people over the experience of her sister's death in physical, non-verbal, untraditional ways helped to ground her after a wildly destabilizing time. As she shifted her relationship to her grief, she made the hard call to shut down Rita Project, a move that is a lesson in itself because we exist in a world where stopping something that's successful can be seen as "quitting." The Dinner Party has had its own moments of near death, as we've wrestled with how to create a non-transactional community of support while still meeting payroll. But what if these endings, these moments of destruction, weren't always framed as a failure? We can't force things to last forever. Nothing does. We can't expect the practice that held us together last month will heal us today. Maybe the ultimate medicine in grief is learning how to love hard with a loose grip.

In the years after my dad died, I developed a deep affinity for a particular blue-skinned, machete-wielding, blood-guzzling goddess. I joined, in my own small and private-until-now way, the many millions of people who worship Kali, Hindu goddess of death and destruction, taking her privately as a bit of a patron saint. I have zero connections to Hindu culture, don't know Sanskrit beyond your entry-level yoga vocabulary, or have any drop of authority on the subject—and yet, looking at her image, something within me quaked.

I've always had my eyes peeled for female role models, archetypes to look up to in a Western world predominated by male-bodied gods and leaders. While over time I've also grown to love the devotion of the

Virgin Mary and the wildness of Artemis, in the years getting used to the g-force of grief, Kali was the deity who reached out her hand, slapped me across the face, and helped me get back on my feet.

Part of coming into a relationship with grief has always been an intimacy with the way life can be absolutely brutal. That for as much as our time on earth can be filled with softness and cookies and orgasms and the fresh-baked-bread smell of a baby, it is also violent and bone-breaking and unjust. Oftentimes, those of us who are grieving have come really close to that sharp knife's edge, the part that destroys, that takes a life sooner than we thought warranted, that tears a family in two, that detonates our plans with no warning and certainly no apology.

I've always been perplexed by the argument that, if there is a God, "he" wouldn't allow terrible things to happen to people. That no benevolent creator would ever allow for famine or cancer, mass shootings or the countless other atrocities that launch us into grief. Kali wears a garland of skulls around her neck, and her foot is usually hoisted on the back of a man she's seemingly knocked to the ground. I've learned that he's often Shiva, her husband, who has rightly surrendered to her wrath. In studying Kali, I found a role model who didn't distract from the pain of destruction, but who wears it as an accessory, who sticks her tongue out, cheeky and terrifying.

Many people interpret her collection of heads as a representation of killing the ego, the part of us that feels superior to the world around us; the part of us that feels separate from the natural system, which is the same part of us that likes to pretend we can outsmart death. In grief, we feel the swift slice of her sword; the rolling skull, the part of us that hoped our nearest and dearest were immune from mortality. We come into direct contact with the universe belly-laughing for thinking we were so special; pointing to our still-beating heart and asking us what we'll make of our remaining breath.

Kali helped me realize there's a way of relating to grief that isn't a hand-wringing lamentation, a sadness to be gotten over. It doesn't have to be met with the blank look thrown at me by so many adults in my life who didn't know what to say in the months after my dad's death. With Kali, grief is met with the opposite of a blank state; it's a stuck-out tongue, a pat on the head, a slap on the ass. What I was looking for wasn't timidness or pity, but tough love. Someone, *anyone*, who could represent the part of the human spirit that can hold the totality of life and death in one image; who could recognize that the thing that had happened to my family—that happens eventually in every family—wasn't some freakish aberration, but an extraordinarily ordinary part of life.

Part of destruction as a care practice means accepting the reality and the fragileness of our existence, which will leave us someday as dust. In Kali, I found a role model who could clean the blood off her blade and ask, *So what?* Who could put me in my place—and put my grief in perspective—as another step in the cosmic choreography. Someone who modeled facing dead-on the hardship of loss, and yet didn't give up on life.

So what will you break, burn, bury, or otherwise destroy? What will you let go of, with the kind of dramatic flare that mirrors what you're feeling inside? And who are the people you can find to cheer you on, as you see just how much power you're packing, even in, especially in, your grief?

# NAVIGATING BIG DAYS

THE END-OF-YEAR HOLIDAYS HAVE BEEN referred to as the Bermuda Triangle of Grief, a stretch of the ocean that's as harrowing as it gets for boats and planes trying to make the trip. Getting through Halloween clear into the New Year can be a grin-and-bear-it time of year for people with empty chairs at the family table, or no family table to return to at all. Then there are the death anniversaries and birthdays of our lates and greats scattered like rogue waves and whirlpools across the rest of the year.

Given what a gnarly time these occasions can be, a frequently asked question at Dinner Party Tables is how to handle the Big Days? Over the years, we've heard of so many ways that people handle events or celebrate anniversaries following a loss. Some people end up stumbling their way, over time, to a new version of an old tradition. Others buck the old ways for new ones. Either way, embracing Renegade Grief is finding a version of marking these days that works for you—whether you decide to re-create, remix, or revolt.

One way I see grievers approach Big Days is to stay true and steady to the ways they used to celebrate with their person by re-creating traditions to the best of their ability despite their gaping absence. They might not be physically present, but it can feel really good to have the consistency of that pastime continue. To know that, even if someone's not there, you can still go back to familiar places.

And then there are the traditions that we've been expecting to participate in our whole lives, which might look a lot different when we arrive there if our person isn't present. When I got married, it felt like arriving at the highest level of the Grief Video Game, the face-off with the Big Boss of Father Loss. As a ritual, weddings are remarkably oriented around the bride being "given away" by her dad. At countless Dinner Party Tables, I've heard the inner musings of women who had lost their fathers and wondered, *But what about my wedding day?*, and I had wondered the same thing too.

It was not Pinterest or a wedding planner's to-do list that helped me prepare for the grief-dimension of our wedding. It was the friends I met through The Dinner Party who were ready and able to think through re-creating these traditions in a way that felt true to me, mostly because they had grappled with them too. Conversations with fellow grievers normalized the part of the process that was sometimes serrated with the sharpness of loss, and who inspired me with their own renegade variations of wedding traditions. I learned that there's so much more to do than just a moment of silence or an empty seat; rituals that go beyond recognizing their absence, and instead, invite in their presence.

I learned about art pieces hung at ceremony sites, and excerpts in ceremony programs. I heard about incorporating a sentimental object into a floral bouquet, or picking a wedding date or venue that reminded you of them in some way. There were nontraditional responses to the "first dance question," and stories of being walked down the aisle not by a father, but by a brother, a beloved pet, a group of friends. And then there was always the option to not do anything—to do you, whether that meant eloping or opting out of any kind of recognition of the loss. At all these intersections we're met with options, and as renegade grievers, we get to choose.

In the end, our wedding was not without grief, but it was also sublime. Both can be true at the same time. My dad found his way into our wedding in ways that were very planned—that favorite email about the expanding universe was read during our ceremony, that favorite family dish of arroz con pollo served as our main course, his grandmother's crochet work hung over our altar. There were also some quiet surprises. A seventy-degree day in October after six weeks of rain. A bald eagle, with its bird's-eye view and majesty, circling the ceremony site. And the biggest blessing of them all, my husband, the person who has become my fiercest supporter and my dearest sense of home, in it with me.

When I close my eyes and wonder if my dad approves, never having met my husband—I see an enthusiastic thumbs-up, and strangely, the face he made while playing the piano or in the midst of a really good meal; the face of savoring life, of losing himself in the acts he loved; encouraging me to keep doing the same.

* * *

Sometimes we're forced to rethink a day and what we want it to represent. Re-creating it, no longer an option. Forgetting it, impossible. At those times, the thing we might want to do is remix. Take some elements of what worked in the past, or what we remember doing with our person, but transmute it into something new altogether.

A moving example of the remix happens every Valentine's Day in Parkland, Florida. Before 2018, February 14 was a day full of fun and affection on campus, with students exchanging candy, cards, and flowers. But after seventeen students and staff members were killed on campus one Valentine's Day, the holiday would never be the same.

As the first Valentine's Day after the shooting approached, school officials worked closely with Dr. David Schonfeld, a leading pediatric bereavement doctor and founder of the National Center for School Crisis and Bereavement. Dr. Schonfeld, a father himself, is often on the next plane with colleagues of his when a school shooting happens, supporting students and school communities in how to find their way back together after a shattering tragedy.

But what to do now? Should the school close for the anniversary of the shooting, giving everyone the day off? In many ways this would have been the easiest path forward. But it would have denied students access to much-needed counseling and the community that many might need. It is difficult for educators to support students when they themselves are feeling many of the same painful emotions, but if the school shut its doors, then what? They were eager to find a way to honor the day that served the various needs of community members.

That's when the idea of a Day of Service and Love emerged, and which is now a yearly event. Instead of classes, students at Marjory Stoneman Douglas High School and schools across the district—Broward County Public Schools serve over 250,000[17] students and is one of the largest districts in the country—would participate in a service-learning day, taking part in projects inspired by the memory of the seventeen victims. The Day of Service and Love[18] was districtwide, and they have made this a yearly event. Attendance was optional, but across the course of the day, students at Marjory Stoneman Douglas hosted a gratitude breakfast for first responders, and dug into service projects to honor victims, such as cleaning up a beach to honor a victim's love of the ocean. Students, staff, and the broader community gathered in a local park for commemorative activities and additional service projects, including hand-packing specifically formulated meals for undernourished children for distribution to a network of more than sixty countries.

The school, with guidance from the National Center for School Crisis and Bereavement, informed parents of the range of responses they might expect from their kids on this day. Some kids might present as fine but be wracked with fear and anxiety on the inside. For others, this loss experience might compound the grief they feel related to a different loss—such as an unrelated death of a close family member or friend. They might be embarrassed to mention that they're feeling sad, feeling like they should be "over it by now." Parents were advised not to force their kids to talk, but to be open to their emotions and fears. And that distress might present itself in different ways—lack of sleep, loss of appetite, irritability, risky behaviors—not just in the expected personification of grief, such as tears and sadness.

In many ways, the ongoing work happening at Marjory Stoneman Douglas is creating a new case study of how communities respond to the ongoing impacts of a major loss experience—how not to default to the easier path of avoiding hard memories by canceling classes for the day, but to create a space for the collective to bring forth something meaningful and good. Instead of processing alone, they're processing together. Instead of a passive memorial, they're creating something together. Instead of focusing on death, they focus on life.

And then, let us not forget, there's the revolt option for Big Days. The "Fuck it. Let's throw it in the wind." The invitation to recognize that there's a completely different way to spend such days, ways that might intentionally not carry any reminders of the past.

After spending some years trying to celebrate Christmas the way it used to be, my brother, cousin, and I opted for a Christmas Day that my dad would have likely been horrified by. We subbed out the nostalgic tradition of a long walk and an even longer cooked meal, Christmas albums and slow present unwrapping, stockings hung with care and stuffed with his childhood ritual of walnuts and clementines, for some mainstream theme park energy.

Throwing tradition to the wind, we washed down weed gummies with lattes and pastries, before being one of the first families in line at Universal Studios on Christmas morning. We dallied in The Wizarding World of Harry Potter, chugging Butterbeers and riding roller coasters. We played trivia games in line, and instead of exchanging presents, we each got magic wands from the gift shop. Later that night, we made coq au vin in an Instant Pot, cracked open a big red, and danced to Chaka Khan.

Our sadness at his absence was still there, but there was a new sense of freedom, too, because together we were rewriting the rules of what would make the holiday meaningful. Continuing with the old way of doing things had felt less like a touchstone of tradition and more like a burden. When approaching these Big Days, you have to be willing to actively ask, *What are the things that I want or need to let go of? And is there a different way to go about this day, that might feel foreign, but could be a whole new tradition in the making?*

There are other kinds of Big Days too. The ones that we don't see looming on the calendars, and that we step into thinking it'll be fine, but then find ourselves sinking as the day goes on, quicksand-style. You find out that you are pregnant and due the same week as your mom's death anniversary. You step in for the daddy-daughter dance at your twin sister's wedding since your dad has been dead for years, and after being strong for her big day, the wave of grief hits you when you're back in your Brooklyn apartment, alone. You spend time with your sister's new baby on a random Tuesday, and your heart feels like it could just stop beating because your daughter should be there too.

All of these are examples of the "Surprise!" days of grief, and they can fall even when we're years out from our loss event. It's on these days that we need our people; the numbers in our phone that we can ring as we walk home from a family event where we felt like the only path forward was forcing a smile, or sitting in the car, waylaid by a wave of grief that seemed to come from nowhere.

On these days, we have our grief emergency kits—the things we know give us comfort, the friendships we've cultivated who get it, and if we have neither of those things squared away, we do our best to find them, like preparing for a rainy day.

So as you prepare for the next grief holiday, with whatever ritual you might be inspired by, or whether you're giving yourself permission to go totally off script, do this one thing for yourself: Lean into a friendship with someone who can sit with you in your grief. Find a buddy who you can reflect with before, during, and after, even if over text, because while those days of grief might catch us off guard, we don't have to go them alone. And give yourself the grace of knowing the brutal truth: there will only ever be more anniversaries, holidays, and annual reminders of your loss—so you've got plenty of time to try something new, rework what feels terrible, lean into what feels good, and get ever more skilled at navigating waters when they're choppy, and appreciating the days that are glassy and smooth.

# GRIEF QUESTING

SOMETIMES THE WAY TO HONOR our past requires us to get out of the same four walls we've been living in during an illness; to break out of a routine; to push back against the idea that our grief is something we need to tend to in privacy. What if, along with turning inward during times of loss, we let ourselves turn outward, to sun our innermost folds of grief in the bright sunlight of the wild, wide world we live in?

There's a genre of story that I file under a slightly nerdy frame of *grief quest*. They differ in particulars, but all revolve around a person who's experienced a significant loss, embarking on some outing with a spirit of adventure.

The grief quests I've been captivated by are ones where someone embarks on a trip with a specific intention around their loss, be it a piece of unfinished business they want to complete, a memory that feels important for them to make, or tracking down some experience they crave. In accepting the mission of the grief quest, they unlock a new way of relating to themselves, the person they lost, as well as to other living people who are navigating through their own parallel grief quest, knowingly or otherwise.

Don't get me wrong though; our grief doesn't get stopped at customs. We can't throw it off our scent as we leap across time zones or leave it at basecamp while we summit a mountain. This isn't a high-speed car chase, with our grief trailing us until we finally shake it. Grief quests are about finding a new angle to our grief because being in motion, as well as the exposure to new people and ways of thinking, might be the only way we can get in the right frame of mind to tend to our grief. Honoring our past doesn't mean we need to stay in the last place we saw our person; honoring our past often asks us to retrace steps or find a new setting where we can feel we are in our relationship with them on the other side of their death, anew.

When it comes to a grief quest, it really doesn't matter whether it's a day trip or a monthslong sojourn; whether you're journeying to a place that's already familiar or visiting it for the first time; whether it's rugged and intense, or the kind of quest where you're stretched out on a picnic blanket watching the clouds pass overhead. What matters is that we embark with a clear intention around the question we're exploring, without an attachment to the outcome.

But before we can take a grief quest, we'll need to reckon with the ways in which it can be hard to get away. For many of us, a particular aftershock of a death loss is a debilitating financial strain. When you're scrambling to make up for a lost paycheck or to cover medical and funerary costs, there's often no extra capacity for time away, even when it's sorely needed.

Given there is no federal mandate around bereavement leave, someone working a job can be fired for missing work, even if the reason for their absence is the death of someone dear to them. The system we live in doesn't encourage us to get space and perspective around a loss; instead, it encourages us to keep up. While many states are getting better at protecting families at the beginning of life, in the form of parental leave, we're still working on how to support families dealing with the other side of life. At the time of writing, thirteen states had a paid leave policy to take care of sick family members, and yet "there is currently no federal law providing or guaranteeing access to paid family and medical leave for workers in the private sector."[19]

While many major airlines offer bereavement fares, those aren't likely to apply for "grief quests"—and there's, alas, still no Make a Wish Foundation for people who are grieving. What might our world look like if everyone who experienced a loss got the space and time they needed to be present with their grief and heal? How much more "productive" and peaceful might we be if, in the seasons of our life where we get the wind knocked out of us, we don't have to pretend to be able to breathe?

I've always been amazed by the stories of renegade grievers who do what they need to do to get the space they're longing for. Whether it's a day off or a month, it's powerful to find ways to slip out of the grind and honor this person's impact on your life, and to answer the call to adventure that their absence might bring.

Going back to work after their mom's passing, Becca realized that waking up to the sound of their alarm, getting dressed and taking the train to their job in higher education, commuting back on the same train line to eat dinner at home followed by an episode or two of reality TV, then waking up and doing it all over again, was an excruciating Groundhog Day.

*Now what?* was the question Becca was asking themselves after their mother, Deborah, died of frontotemporal dementia and ALS. Years of caretaking, of flying between their home city of Chicago and Philadelphia, where they lived; years of living with a diagnosis that had zero possibility of recovery; years of watching their mother, a feminist and an academic and an all-round fierce woman, transform into an unrecognizable mind and brittle body. Their mother's death meant that their whole world had changed because they had been altered by both the experience of losing her, as well as by the years of caretaking that had come before. And yet the rinse-repeat feeling of their life was not reflecting the immense shift that had taken place. So Becca, in their mid-twenties, with no dependents and some savings tucked away and the privilege to spend part of the upcoming year not prioritizing an income, pulled the ripcord.

As they put it to me, "There are times in life when we don't have to be in the grind. Being able to feel and recognize those moments is really powerful. I was in full-on survival mode and needed to make a change."

If you're contemplating a grief quest, there might be some bread-crumbs your person left for you. For one friend, his quest instructions were explicit—his mother asked him to scatter her ashes in three places she held dear, a framework for the different trips he'll take over the course of his life.

For another friend named Angel, in the months after her husband Rob's death, the only thing that sounded slightly enticing was a road trip through the Scottish Highlands, visiting towns she'd read about in *Outlander*. She had postponed her destination wedding when Rob was diagnosed with cancer. She explained that "on a day of willful defiance against his illness, we officially got married in a small ceremony. It was so spur-of-the-moment that the only person from my family in atten-dance was my mother. Rob died ten days later." Left with the budget for a wedding and honeymoon that never happened, she decided to visit the places in the historical fiction book series whose pages kept her company during the long, lonely weeks at the hospital.

In other instances, we're left wondering, *Where do we go? Which di-rection to drive in?* Even just asking can help you get a clear answer on what is calling for your honoring and attention.

Part of what inspired Becca to leave their job was a brown leather journal that their mother had kept while on a trip to Europe when she herself was in her twenties. In the journal's pages, filled with their mother's familiar handwriting, Becca found the inspiration for how they wanted to spend this time in their life—to create space for their grief.

"Deborah's European Adventure" was something Becca had heard about growing up, but in the pages of the journal, different sides of their mom's story revealed themselves. There was the love affair with a Palestinian man, whom Becca's ardently Jewish mom had fallen for while in London. A harrowing incident in Rome that Becca had never heard about. And along the way, the colorful day-to-day detailing of the trials and tribulations of traveling with close friends in the days before email or cell phones.

Becca taught me how traveling after times of loss can be revelatory, healing, and right. In the blog they kept over their two months on the road, they oscillated between updating friends and family, and writing directly to their mom: "In this moment, I feel extraordinarily grateful to have this time, to intentionally reflect on everything that's happened over the last few years (and the twentysomething years before that). Thank you for taking copious notes on your life—and this trip—so that thirty-eight years later, most unexpectedly, I could trace your steps and live my way into the answers."

Becca's own trip had complicated aspects. They were both mourning their mother and also facing some of the complicated aspects of their relationship. With this trip, Becca saw another way to know their mother. "I wanted to understand who she was before things got really hard in her own life," they told me. The trip also allowed Becca to process their grief in unexpected ways. Writing directly to Deborah, they explained the effect of physically visiting the same places their mother had traveled:

> One thing I've noticed is that some of my strongest waves of grief come from a sensory experience—a smell, a taste, a sound. It's why so often on this trip, the moments when I feel most connected to you consist of a particularly good bite of roast chicken from the Rotisserie counter at Harrods, the sound of an Ella Fitzgerald or Bob Dylan song streaming through a window, the smell of an old book at a bookstore (I went to your favorite, Shakespeare and Co., this afternoon and left you a little note on a wall where people write from all over the world).

Oftentimes when we think of a quest, we think of a solo journey, a lone soul out on the open road. However, solitude was the last thing Becca wanted. A highlight of the trip was when Becca's dad and sibling joined them on the trip for some silly sibling shenanigans that years of caretaking for their dying mom had made it hard to access.

Laughing, Becca shares with me how the siblings found a red pepper at a market in Italy and decided to carve a face on it, naming the pepper Deborah. "We decided we were going to show our mom Italy in the form of this pepper, and we carried it around for the rest of the day."

It's weird as hell, but to me, this is the exact type of place we can get to when we slip out of the grind of our default world. Playful, funny, creative, and weird, writing our own version of the story, finding out our own silly, quirky, lighthearted ways of continuing bonds. It can be our own version of the hero's journey, our own epic story of how we managed to have fun, even in the face of such sadness.

Sometimes, when we hear the call to quest, to explore a part of ourselves while out in the world around us, it's not pretty or easy or chill. There are lots of ways that grief quests can test us. But that doesn't mean we shouldn't heed the call. It's just good to go into them ready to stay alert for the watch-outs.

We might find that our quests sort of let us down, that the thing we think we're going to find isn't there after all. One Dinner Partier flew to China, hoping for a cathartic release in the arms of his mother's blood relatives. He was sure that he'd find a transcendent connection to the ancestral home, cinematic soundtrack playing in the background and all. But his trip to his late mother's homeland kind of sucked. His grandmother sobbed for the first ten minutes they were there, and then his mom didn't get mentioned for the rest of the trip. His dad had also since remarried, but he hadn't shared the news with his mother's family, and they had to keep that whole new-wife thing a secret. While it was beautiful to taste the flavors that reminded him of his mother's kitchen, he didn't leave feeling like some big blockage had been moved in the interior of his grief. It was during a later trip with friends to South America, however, where he found the relief he had been searching for and from which he returned home ready to set up his own kitchen, where he could then continue his mom's recipes. His trip to China wasn't what he wanted, but it helped him get to where he inevitably wanted to go.

In some instances, we might not get external validation for the quest we are longing for, or we might get criticized by people who usually tend to care. Rachel Alger, a writer grappling with the depths of despair after losing her sister, felt like the only place that might take the edge off her grief was the corporate, clean, color-pop world of Disney World. At first she resisted the idea. Disney wasn't her thing. It wasn't even a multiverse she particularly associated with her sister, beyond watching some Disney films together as girls. She assumed going there, being in a crowd of happy families skipping around with rainbow-swirl lollipops and smiles, would be an absolute nightmare. She was sure that the "happiest place on earth" would be a grave reminder of her sorrow. She also despised the capitalism of it. And she didn't have kids who she could justify the trip for. But in the dark cave of her grief, something about the magic castle kept calling to her. So she decided that she needed to go.

Going from living in the shadows of her home to a summer day at the park felt like reentering the world of the living. The sounds, smells, colors, and lights overwhelmed her. She needed to yank herself out of her shock. A safe reentry, where stakes were low, where snacks were abundant, and where everywhere you looked, something or someone was strategically placed to surprise and delight. There was something about the container of that place that felt safe, and safe was what she needed. She's since returned several times. She feels connected to her sister there, not because they have memories littered throughout the park, but because of the opposite. Because in this hyperreality, something happens that lets her wake up a little more to the reality of life without her sister, candy-coating and all. Her family and friends don't get it—and side-eye at her now-annual trip to Disney—but she persists.

Grief quests don't have to be as elaborate as going to Europe or planning an annual trip to Disney. Not everyone has the privilege, financial means, or life flexibility to go on their preferred quest, so sometimes we must get creative with what's available to us. For one of our community members, COVID-era travel restrictions meant that she couldn't fly to the Philippines where her dad was facing his final days; and even after travel restrictions were lifted, the cost was too prohibitive for her to take the time off work and be there in person. She's now saving up for the trip, which she knows she'll take one day, but in the meantime, she's found a local version of a quest that she does on her days off work.

She goes to her local beach with a towel and her journal, a thermos of tea and layers, depending on the time of day. She sits facing the ocean and checks in with her dad. Memories wash in with the surf, and the waves carry out her heavy exhales. She takes breaks from journaling to stare out to the horizon line, and even though she's not on her ancestral lands, looking at the place where the sea knits into the sky gives her the feeling of safety and calm that her father's presence once provided.

In mythologist Joseph Campbell's definition of a hero's journey,[20] the hero returns but they're never quite the same afterward. There's a homecoming, but there's still some separation from the familiar sights and people they find there. Grief feels a lot like this too. We might return home, but our world is a little tilted in a new way. Over time, though, we reorient, and what was tilted becomes our new upright. Holding that paradox, we can arrive at a place of some Jedi-ability. When we return home, we realize that the form has shifted, once when our person died, and again upon our return. Change is the one thing we can rely on.

Becca wrote about it beautifully: "The dictionary definition of resilience reads: 'the capacity to recover quickly from difficulties.' I know now that I will not recover quickly from my mom's death. I may not even 'recover' at all. What I do know is that her death has taught me how I want to live—with joy, gratitude, adventure, and hope. This trip is only the beginning."

Now, years after that first trip, Becca is no longer in "quest mode." They're grateful for the closure they got on that trip and say that they would do it again one thousand times over. However, questing is no longer the way they're tending to their grief. They're settling down after a move back to their native city of Chicago. Older now, the idea of sleeping in hostels with a bunch of strangers is no longer appealing. "I was in survival mode. Now I'm in building mode," they tell me. But that's not to say that grief quests need to happen in a certain phase of life. Becca's starting a family of their own, and dreams of the day they'll take their own kids to some of Deborah's favorite haunts, embarking on a quest with a different intention.

In one of the top corners of her brown leather journal, Deborah had scribbled the lyrics to the Barbra Streisand song "The Way We Were" in red ink across the top of a page: "And if we had the chance to do it all again, tell me—would we? Could we?" It's what we all often wonder. Grief quests require a leap into some kind of unknown, a carving out of space for our own curiosity, pleasure, and healing. Might they be challenging? Certainly. Will we regret them? The bigger regret might be never seeing what there is to learn from our loss, and ourselves, in the backdrop of a different place.

Honoring our past is not a stage that's ever completed, a box fully checked. To really defy the cultural norms that whisper to us that grief is something to get over, that bonds are worth breaking, we spend time over the course of our lives honoring those who have come before us. We look for stories, the pathways to stay connected to the recently departed, and those departed long before them. We spend time remembering our ancestors, because within each of our histories is a great-great-grandparent practiced in ways of holding grief that we might miss, deep in our bones, even if it's new information to our brains.

Each time we look in the rearview mirror, we revisit the wisdom that's there for us, and it mirrors back our own transformation in the miles we've traveled. We've grown, and our relationship to the past shifts and deepens. We learn how to use our rearview mirror as a tool to navigate our loss; yet our gaze never fully rests there, lest we miss the exit on the road ahead. Because once we've spent time sitting with the histories and relationships and realizations of the past, it's time to tend to our grief in the present tense.

# ACT 2

# BEING WITH YOUR PRESENT

IN THE EARLY DAYS OF The Dinner Party, we'd invite people to introduce themselves with their name and whose death—well, life, really—had brought them to the Table. Later, we added a question: "Where are you at with your loss right now?"

This addition was inspired by one of our first hosts in the Bay Area, a tattooed bicycle messenger named Lindsay. With an impeccable nose for bullshit, Lindsay had noticed that stories shared around the table had started sounding a little rehearsed. Understandable enough. People were likely a little nervous, having accepted an invitation to a stranger's house to talk about a thing they had gotten good at avoiding. Instead of a one-off gathering, Dinner Partiers were signing up to be a part of the same Table of people gathering consistently over time, often monthly, or every other month. After dinner three of four, it was no longer the time to rehash the overdose, the diagnosis, the death, but turn our attention toward the present tense.

What Lindsay was tuning into was the sort of narrative autopilot we can slip into when we share certain stories—always telling them the same way, with the same beats. You know the ones, the stories where there might once have been real emotion attached to it, but whatever it was, it's drained away in all the anticipatory rehearsing and retelling. Lindsay's suggestion allowed everyone at the Table to confront their grief as it existed in the present tense. Instead of rehashing a story from the past—like that unbelievable thing my great-aunt said at the funeral; or imagining the future, like, how I am going to become a mom someday without my mom—but to ask, *Where is my grief within this moment of my life?*

In shifting from autopilot to authentic updates, what Lindsay was uncovering was a simple question that sets a poignant tone, one that dismisses the pretending we do in grief from the Table. And by leading with her answer, everyone else is given the social permission to stop brushing off or holding back too. Suddenly, the airwaves are open for a new and powerful kind of connection, the ones that so many of us are craving. These bonds, the real antidotes to the loneliness and disconnection at the root of our struggles with grief culture, are often just a question away.

Try it. Think of your loss experience. Replay the versions of the story you've gotten comfortable sharing on first dates or during conversations with friends. Notice the way you might soften the experience or segue out of your story to minimize making the other person uncomfortable. It might even feel cemented into your mouth like the Pledge of Allegiance or a poem you've memorized. How does it feel to share it? Is it coming more from your head or from your heart? How many times have you said that same string of words?

And then ask, what's coming up for me today? As I read this page? Over the past couple weeks? What are the quiet or loud ways grief is presenting itself in this intersection of my life? Are there things happening in my world that maybe don't lead with a story of grief, but when I take a breath and a deeper look, I can see how my response is tinted with my loss? The question "Where are you at with your loss right now?" is really an invitation to be present. It requires us to not only listen to other people, but to more thoughtfully listen to ourselves.

Often, when we take the time to assess, our responses can surprise us. We might grow more conscious of how deeply sad we feel, despite our attempts to make everything okay, or we may find we are oddly detached. The thing that's bugging us at work, the family dynamics that feel haggard, the friendship that feels distant, humming with grief. When we don't slip into our rehearsed stories, we can be present to the truths we might be hurrying over or avoiding. As they get clarified and verbalized, something inside us can shift. By shining a light on our present-tense inner landscape, we can stop expending the energy to avoid or ignore, to force or pretend, and come face-to-face with where we're really at and what is really true.

If I tell you about my grief, I can relay the moment of my dad's passing, the cancer diagnosis, the seizures, the tears, the tequila we had saved for his remission celebration that we drank straight from the bottle around his deathbed, the rough grappling with life in the immediate after. And admittedly, I can tell you all of that without really feeling much. I've had years of practice. And that's not a bad thing. Over the years, I've come to a place of greater acceptance and sensitization—it's relatively great to be asked about my parents, and to be able to calmly respond that my dad is dead, without needing to expend any emotional energy. It's become a fact of my life, like my social security number or that my hair is red.

But if you ask me about where my grief is today, it currently lives in smaller details of my life. Like planning a trip to meet my newborn nephew, José Fernandez V, and feeling the gravitas of inheriting his grandfather's grandfather's name. It's in the details of planning a wedding, and the quiet question my mom asked me of who would be walking me down the aisle. It's in the part of me that's writing this book and recognizing the twisted wish that he was around to be my first reader.

The grief has diffused, no longer a poignant headline, but a backdrop to everything else; occasionally it's an ache, but more often it's a low frequency I can tune in to at almost any time. I'm sure new chapters of my grief story will sprout up, likely until the end of my own life. I've learned that if I don't take the time to honor them for what they are, the feelings will come spewing out in other ways. Keeping myself from blowing up unexpectedly means taking moments to slow down and return to the present moment; acknowledging the feeling when it arises, an old friend by now, often presenting itself in new or nuanced ways.

So the question for us is how do we find ways to stay in the present moment—to tend to it like the companion it inevitably becomes, without trying to fix it. Dr. Mary-Frances O'Connor calls this "accepting," which she describes as a process of self-observation, not to be confused with "acceptance," which implies at a certain point we permanently change how a situation is viewed and move on. For Dr. O'Connor, "the key to accepting is not doing anything with what you are experiencing; not asking what your feelings mean, or how long they will last. Accepting is not about pushing them away and saying that you cannot bear it. It is not about believing that you are now a broken person." It's about building a practice of tending to your grief when it shows up—and the stories in the following chapters are ways of doing just that.

After many years of supporting individual Tables or hosting small retreats of a dozen or so Partiers, The Dinner Party staff pulled off a triumphant feat a few years back and brought more than one hundred people from our community together, from across the country and loss types and lived experiences, at an old-school family camp in the Wisconsin woods for a weekend of very much being in the present moment. In the closing ceremony, before folks piled back onto buses and headed to the airport, one of our hosts from Philadelphia, Mark, made a rousing speech. During it, Mark honored Dinner Partiers for the ways in which grief has forced us to, in the words of comedian Jaboukie, "raw dog reality." A reference to unprotected intercourse became a lewd and exquisite comparison to living with loss—no longer protected, no longer holding back, crystal clear about the stakes of our own mortality. Feelings of innocence and safety are often a little harder to access after a major loss. His congratulations to the hundred other campers in the room came from a place of real acknowledgment of how hard-core it can be to show up for yourself and care for your grief. The room clapped and howled back at Mark. Everybody got it.

Being present with grief is being present with some of the deepest, most aching realities of life. It is both tender and metal, all in one breath. By being here, you are actively engaged in this work. By finding your people to be present with, in your own answer to our question, and in their responses, too, you are also raw dogging reality; and you too are deserving of a roomful of applause.

I recently received a group email from Lindsay, whose insight about staying in the present moment of grief forever changed how I see this work. The email was sent out the afternoon of her forty-fourth birthday. It was a big one, as she was turning the age her mother was when she died. Becoming "that age" is one of those grief milestones that, as Lindsay discovered, you can anticipate in all kinds of ways, but you won't know it until it arrives. Until you're in its presence.

She wrote, real as ever, that it was "surreal and sad to look at our dying parent's life through eyes that have lived the same number of years they had." She shared some of the questions she was holding, that she would ask her mom if she could: "What was she most worried about? Did she feel cheated? What is it like to plan and work toward a life and then lose it? Was she scared to leave her children behind? Did she find peace within the chaos?"

In this email, written to a group of us in the club, Lindsay was letting herself sit with the real sadness of the day, knowing "it will not be permanent. I will turn toward the excitement I feel at being like her: strong-minded, smart, funny, and determined to forge my own path."

But she's not sugarcoating it. She recognized just how much the temperature of her grief might be turned up as she takes this particular lap around the sun, and the one to follow—surpassing her mother's lifespan. A flurry of photos of her adorable preschooler followed. A head nodding as each of us read, wondering, too, how it will feel to hit that age. A knowledge that, when the time comes, we'll have people who can be present with us in it, whatever it brings.

# ESCAPING

THE IDEA OF BEING PRESENT with your grief might evoke virtuous images of letting ashes blow in the wind like dandelion seeds; days spent flipping through family photo albums; or crossing the finish line of a charity run in honor of your person. Yes, Renegade Grief at different times in your journey might look like all those things to you.

But it's also renegade to recognize that the thing your grief might be calling for is to find the off switch. Or if there's not one to be found, to turn the volume up on something else in your life to drown out the noise that all this grappling with death can stir up. Fantasy football. National politics. *FBoy Island.* Sometimes the best next thing we can do to tend to our grief is find a way to change the channel, in whatever form that takes.

You might be relieved to get this permission to turn away. You might be doubly relieved to hear that it's not just self-help conjecture but backed by some field-changing psychology research led by scholars Margaret Stroebe and Henk Schut.

Their theory, known as the dual-process model[1] of coping with bereavement, is rooted in the observation that in grief we oscillate between two different modes of being: one where we are actively working through the real-life stressors of losing someone (like cleaning out our dead cousin's dorm room), and another where we're seeking a break from grief, even actively avoiding having to deal. As Stroebe and Schut argue, the second mode isn't some kind of failure. It's a critical part of how we learn to live with our loss.

This likely feels intuitively true to you. Some days you're vibrating with all the feelings and looking for better ways to find meaning with what's happened, and some days you're absolutely wrecked. And on other days, you might just want to shout "Check please!" at the grief buffet and get out. What's so helpful about Stroebe and Schut's model is knowing that oscillating back and forth isn't something to fight, but to embrace.

When we can find ways to healthfully escape, oftentimes that is paradoxically where we can also find the heart of our healing. Escaping is just as much the work of grief as is weeping. That in grief we're learning how to titrate our emotions, find the ways to lift up and out of it, and then reenter back into it, refueled by the reasons we love to be alive, no matter how outrageous or niche or nerdy that escape may be.

For my sibling Claire (they/them), their escape came in the form of fantasy worlds. On the surface, the fantasy genre might present itself as a reprieve. Upon deeper investigation, Claire's escape revealed a kaleidoscope of myths and lessons helping them make sense of their darkest days and sourcing the strength through fiction to get through challenging passageways in the default world.

Claire was a fan of fantastical worlds long before our dad died. When other students at their Catholic school dressed up as cheerleaders and football players on Halloween, they opted for a spooky werewolf mask and didn't take it off all day. While other kids spent summers in mesh scrimmage vests at soccer camp, Claire preferred a chain-mail overshirt worn to the local Ren Faire, where they learned how to shoot a bullseye with a bow and arrow, and developed a taste for mead.

A.D., or "after our dad's death," fantastical worlds became an even bigger refuge for Claire. Yet Tolkien novels had finite pages, and Star Trek made only so many episodes of the original season. Fan fiction forums, where fellow lovers of far-out worlds could elaborate on characters and themes, allowed Claire a never-ending supply of their favorite escape. Whether reading, or writing, Claire was hooked. I asked Claire later if this was smutty stuff, assuming the lure was tied up in the potential erotic tension between Star Trek's Spock and Captain Kirk. But it wasn't that. "Writing about how my favorite characters dealt with situations that mirrored my own—whether it was my first breakup, or Dad dying, gave me a way to experiment with my own choice and response," they told me. For Claire, fantastical storylines allowed them to play out different scenarios, removed from the specificity and personal attachments of their own life.

When Claire first played Dungeons & Dragons, the cult-classic tabletop game from the 1970s, now deep in its grand twenty-first-century resurgence, they were pulled in by the way in which one game could go in an infinite number of directions. The premise is simple, the outcomes limitless. You play with a board and dice and set characters to navigate a plot narrated by the Dungeon Master, a role of container-setter and conversation engine that's not dissimilar to the role of host at our Dinner Party Tables. What Claire loved about D&D was the expansiveness of the worlds, the characters, the storylines. Anything could happen. Anything might. Video games could only take you as far as the developer had designed; there is always an external wall in that world, a place where your character could try to march forward but might end up running in place—something that if you're deep in grief can feel like way too direct of a metaphor. And in connecting with a local weekly D&D table, the game offered the opposite of those walls and the isolation of single-player games.

A game of D&D represents a shared experience with at least three other humans at the table who are all open to improvising, listening, and responding. The game requires its players to lean on one another, to hold a shared image of an imagined world in their mind's eye, and to decide how to navigate conflict together. Whether the conflict on the board was directly related to navigating a death, or simply a way to weave a social safety net more tightly between a group of players, it was through these unseen worlds that Claire found their most solid footing in grief.

After hearing stories told of Claire's fantastical favorites, our brother José and I asked to join in. Without our dad in his family role of initiating time together, it was up to us kids to find time to connect. A weird silver lining meant that instead of doing the yacht-rock activities he enjoyed—unnecessarily long walks, alphabetizing his CDs, washing his car in the driveway—we now got to take turns picking the agenda.

I had moved from Los Angeles out to the Mojave Desert, and my siblings came to stay with me for the weekend. But our real destination? The Lost Mines of Phandelver, a day's walk outside the town of Phandalin, where a few good townsmen had gone missing, or so posited Claire, our Dungeon Master. We named characters, defined our skills, and blew good luck breath on the litany of dice.

It was the first time we were dedicating a day to play together since our dad died, and it felt radical. We opted out of the default conversations of sibling time: catching up on work and relationships, shooting the shit about movies we'd seen, venting about family dynamics, all topics inevitably circling the newly gaping hole at the center of our world. Instead, we played in this imaginary world where anything was possible and nothing off-limits, and it was surprisingly liberating. That weekend, we weren't just three grieving siblings. Two of us were crusaders, an orc and a Druid, attempting to rescue strangers from goblins, and one of us was a Dungeon Master, keeping score.

After hours of campaigning inside, splayed on the floor amid a litter of note pads, chip bags and seltzer cans, we would move the game outside in the evening. All was quiet except for the occasional heckle of coyotes hunting cottontail in the darkness behind my house. The wind rustled the sprawl of character sheets in front of us, breezing through the inky darkness all around. We had laughed so hard together at the absurdity and ridiculousness of getting into character, bizarro accents and all. And then we were laughing about the situations we were in, why José, or as he named himself in the game, Orkukromulon, had decided to blow up the bridge we were meant to walk over in a moment of revelry with his fireball powers. This weekend everything was possible. Casting spells to bring someone back from the brink of death, an actual option. The road ahead was as clear as a single call to adventure.

As a community builder, curious about the ways we can bring people together for individual and collective healing, that first D&D campaign blew my mind. The conversations we ended up having in the game, as our characters, felt deeper and more present than the default conversation of those days, even if the subject matter was which spell I could invoke to turn leaves into razor blades, or the number of ale casks José could carry on his back, or what the characters that Claire seamlessly morphed into as our Dungeon Master, with different accents and shifts in body language, had to tell us about our campaign.

There were times since our dad died where the three of us would have opposite responses to the same situation: whether we thought our dad should be buried or cremated (he had died without ever voicing his requests); whether we should encourage our stepmom to get rid of his clothes in the closet, or sweetly smile at the lines of suit jackets that gave her comfort. While we were siblings, we were very different people, and had very distinct relationships with our dad. The uniqueness of how we knew him impacted how we each experienced his passing. We didn't always understand each other. In the tenderness of grief, our inherent differences were confusing, and sometimes unintentionally hurtful. But in this role-playing world, we were able to be explicit about our preferences. And having a diversity of skills on the team actually helped, not hindered, the quest.

Once we finally snapped out of the Mines of Phandelver and drove to our neighborhood saloon for burgers and beers, I noticed that we could be with each other a little bit differently. By spending the afternoon not talking about the normal swirl we usually landed on, we were able to get to know one another in new ways. Sitting in a booth, stealing fries from each other's plates, we had gone from three siblings to a party of six. Our day-to-day selves and our alternate-reality selves had all sat down to dinner, and we were closer for it.

Gandalf gets taken out on the Bridge of Khazad-dûm, at the hands of a Balrog. Mufasa, by a wildebeest stampede incited by his enemy Scar. Yoda, in his bed, at nine hundred years of old age. Our father, at home in San Francisco, brain cancer. Each fantastical epic has a storyline where the father figure dies. According to mythologist Joseph Campbell, it's almost a prerequisite to beginning a process of becoming. And in those nights together, our father dying felt less like the ending of a tragic tale, and more like the beginning of an adventure we were embarking on together, fears and flaws and freak-outs and all.

One thing I've learned around The Dinner Party Table is that you can't just expect people to plop down and "go there"—to connect immediately over a shared story of loss. Leaping head-on into hard conversations can have the opposite effect of what we may have intended, shutting everything down instead of opening us up. We all have scripts that are easy to repeat, the autoplay description that skims the surface of the thoughts and emotions that bubble beneath. They keep us safe from getting vulnerable in times where we don't feel the proper safety net has been set. You can ask Lindsay's question of "Where are you at with your loss right now?" but the room can't genuinely respond until people feel like there's the social safety to go there.

After many dinners, Lennon and I realized that instead of racing to have everything perfectly prepped, we could leave some things un- done and have small tasks for people to do as they arrived. This gave first-timers and recent joiners a way to busy their hands and a period to settle in as they chopped cucumbers for a salad, set the table, or made a round of cocktails. Another term for this approach is "entering at a slant," which Parker Palmer, Quaker leader and early mentor to The Dinner Party, introduced me to. Parker described the soul "like a wild animal—tough, resilient, savvy, self-sufficient, and yet exceedingly shy. If we want to see a wild animal, the last thing we should do is go crashing through the woods, shouting for the creature to come out."[2] So he uses "third things"—usually poems for groups coming together around a shared conversation to read together, to start to untangle the themes of the discussion, without starting from a place of forced vulnerability or personal sharing.

I realized that D&D served as a holy motherload of a third thing for me and my siblings. Fantasy realms offer us both a place to escape and an alternate reality to inhabit when our own is too intense, too boring, too heartbroken. But also, once we're there, it can help us approach our healing from a new angle, experimenting with new neural pathways and narratives in a lower-stakes setting.

Liam O'Brien of Critical Role, a live streamed Dungeons & Dragons game played by professional voice actors who've turned a tabletop game into a spectator sport, has cracked this open. In the months following his mother's passing, O'Brien spoke bravely about the way that his table became the linchpin in his grief process on X. For Liam, incorporating the themes he was grappling with into the game itself became a powerful tool in processing his grief.

He shared on X, "It was exactly at that moment a snap decision in this little game of ours led the story into a direction heavily layered with death and dying. One that lasted to the end of the campaign. The intersection of life and the game was uncanny to me, and the two bled into each other. In the weeks following her passing, I felt pretty swelled up by loss, but spending time with my trusted friends every week, exploring the very thing that I was haunted by, taught me volumes. Sometimes art is just entertainment. But it's often much more."[3]

In most games, death is simply handled by rebooting. But in

D&D, when characters that you've fallen in love with over the course of many hours of play fall in battle, there can be genuine sadness followed by a real emotional release that can act as a sort of catch-it-where-you-can catharsis. By the traditional rules of the game, characters can't just restart. The living characters must reconcile with the absence of a formerly key member of their group. They must roll the dice and decide on their next move. They must figure out a new path forward.

For Claire, and for so many others, fantasy worlds aren't just about escaping into some Fortress of Solitude, they're also about finding a community of people to anchor them during a time of loss and rapid transition. Their now weekly game, hosted every Saturday at their apartment in Alameda, has become a ritual that they're as devoted to as our Catholic grandmother's commitment to church. Just swap the wafers for salt-and-vinegar chips; the wine for taro boba; the hymns for a tavern music playlist; and the pews for cozy couches, with their cat Potato curled up and watching every move.

Their D&D table is filled with people who are also reckoning with big questions of life and loss, and who find that unpacking those quandaries through the lens of characters and quests paradoxically lets them go deeper. Curious how to work through it? Develop a character who's jousting with that question in their own way. Claire's played a philosophically disassociated elf monk raised by orcs, a dragonborn surfer-bro barbarian on a quest to reach the top of every mountain, and an emo fairy warlock, exploring different parts of themselves through the process.

Play a campaign. Experiment with responses. See what you learn about the characters, and about yourself. This blurry line between self and character is referred to as "the bleed" by counselors who use fantasy realms in their therapy.[4] Claire's D&D table is where they can be most themselves by paradoxically being different characters. And in each character, there's some thread of understanding that Claire gets to express, some part of themselves that comes into greater focus, around a table with people who are becoming more and more their home.

Making myths to help make sense of tragedy is one of our most tried-and-true care practices. Humans have always told stories normalizing just how hard a loss can hit, with cautionary tales of how to navigate them with grace. Orpheus finds his way to hell and back, in hopes of reviving his one true love, Eurydice. Isis cries tears over her husband, willing him back to life. Demeter, the Greek Goddess of the Harvest, so devastated by her daughter Persephone's abduction to the underworld, halts the fertile fields of nature and wills the world's first winter.

If the ancient world turned to its myths, many modern-day humans turn instead to comics. There, we find a storytelling tradition that's just as knowledgeable about the byways of loss, and that present just as many case studies for how to move through hardship with courage and care—tracing back to the earliest days of comics and the genre's forefathers.

In 1932, the owner of a clothing store died of a heart attack after being mugged. The shopkeeper's son, grappling with the loss, wrote an alternate version of the story with a buddy of his, where instead of the shopkeeper dying, an invincible protector came in to prevent the crime. Jerry Siegel and Joseph Shuster invented Superman as an act of Renegade Grief—reimagining how else the story could have gone, and through the power of imagination, willing another world into being. As author Brad Metzler[5] observes, "America did not get Superman from our greatest legends, but because a boy lost his father. Superman came not out of our strength, but out of our vulnerability."

So many of our superheroes' stories—the wise characters we aspire to and dress up like on Halloween and see plastered on buses when the latest blockbusters are released—are, at their cores, about grief and loss. Once you start noticing it, you can't unsee it. Wonder Woman longs for her late army general love, Steve Trevor. The way that Iron Man flashes back to his parents' deaths could be signaling Complicated Grief, a controversial classification for an ongoing grief response that prevents a person from living their life. In Black Panther, we're faced with the volume of violence against Black men and a young man coming to terms with losing his father. If you're ever feeling alone in your grief, get yourself to a comic bookstore or cue up a movie marathon. Our superheroes are card-carrying members of this club.

Dr. Jill Harrington, a social worker and leading researcher in the field of bereavement, doubled down on an ongoing interest in superhero grief while counseling kids bereaved after the attacks of 9/11. One young boy in particular was having a hard time opening up about his uncle's violent passing. After twelve weeks of lots of silence, he came into Jill's office wearing a Batman shirt. This was the crack in the door she had been waiting for. "You know, Bruce Wayne was a grieving boy too," she said. The floodgates opened.

She's since released a book, co-edited with grief researcher Robert Neimeyer, called *Superhero Grief*,[6] in which she observes that the origin story of nearly all superheroes "is a story of profound trauma, most notably the violent death of a parent or loved one, and the emergence from the vulnerability of traumatic loss through a transformative process—one that often involves facing the overwhelming force of heartbreak, loss, devastation, and walking through the forging fire of grief."

Having superhero powers doesn't allow the possessor to avoid grief or be "impervious to it." Rather, what we get with superhero narratives is the chance to follow the "often messy and complex journey" the characters are sent on by their loss. And, as Harrington points to, it is through observing these fictional forays into grief "that we can learn lessons of profound pain, survival, transformation, and growth." Grief readiness training, in the comics section.

Members of the mortal realm seem to have shown superhuman ability to weather the storm of hard times. While I like Superman, I love Madonna, whose mother died of breast cancer when she was just five years old. The superstar once admitted to *Interview* magazine that if her mother "were alive, I would be someone else. I would be a completely different person." It's her mother's death that she harnessed as a motivating force. "I became very obsessed with death, and the idea that you never know when death will arrive, so one has to do as much as possible all the time to get the most out of life."[7] As someone who has googled "celebrities with dead relatives" more times than I like to recount, I'm always amazed. They—the Venus and Serena Williamses, and Stephen Colberts, the Regina Kings and Leonard Cohens—have not only survived, but worked hard to make the world a more hospitable, inspired, art-filled place.

Indeed, there's almost an uncanny number of people who fall into the category of "eminent orphans,"[8] the term Malcolm Gladwell coined in his book *David and Goliath* for the unusually high number of highly successful people who lost a parent early in life. Nearly a third of all American presidents lost a father at a young age. Over 67 percent of British prime ministers had a parent dead before sixteen. Writing about this for NPR, Robert Krulwich[9] observed, it's possible that "the death of a mother or father is a spur, a propellant that sends them catapulting into life. Because they are on their own, they are forced to persist, to invent, to chart their own way."

Krulwich notes that it's a "touchy subject"—not wanting to equate catastrophe to a career booster. I'm not suggesting that we should all use our grief stories to launch ourselves to the Oval Office or the Grammys. I'm simply pointing out that the members of our club are everywhere, and at times of uncertainty it can help to scan the horizon line. Basically, to figure out who our grief role models are and whether it's their conical bra and Voguing, or their two-term presidency, or their bodysuit and hoverboard that might serve as inspiration for plotting how our grief might inform the way we live, rather than impede it.

I like to believe that in some ways grief isn't our kryptonite, but instead it amplifies our powers. When the hardest thing has happened to us, the small tantrums of the world seem survivable, even laughable. In our grief, we also might have to find the courage to do the hard thing, such as rescue our relationships with the people around us (even if they are pushing us away), or choose to be present for our families (even though we want to hide), or force ourselves to fully answer the question, "Where are you at with your loss right now?" It gives us the power to connect to people in new, profound ways. We may very well wish we didn't have to be the resilient one, but there we find ourselves, nonetheless, forevermore.

Which escapes, and corresponding fandoms, speak to you? It might be your neighborhood knitting circle, or an NBA team that is your favorite escape. It might be reuniting with a childhood obsession, like Legos or coloring books, that can lift you up and out of your swirling, grief-laden thoughts. It might be something totally new, like the ax-throwing bar that just opened across town, or the watercolor class that'll be mostly old ladies and you. Consider this your hall pass to explore whatever makes you feel like you want to rub your hands together with glee, or that serves as the remote control to change the channel in your mind, or helps you find people who share the same niche interests.

Forget productivity, or healing head-on. Find the thing that lights you up, that sweeps you off your feet, and let it take you there. When my siblings and I were playing Dungeons and Dragons, we felt unhinged from the rigidity of responsibilities in life, of caretaking, of hard conversations, of figuring out how to father ourselves. In our anchorlessness, we were finding a new kind of way to be present, and through our presence, be both together and be free.

# LETTING IT OUT

AMID A PARTICULARLY TEARY-EYED DAY in a season marked by loss and sorrow, photographer Rose-Lynn Fisher found herself wondering: *What actually are tears?* These types of questions have driven Rose-Lynn to explore the world from behind her camera lens, photographing bees inside a microscope or the landscape below airplane windows; this time, however, her question led her to capture, magnify, and photograph tears—mainly her own, and some from friends and family.

Rose-Lynn's project reminded me of the curious kind of perspective we get when we overload on an experience that we haven't considered before in depth: like contemplating how a hundred-ton cruise ship can float in water or investigating what it is that makes a can of soup shelf-stable for years. Something that seemed common and mundane before suddenly becomes alive and new and strange. Crying, the first thing we come out of the womb doing, isn't something most of us have spent time understanding.

Good thing we have artists like Rose-Lynn, who take curious questions and turn them into creative obsessions. Each photomicrograph in her collection is captioned—some with explicit descriptions like ONION TEARS, others with labels that insinuate a story not fully revealed, such AS THE LAST TEAR I EVER CRY FOR YOU. And each image reveals a wild landscape, reminiscent of her aerial photographs; this time, images of her emotional terrain. All of them look like satellite imagery taken of some remote place on earth. Rose-Lynn leads off the collection and book, titled *The Topography of Tears*,[10] with a quote from Antoine de

Saint-Exupéry's *The Little Prince*, which gets to the heart of her project: "It is such a secret place, the land of tears."

I picked up a piece of "grief etiquette" somewhere along this road that handing someone a tissue when they're crying is not the right thing to do; that by rushing to get the little cube box and dropping it in a crier's lap, or dangling a starchy white paper in their face when they're in the midst of revealing some insight that's bursting through with such life force to demand a sob, that you're rejecting their grief. That you're quietly insisting that what they need to do is clean up the spill happening all over their face and stop being such a mess.

I don't always agree with this rule and know that tissues are quite literally made for snot; for many people, offering a tissue signifies care and concern, a listening, patient ear; but it does speak to the larger question of how we react to our own tears and the tears of others. Do we let them flow, or do we rush to clean them up? Maybe they're stifled all together? And how might our culture change if tears weren't something that we wiped away, or hid from the rest of the room by sprinting to the bathroom stall? What if, inspired by Rose-Lynn, we could get curious about our tears, and really ask them, what do you have to tell me? In resisting cultural pressure to not cry, to clean it up, to move on, we can enter into a renegade relationship to our tears: trusting our body's ability to deploy this function, to take the dark cloud of feelings on the inside, and through this miraculous act of condensation, let them go.

\* \* \*

Tears are a human universal, but their actual function in our bodies remains something of a mystery. Some researchers posit they're a way for the body to release stress hormones, and that if we don't let them out, that build-up over time can be harmful.[11] There's also the claim that it's a core way of signaling the need for human connection, learned as a baby to draw attention to ourselves when we're hungry or wet; and as adults, a way to signal to ourselves or others that something just isn't right.[12] Tears of irritation are a different chemical compound than tears of sorrow.[13]

While science hasn't yet aligned on their physical function, what we do know is that crying is a grief care practice so ancient that it's embedded in our physiology. Weeping is a feature of nearly every culture's funeral rituals. Still, in the aftermath of a long era when "breaking bonds"—that is, ignoring grief and marching on—reigned as the psychological best practice, it may be that we've lost touch with one of our most salient ways to process emotions. Instead of seeing tears as a symptom of something wrong, or an action to be ashamed of, what if we saw our tears and other active lamentations as the pathway through? What if our tears were a sign that there isn't anything wrong with us, but that something outside of us is tragic, off, or unwell?

When we tune in to humans expressing grief over the ages, it hasn't always been a nod at the "sorry for your loss" in the memorial greeting line, or the forced smile to the coworker on their first day back from bereavement leave. Actually, during less stifled times, grief used to be loud.

Crying about our dead is not the stuff of sissies but of gods. In present-day Syria, researchers found a sixteen-thousand-year-old stone tablet with the earliest written record of tears.[14] On the tablet, the goddess Anat laments the death of her brother, Ba'al, an earth god worshiped by several Middle Eastern cultures. In this early sibling loss story, Anat "continued sating herself with weeping, to drink tears like wine." And the tears actually bring Ba'al back to life. In the mythic fabric of our species, there's a feeling that through our tears, the boundary between life and death becomes blurry.

I looked into some of the practices that were perhaps native to my great-great-grandparents from the southern tip of Ireland, to see if there's any resonance in my own bones with mostly forgotten rituals. There I came across the Irish art of keening. Keening is derived from the Gaelic word for crying, or expressing the lament for loss, and is a practice that mostly faded into black in the mid-twentieth century. When I first heard old recordings of keening, I was taken back to my first encounter with death, when a boy from high school died in a car accident while speeding down a curving forest road. The evening of the accident, a crowd of friends made their way to the cul-de-sac where he lived and sat in shock on truck tailgates outside. I'll never forget the sound of his mother wailing from her room, crystal clear even through the thickness of an adobe-walled home. It was an unforgettable sound: feral, making my blood run cold. There weren't any words to say that night, but there was that sound.

The recording I listened to can be found in the Irish Traditional Music Archive in Dublin, and I learned about it through the research of Marie-Louise Muir, an Irish arts presenter and radio host. In her BBC documentary, *Songs for the Dead*,[15] Muir talks about how grief has become much quieter, and without places to gather to honor the feelings related to a loss, much more isolated than when she was a girl. She said: "The way we deal with death has changed. When I was young, wakes were common. The body would lay at home for three days. Hundreds would visit the house. Communities would gather round for the burden of grief. But my own daughters have never seen a wake." In her coverage of Ireland's keeners, Muir encountered a different way to process a loss. A community, coming together. Sadness proudly expressed. Music, and a minor key, to express the agony at the stone-pit center of the feeling.

Why was keening lost? Muir recounts how keening got muffled gradually by church authorities as funerals were presided over by priests and administered in a more orderly fashion, with the person at the pulpit the only one making a peep. "It was practically outlawed in Ireland,"[16] she shared with the *Irish Examiner*. Keening was seen as women's work, sort of old-fashioned, too raw and wild. And if the people we mourned were heaven-bound, as was promised by church doctrine, why were we weeping for them? After all, the pearly gates awaited. They were in the divine company of God. Expressing grief implied a distrust in the doctrine around a specific type of afterlife. The retirement of the ritual keening silenced grief, a strong spiritual bypass. To be good, we got quiet. Never mind that even when you believed with all your heart that your person was in heaven, it didn't change the fact that you still might want to howl at their absence earthside. To honor the real power of the present moment, sometimes the only thing we can reasonably do is cry like wild.

Stigmas around crying are even more of a burden for men, particularly men of color. In his *Esquire* article "How (Not) To Grieve,"[17] author Mitchell S. Jackson recounts how he was "taught to not cry at death, and admittedly, how it 'fucked [him] up.'" Writing about the violent death of a friend, and the near death of a cousin, he explains the decision point his friends and him reached about how to handle the loss: "To grieve or not to grieve? Often the answer was a mandate: Shake that shit off pronto."

For Jackson, this isn't as simple as shaking off a trope. "Yeah, slavery was ages ago, but if epigenetics is true, how might those traumas have shaped the descendants of the once enslaved?" As the study of epigenetics further reveals that we inherit the lived experiences of our ancestors in our DNA, the pressure to keep emotions on the inside and not let the world see how its harshness might be getting to you is a deeply embedded survival mechanism. Peeling back the layers on why it is that after a loss we cry—and why it is we don't, or can't, or have this unspoken knowing that we shouldn't—reveals much more than just a story of biological function, but one of historical oppression.

In his article, Jackson writes about the times when he really lets himself feel it: fresh off a transatlantic flight, when he got the call that his father died; saying a prayer around his grandfather's deathbed; and when reading a journal he had bought for his late aunt, who had aspirations of being a writer and had expressed in those pages how his support had meant something to her. "Because I was alone, I let myself weep without reserve, the last I lamented her passing without wondering if it had lasted too long."

Think about how often people, when they are expressing emotion, apologize for crying as if they're doing something that requires forgiveness. That's why, for many of us, the hard thing is getting in the mood to let the tears flow—to transmute the feeling of being stuck, or in discomfort, or the ache of grief into the release of tears. Humans, however, have found a solution for that. For thousands of years, we've made it someone else's job to help us mourn.

Moirologists, or hired mourners, are people—mostly women—who are paid, according to Muir's research, "to cry, sing, wail over the dead, to publicly display, to articulate and channel the grief of a whole community." You'll find this practice rooted in the history of Great Britain and Ireland, but it's also just as strongly rooted in other cultures spanning the globe, including Ghana, Egypt, China, and India. The Bible even makes mention of "the mourning women," instructing parents to "teach your daughters to wail; teach one another how to lament."[18] I definitely missed that class in Sunday school.

Apart from hiring a moirologist, there are so many other creative ways people are finding the catharsis they're longing for. The writing staff of *This Is Us*, a TV show known for its tear-jerking storylines, would receive angry comments from fans after episodes that weren't exceedingly emotional, feeling deprived of their weekly cry. In Japan, there are "crying clubs" called rui-katsu—meaning "tear seeking"—where people come together for sobfests, usually sparked by sad movies or the reading of sentimental stories or letters. Filled with people from all walks of life, and led by people called tear teachers, these are spaces where the name of the game is crying.

"If you don't cry it out, you'll get sick" is what Ami Dokli, a professional mourner in present day Ghana, told the BBC.[19] So follow Ami's advice, and the next time you feel a lump in your throat, resist the urge to apologize, stifle, or run to the bathroom, and see what happens. You might be giving whoever is with you permission to feel their own feelings too.

★ ★ ★

If your local search results are coming up blank for a neighborhood moirologist, or there isn't a crying club on your campus, or you know there are some feelings that could use some releasing but you just can't find the valve, there's another miracle tool that I would love to bring to your attention, one that you already know well. It's so obvious sometimes, we forget its transcendence. It's simply, with all of its complexity, music.

The more research that's done on how music relates to our brain, the more we learn that music operates like a key to a bank of memories that we can lose access to in our normal nonmusical life. Activating the unconscious, it slips into a lock and clicks open places, faces, moments, and times that were collecting dust. A bereavement program in North Carolina surveyed grievers across ages, loss types, and faith backgrounds, and they found that 94 percent of respondents reported that they turned to music as a part of their grief journey.[20] Science is starting to prove the things our bodies already knew to be true. That music and singing are medicine. That for half of us, listening to music triggers unignorable physical reactions, like diminishing the stress chemicals coursing through our veins.[21] That listening to music we love increases our dopamine levels by almost 10 percent. And research has shown that hearing music in the operating room acts as an anti-anxiety intervention, and can even reduce the quantity of painkillers or anesthesia needed during surgery.[22] If we can own the fact that music is a secret weapon that collaborates with our body in its own longing to heal, how might we listen to it differently?

I've learned so much from conversations with grievers about the ways that we can use music to shift the way we're feeling. Whether you're ready to belt out the song you shared with your person or you are hearing something on the radio for the first time and it's hitting a nerve you didn't know was there. Whether you're into ancient funeral dirges or religious hymns, or your version of go-to grief music is rap or trance or grunge or ambient spa, sound is a conduit for grief. I invite you to listen for the ways your grief wants to move—to wrestle, to waltz, to be lulled, or to mosh—with the music that's in and around your life.

One of my favorite practices to see what kind of emotion may be lurking in the wings, waiting for its cue, is the curation of playlists. Playlists, plural, because there are so many types. There can be sentimental ones designed to confront the pain of our grief or continue the bonds. (For me, always centered around Paul Simon's album *Graceland*.) I recommend a "plate-smashing playlist" for when that anger wave is cresting and you need to roll down the windows of your car and scream along. (Think: Alanis Morissette's *Jagged Little Pill*.) The "I have to pull my shit together today and give this big work presentation even though I feel like the earth is quicksand under my feet" playlist. (À la Notorious B.I.G.'s *Ready to Die*.) And then there's the playlist of songs written from someone else's place of grief, like Mustafa the Poet's "Stay Alive," a ballad written by the artist after he lost a friend to gang violence in his hometown of Toronto. The song brought attention to a crisis of gun violence that had been dehumanized by biased news coverage. In this case, music could cut through in a way that news headlines couldn't.

At workshops and retreats over the years, we've recommended developing these personal mixtapes, like emergency kits at the ready. Even just the act of creating them can be helpful because it makes you stop and ask: *What am I actually craving to hear? What is the music that's going to help me let it out, in whatever way feels right to me?*

Beyond just making the playlist, it is important to find a place where you can listen and feel open to going with the flow of whatever comes out. My personal favorite is my car in a place I don't already know, on some stretch of highway. You might have a trail or a neighborhood where you feel safe and anonymous. Maybe it's multitasking, home alone doing or with your Dinner Party Table. Maybe it's your bedroom, with the door shut and a candle lit, or with your best friend. Wherever it is, it's about setting the intention—a simple statement of why you're turning to the music you're tuning into—and then seeing what comes up.

Sometimes, certain music can be too much; hitting play becomes the same as staring into the white-hot heat of the sun. The songs that remind us of our people, too raw in our hearts, a Pandora's box we don't have the capacity to deal with on a given day. If you're not ready, know that the time capsule effect music can have on our brains will mean the song and the memories will be there when the time is right, so put it on a playlist for a time where there's a little more cloud cover between you and the intensity of your grief.

My father and his three siblings, his parents before him, and his grandparents before them, had an affinity for an old folksong that you've likely heard performed mariachi-style. Or if you're from a family like mine, sung at weddings and funerals, glasses held in the air. The tune, "Cielito Lindo," is a singsongy melody with a chorus built for belting, the words "ay, ay, ay, ay, Canta y no llores" perfect for a group sing-along. The lyrics, ironically, urge us to sing, and not cry. It's a song that, growing up, I'd sung so many damn times it had become annoying and rote, a weird and awkward thing the old people in my family insisted we do.

But that all changed when my family and I stood around our dad's hospital bed on his last day, wondering what to say or do or where to place our hands as we watched him struggle with his final breaths. It occurred to me that there was one way we could comfort him. They say that the last sense to go is hearing, so I suggested we give him something to listen to other than our panicked lamentations. We started humming "Cielito Lindo," and then singing with wavering voices, and before we knew it, he was gone. It ended up serving as his send-off song, creating a sonic link between core moments of his life—birthdays, weddings, family reunions—all the way until his last.

Singing "Cielito Lindo" used to feel more obligatory than personal, until I entered a time in my life when knowing traditions to connect me with my ancestors wasn't just quaint, but critical. Now when the song starts playing at family events, I don't roll my eyes and cringe, I get into it. It feels like a way of bringing him into the room; instead of an empty chair or an altar with photos, it's a "Cielito Lindo" sing-along. I can't help but think of all the other voices who've sung it loud too.

There's a way of listening to music in grief that sounds like the universe is talking back to you. After my father's death, "Cielito Lindo" began showing up at some uncanny times and places for my siblings and me—warbling by on a food truck when my brother and his new wife stepped outside city hall, making it official just minutes before; or playing over the restaurant sound system when I was feeling a little out of place in a new town.

At such times, I experience the song as both a glorious coincidence and a kind of spiritual intercom. I wonder if it's quantum physics or angelic intervention; whether I'm hearing it everywhere because of frequency bias, or wishful thinking. I'm not sure, and at this point, I don't care. I've stopped trying to figure out whether my dad is hitting play on some kind of cosmic jukebox to let me know he's still listening. When I hear it, time folds in on itself. When I hear it, he's beaming in from the edge of an expanding universe, reminding me there are things I can do to find joy even in the face of brutal loss. I can start by singing, and oftentimes it's the song that helps to loosen up my tears.

✳ ✳ ✳

Even with a family anthem that discourages crying, I still think it's a radical release. And spending time with Rose-Lynn Fisher and her photographs of tears has deepened my respect for the relationship between our emotions and our physical selves. In our conversation, she reminded me that people who are grieving can be renegade, but that grief itself is renegade too—unpredictable, defying containment, does what it wants. No two images of tears are the same—the internal landscape is always shifting, and sometimes we're left holding on.

Sheer cliffs. Marshy bogs. Mountain ranges that collapse into a quiet sea. In Rose-Lynn Fisher's photographs, tears under the microscope aren't just tiny puddles, they are wild worlds. In the microcosm of a tear, she's found the kind of perspective only satellites can capture. Vistas that take millennia to form on the face of the earth through the long, slow, shifting of tectonic plates are spurred into being within a split second. In the case of tears, it's a comment, a song, a memory that builds the terrain.

Spending time with her photographs has changed the way I cry, whether it's a tear inspired by a song I hear, or a hysterical slice of dark humor, or a rogue grief wave that knocks me down. Now, in the lead up to what I know is a storm brewing inside me, I'm more watchful: the sharp comments I make to loved ones, the feeling of being overwhelmed, the holding of breath; the final tip-over when I sense the incoming tide; the last straw never really being what the crying is over; the hot relief. I watch, most often now, for the quick reflex to touch my face; no longer to wipe my tears away, but to catch on my fingertips these little panoramas from inside, the hard-earned landscapes of my life.

And while sitting around The Dinner Party Table is much less sad than it sounds, usually filled with howls of laughter and knee slaps of recognition, tears are very much welcome there. It's our own cry club, in a way. Being in the presence of a group of people moved to tears—not because of the insularity of one person's experience, but because of the resonance across the table—is one of the most numinous things I've ever experienced. Glistening eyes locking across the table, filled with tears that no longer come from a place of feeling alone in the world or hungry for connection, but a feeling of having been fed. It's an exchange that doesn't require words. We get it. We're right here.

# TENDING PAIN,
# FOLLOWING PLEASURE

IT'S EASY TO SHAKE A fist at the people who weren't "grief literate" enough for us when we were experiencing a loss. Sometimes those complaints are warranted, like the boss who asked a friend to finish her shift at a bakery, and the rest of her shifts that week, even though the friend got the surprising news that her dad had just dropped dead; or the friends who criticized Rachel's trips to Disney World; or the former high school buddy who came up to me at our ten-year reunion and expressed her apparently long-held disappointment that I'd never reached out to her when my dad was sick, as if I had erred in not tending to her need for connection. What a world.

But to be honest, my biggest grief bully has been my own mind. In grief, it's been hard for me to get out of my head. When the emotions we're feeling in our bodies are extreme, we can retreat to the comfortable corners of our minds and do the things that our brains like to do—count, measure, solve, explain, categorize—all in an attempt to regain control in times of chaos and pain. And in many passages of life after a major loss, letting our hard-driving heads lead is critical to maintaining the job we depend on, or to stabilizing a home for children who are also grieving, or to otherwise keep a foot in the world of the living.

But over time, we learn how to disarm the grief bully, to slip underneath the part of our consciousness that's so busy being a know-it-all and skating over how we're really feeling inside, and instead connect to the depth and brilliance of our bodies. It's alarming how instinctual it is to do the opposite of that. I will confess that even as I write this, I feel a little tense. I can hear the voice of my Brooklyn-bred ancestors eye-rolling at the question: "Where does grief live in your body?" Even with *The Body Keeps the Score* topping bestseller lists for hundreds of weeks, and cascades of research proving that the "I think, therefore I am" paradigm that's pervaded our medical system is an incomplete picture, I still feel a little squeamish. But this inner critic leaves me suspicious. Why does she protest so much?

We now know that grief manifests through physical symptoms, beyond just fatigue and tears. Loss can cause our body to inflame, and it weakens our immune systems.[23] Ever forget to turn off the tap after washing your hands, or find yourself standing in the garage with no recollection of why you walked out there in the first place? Remind yourself, your grieving brain is working overtime. The brain fog you might feel isn't a choice, but a neurological reaction to impossible-to-process information. A neurologist and griever herself, Dr. Lisa Schulman has studied the ways in which our grieving brains experience a flood of hormones like cortisol, which literally reshapes and rewires us. It's not a personal insufficiency, it's a protective mechanism.[24]

So if you have your own version of an internal bully, sit them down and tell them that grief is a full-body, physical experience, not something that can be processed alone through rehashing and ruminating. Whether your loss is directly tied to a capital *T* trauma (an event where your life or bodily integrity was threatened) or a lowercase *t* trauma, such as "an event that is beyond a person's ability to master at the time of the event,"[25] and which can be as simple as a child getting separated from their parents in a grocery store for a few minutes, our subconscious minds and bodies hold on to the impact. So much so that healing demands that we focus our attention not just on the mind chatter, but in the depth of our breath, the folds of our flesh, and from these places, we need to listen to what our bodies have to say about it all.

As I'm writing this, I can hear a raven calling in the canyon behind my house, and see a bee buzzing by, its shadow darting across a diamond of light falling on the outdoor table where I sit. The smell of food heating up in the kitchen, a midday breeze on my bare feet. Through my senses, I can come back to a moment that is outside the worry, the stress, the brain's relentless attempts to figure out something that, in the case of grief and loss, is more mystery than math problem. The hours I've spent thinking about what I need, and why he died, and where he is now, is futile—because there is no answer that'll ever satisfy my rational mind. It's beyond comprehension. The part of my being that can comprehend that truth is not the drill sergeant sitting between my temples, but lives in the quiet, sensing part of me that can hold the spectrum of sadness and joy in a broader periphery.

So what do I sense when I ask myself the question of where grief lives in my body? Well, my grief lives in my shoulders, which were often tense or armor-like as I moved through the last decade of learning how to father myself. I feel it in my lungs, when I too often find myself holding my breath, which reminds me of my long-time smoker grandmother who died from emphysema. And perhaps grief was in the migraine I had this weekend, which brought me to my knees and reminded me that our bodies will tap us on the shoulder—and if we *still* don't listen, it might even tackle us to the ground.

This brings me to the question, where do you feel it in yours? And what are the ways that help you tap into your body, to not just locate where you're holding the tension of it all, but to tend to it, express it, move it, care for it so that your version of the armor, the held breath, can be released?

As you sit with those questions, I want to introduce you to three stories that have forever changed my lens on navigating the relationship between pleasure and pain in times of loss; the ache of grief in our bodies and the medicine of letting what feels good to our flesh guide us through our healing. They are a hot springs hopper, a dancer, and a clown. I wonder what stories you've come across that you would add to the stack, your own included.

The first is Eva, our first-ever host of an LGBTQ+ table. Eva was one of the brave souls who started a Table with us in the early days, when the way we approached running our organization was more punk rock than polished nonprofit. Soft-spoken and sincerely kind, with a pixie haircut and nose ring, Eva is a honey bear of a human who you just want to hug forever. For many of us, the physical cause of death of our person might be something that lingers in the room with us as we grieve, because it's in our bodies too. That was the case with Eva, who, after losing her mom to breast cancer, had to address her own risk of contracting the disease.

I really got to know Eva in the alpine town of Truckee in the off-season, at an annual gathering for hosts. She'd joined our community after losing both parents, Mona and Jerry, by the age of nineteen. But as the last drifts of snow melted and early spring sunlight made for fragrant pine forests, it was Eva's relationship to Mona's life that was at the forefront for her during that weekend.

A year before, Eva had taken a test her mom never had the chance to receive: a BRCA gene test. The results were positive, showing that she had at least an 86 percent chance of developing the highly aggressive breast cancer that her mother had died from. After deliberating, Eva made the decision to have a double mastectomy. A series of massive surgeries were involved, which would require months of healing in bed.

Instead of missing the retreat, our community arranged for Eva to be transported from her apartment in Oakland to the king-sized bed of our rental, where she recuperated for three days while a bustling room of fellow hosts cared for her. She dozed in and out; we kept her fed and watered and properly propped up with a pile of pillows. Helping was not a hardship. After having sat bedside for my dad, it felt great to be a caretaker for someone who had made the decision to remain very much alive. I remember the weird pleasure in cutting long strips of bandages, tenderly removing old cotton pads from newly sewn up skin, smiling and chuckling at how this all felt so adult. Eva went home from the hospital with the chosen family and community that she'd cultivated and nourished over the years.

Nowadays, Eva talks about this period in her life as a forced reckoning with her body, a time when she had to surrender beyond any surrendering she'd ever done before. I asked Eva how it felt to face the disease that took her mom's life and how she made sense of the way in which that story was transcribed in her own DNA. "It made me grieve for my mother in a whole new way." Mona wasn't comfortable in her body, and didn't end up going to the doctor until her cancer was well on its way. The power of Eva's proactive care for herself feels even more pronounced against the backdrop of her mom's story. Mona's own care was tainted by patriarchal malpractice, her discomfort written off by a doctor who didn't take her case seriously: "He suggested a severely swollen lymph node was actually an ingrown hair, and she didn't get the scans she needed until it was too late." How many people become grievers because of an easily preventable death? How do we metabolize the part of our grief that says, in a muffled voice or a rage-filled scream, *It didn't have to end this way?*

For Eva, grieving her parents has gotten interwoven with figuring out how to provide herself with safety, comfort, and nourishment in their absence. Eva shared what she does to care for herself—other than putting her body through four rounds of surgical intensity to save her own life—and she doesn't have to think hard. She tells me about standing naked at the edge of her favorite hot springs, tucked within the folds of the Eastern Sierras that straddle the California and Nevada border. She makes her way down the slippery ledges of rock to slip into a shallow pool without another soul in sight. The water is stingingly warm on her skin. There's no one there to see how the silvery lines of scars making their way up her back and around her breasts have healed up beautifully.

Some of her earliest childhood memories are from bath time with Mona at their New Jersey home. They are happy memories, imbued with love and safety. By dipping her body under the water in her favorite spots in the Sierras, a part of her can transport back to that bathtub and the feel of getting warm cups of water poured over her scalp. She likes to lie back in the water and float, to take in the grandness of the Eastern Sierra. To be held in mid-float. To prioritize the things that give her pleasure, particularly after the pain of surgery. Her parents, she tells me, would be proud.

Eva's parents were both Jewish, and her grandparents were Holocaust survivors. Did ancestral rituals tie into her care at all? Mikvah, or sacred bathing, is a Jewish tradition thousands of years old, a contemplative practice for purification or release that takes place in pools of water. While Eva knows about Mikvah, it's not what she has in mind while she's slipping into the hot springs. It's almost as if she's found a way to practice a cultural tradition outside of religious prescription. It's entirely her own. Listening to her describe it, I'm reminded of the roundabout routes by which we find our ways to our ancestors' practices. It reminds me of the old parable: lead a horse to water, and they may not drink. But let wild horses run free, and they'll find their own way to the source.

Eva recently retrofitted a van, an old white delivery truck she'd saved up for over the years, so she has a getaway vehicle of her own for trips up to the Sierras. It's a major feat, and it's been inspiring to watch the process unfold. Part of reckoning with her vulnerability—as a human being, as someone with a genetic marker that tilts toward cancer, as an adult orphan—has been investing time in practices that emphasize her resourcefulness and resilience. What's inspiring about Eva is that her bravery and strength isn't in conflict with the part of her that longs for tenderness, community wisdom, and a good long soak—it's an advocate for care, for herself and her people. After tons of research, mastering various power tools, dozens of YouTube tutorials, and asking skilled friends for help, Eva finally has her very own Hot Springs Express.

\* \* \*

The second person who has been a role model for me when it comes to tending to pain through the pleasure of our bodies is Sarah. When I interviewed Sarah, she was on the first day of a professional sabbatical, having just quit her job as partner in a law firm, and for the first time in her adult life she was living life without a plan. She wasn't rushing into some next chapter like she'd always done at every other transition point in her life, a person very familiar with the internal grief bully, pushing herself to work harder lest she unpack the complex feelings related to her grief. Instead, Sarah decided to spend a year seeing what it felt like to just be here, in her living room. The last time she felt like she wasn't drowning was thirty-three years ago, before her sister Tonya died in a car accident when they were both girls.

Needless to say, Tonya's death was hard on Sarah's family, and as a way of controlling her emotions and dealing with the trauma of her sister's death, she focused all her energy on her schoolwork. A+ energy could, for a while at least, give her a brass ring to reach for, a striving that kept her too busy to tumble into deep despair. Workaholism can feel like a perfect antidote to heavy grief; that is, until we find ourselves over-committed and stressed. Then the thing that was a life raft can become weights tied to our ankles. But how do we stay alert enough to know the difference? How do we strike the balance?

In the midst of a hard breakup at thirty-five, two decades after her sister's death, Sarah started therapy to work through some of the issues in the relationship with her now-ex. She'd been in therapy for a few years before she happened to share with the therapist that, by the way, she had a sister who died in a car accident when she was young. That Sarah had been in the car when it happened, and, oh yes, she could still relay the entire accident from start to finish all these years later. The therapist recommended Sarah try a therapeutic style called somatic experiencing, which has been especially useful for people who've gone through major traumatic events and may still be experiencing PTSD symptoms. During her sessions with this alternative type of therapy, Sarah started to shed some of the weight that had been living in her body, weight that she hadn't even been conscious of.

And finally, through the winding road of therapy and somatic experiencing, Sarah found her way to dance. At a host retreat for The Dinner Party, the same one where Eva sat in the room next door getting bandages redressed, Sarah was participating in a dance workshop that put all the notebooks aside and invited us to express where we were with our grief through movement, our facial expressions, the stomping of our feet, or the articulation of our hands through space. She was hooked.

The dance Sarah practices now is called Open Floor and Body Prayer, but no matter the style. All it requires is music, a space to move, and some intention, but physical release can happen at a music festival, or in the dark back room of a club, or during a front-seat dance party at a stoplight. She reached out to a teacher who leads classes in which participants embody different people you want to conjure memories of, or embody people you want to release emotion around. Sarah could dance like Tonya, or like herself at age thirteen; or like her parents, broken after the accident; and stories and images and emotions that she hadn't thought of for years would pop into her head. For her, the dance floor has become a portal. It was the thing that allowed her body to express itself in a way that revealed new information. Now, her time on the dance floor is where she feels most connected to her sister, and not in a sad way. In more sessions than she can count, she's been brought to tears while dancing, moved by this fountain of feelings that is her body.

As she prepares for this big yearlong break, she's curious where else her body will lead her, and now through her dance she's embedded in a community of people to whom she can turn in times of both the ecstasy, the agony, and the in between. Whatever it is, she knows it will include dancing.

*  *  *

The third person who taught me about finding a path through pain via pleasure is someone I met once, briefly, and intimately. In the months after the funeral was wrapped, I spent a few weeks with a friend who was au pairing for a family in Paris. I was numbed-out from caretaking. I remember spending time writing letters in cafes while drinking coffee and wine, trying to preserve memories, lest him being dead meant that I would soon forget. Not a bad life, come to think of it. When my friend got a week off work, we played the Ryanair roulette and found cheap tickets to the Italian island of Sardinia. Swimming in the chilly Mediterranean and driving through offseason farmlands would match my sulking energy and obsession with Edith Hamilton's book on Greek mythology, where I found the dramatic tales of mortals struggling with the decisions of gods more relatable than everyday affairs.

At a bar one night, while my friend with masterful flirtation skills held an entire soccer team in thrall, I counted down the minutes until we could go back to our hostel and get into pajamas. The bartender struck up a conversation with me, I assumed in pity at how miserable I seemed, and within seconds we both heard the cymbal crash of a powerful connection. He was home for the offseason, helping a friend run his bar and would be returning to the mainland the next day where his job was, well, to be a clown. Laugh all you want. He wasn't a red-nose, big-shoe, birthday-party clown—think more Italian busker, hot theater mime. He asked if we could meet up in the morning, and I spent the night at the hostel obsessing over him. What switch had just been flipped in my insides? I thrummed with a voracious hunger for this man. After so many months of chronic dread and living in the death zone, here was my body responding to wanting something, with the added thrill of knowing I could likely have it if I wanted.

My friend accompanied me the next day to meet him at a cafe by the small marina, and the three of us drove in his Fiat (bigger than a clown car, but not by much), with the windows down and wind gusting, and the radio blasting Nancy Sinatra. He took us to the beach where he often went to practice his trumpet, and he serenaded us. Then the two of us dipped off to explore this palpable question posed in the air between us, on a bed of yellow-flower sweet grass by the sea. He had a flight to catch, and my friend and I had a rental car to return, so there was no real chance for lingering. It was a crystal clear, surgical mission, and it defibrillated my heart.

I laughed at the synchronicity that is connecting with a person whose job it is to make people laugh, to poke fun at seriousness, to eye-roll at people in power. To speak, not just with words, but with dramatized gestures that make a crowd laugh at the absurdity of being alive. Clowns, in many cultures, have been the trickster energy who can speak truth to power; the only member of the court allowed to criticize the king. It seemed only appropriate that, of course, in this somber season of my life, the person who would grab my attention would be a clown. The joke was on me, and I took it wholeheartedly.

A few weeks later, back in the States, driving on a long stretch of desert highway, my phone rang with a long number preceded by a plus sign. I answered. "I've been practicing a new song on the trumpet," he told me, and he wanted to play it for me. I could hear him set the phone down and, with my hands on the steering wheel at ten and two, I listened. Within the first few notes, big tears and a bigger grin hit my face. After finishing the song, he picked up the phone again and asked whether I knew the song? "Yes," I told him. It was "Cielito Lindo," and I loved the way he made it sound, even with five thousand miles between us. But apparently no distance was too far to feel the love. I took this moment of resonance as an endorsement for moving through grief not always with stone-cold earnestness, but with letting the body lead. The song reverberating through a trumpet a continent away, and through the generations, a solid sounding yes.

Now, don't get me wrong. I know not all of us feel fired up and ready to go when we're grieving. For many of us, the loss we've experienced might be a long-time libido killer. Others might be dealing with a partner loss that still makes it feel too soon. All this to say that this may very well *not* be your season to have sex on the beach. Trust yourself on that one. But there are so many other ways we can cultivate pleasure—warm socks, molten cake, taking an old friend to a long lunch, lying in the sun and feeling it warm every inch of our skin. It's renegade, in a time of life where things feel miserable, to let your body guide you into its own version of contentment, however fleeting. Over time, the source of that contentment will likely change—and the work becomes listening to what our bodies want—nay, need—next.

My grief bully isn't gone, but I have now heard enough stories and spent enough hours in my own bones to know that grieving isn't something we do neck up, or even heart up. We do it belly up, loins up, knees up, soles up. Our direct line to grieving in a way that doesn't default to harmful or uninformed cultural norms is in getting out of the cerebral sense-making and into the processing only our bodies can achieve as we touch, taste, smell, sweat, and dance our way into clarity. But it can be hard to change your own bandages, and dance parties of one, while great, hit different than dancing with friends. Part of your assignment is prioritizing finding the people who get the pain you're holding, because they've felt it too; who can tell your grief bully to take the day off while you spend time together letting the rest of your being breathe.

# REWIRING THOUGHT PATTERNS

SEVERAL YEARS AGO, LENNON AND I cohosted a collective care retreat for grievers in Los Angeles, during which we spent the weekend experimenting with some of the different practices that now live in this book. At one of the sessions, a participant asked me, "What was most helpful to you in making sense of your grief?" I wavered before answering. Should I be professional and give an endorsement for our organization and the power of gathering around a table for a meal? Or should I tell her the thing that first leapt to mind?

I chose to take off my facilitator hat and give it to her straight. "Honestly? For me, psychedelics," I said. I had always been hesitant to answer this question because it perpetuates the search for the "silver bullet," the idea that somewhere out there exists the one care practice that will reset our emotional landscape to our pre-loss, factory settings. I also hesitated because of the wide array of reactions that mentioning mind-altering substances can elucidate from a participant—ick, awe, distrust, or curiosity, to name a few.

But the truth is that psychedelics helped me cut through my own fears long enough for me to see my dad's passing as something sacred. It introduced into my consciousness the idea that the process of helping him die was an opportunity to honor him, which suggested that life after his death might not be as much of an ass-kick into the void as I was anticipating. And having people with whom I could integrate those learnings—through therapy and peer support— meant that it wasn't just a peak experience, but a new kind of programming.

Nowadays, we're well on our way to reaching mainstream psychedelic therapy, and the discretion that made me hesitate before gabbing about plant medicine is getting blown off its hinges. Michael Pollan, a leading voice who informs what liberals put into their bodies, wrote a whole book celebrating these substances, which you can pick up in any airport bookstore. Prince Harry wrote in his tell-all memoir that he turned to psychedelics "not just to escape reality, but to redefine reality," as he healed from the death of his mother. Something that was illegal and incriminating is now being touted as a miracle worker—when taken in the right setting, with the right space holders.

Psychedelics can help us zoom out and look at the cultural and familial patterns that we're a part of, and then investigate what is and isn't working for us, as well as help us find our way to a different path.

It was in a second-story yoga studio on a bustling intersection in Hollywood, catty-corner to a famous hot-dog stand and a beloved Latin drag bar, where I first participated in a group psychedelic ceremony. My dad was then in his final cancer decline, picking up speed toward death, and I was picking up speed in my anticipatory grief. When I received an invitation from a friend to attend, I thought, *Why not?* I was all out of answers on how to proceed. This was a disaster, and my heart was certainly about to shatter. Might as well slingshot myself into some other version of reality through drinking down two big cups of dirt-water ayahuasca.

I will spare the inevitably clichéd descriptions of someone else's plant medicine awakening, of how at the end of the day the only thing that rightfully matters is love, of how amazed I was at this underground network of people actively pursuing the expansion of consciousness and continuing ancient traditions of ethnobotanic medicine, of how the "ego death" that occurs when properly dosed is terrifying until it's irrevocably illuminating. But I will share this. At one point during the trip, as I sat in a circle of vomiting strangers on sheepskin rugs, I was deep in dialogue with a faceless entity to whom I posed my most burning question and the real reason for my visit: "So, he's going to die, isn't he? How am I going to get through this?"

Whoever this alternative narrator was, whatever spiritual mainframe I had plugged myself into, it gave me an unexpected but transformative answer. What it shared with me wasn't a set of words, but a wink, a nudge, and something else: An A-OK hand gesture. A brush-off. A feeling of *just you wait*.

My reaction must have been like the cocked head of a dog hearing an interesting new noise, ears flopping and eyes widening. *A-OK?* The message seemed to be that somehow, even if this worst-case scenario came to be (which day by day was looking more like the case), I was going to be okay. A-OK. In fact, I could even do with a little lightening up. Sure, my dad was going to die, but in some kind of cosmic joke sort of way, death wasn't that big of a deal in the end. Happens to everyone at some point, but that doesn't mean we can't enjoy the ride until then. We were both going to be fine—him, leaving his body; and me, navigating life afterward.

*Excuse me?* I remember thinking. Never had it occurred to me, or been suggested to me, that my dad's illness was anything other than the most fucked-up, saddest, terrible piece-of-shit thing to ever happen to my family. And here was this entity giving me a flirty little wink, a little pat on the ass, a big smile, and an optimistic nudge. There's always the threat of spiritual bypassing—of overly indexing on a spiritual idea (death's no big deal!) to avoid facing something hard or inconvenient. But this felt different. This felt surprising and refreshing and true. This felt like relief.

We often talk about how we all have the answers inside us, like Dorothy's Ruby Slippers are always on our feet, ready to take us to whatever version of home we're longing for. In that moment, that answer, with its cool confidence that we can survive even the hardest of things, was the home I didn't know I was longing for. What stunned me about this experience was that, in all the months before this, as my brain frantically tried to figure out solutions, cures, a way out, it had never occurred to me to consider death as anything like ease. As an exhalation. Never had it occurred to me to think that this could be both big and hard, but also fine. Be natural. Be both malignant and metastatic, but also mildly benign. In my mind, death had always meant defeat. Failure. It had never occurred to me that death might also be an ecstatic release, or something that I didn't have to battle with grim, anxious determination.

Since the time he got sick, my dad would tell us that "even if everything isn't okay, it's still going to be okay." We would always nod, shrug, and move on, not really accepting that there was a chance he might actually die. Yet underneath the dim lights of this yoga studio with a barf bucket between my knees, I was actually taking that likelihood in. And that realization created a little bit of space in my panicked mind that allowed me to show up differently. It meant that I could spend time at his bedside, mid-seizure or brain-tumor-induced hallucination or immersed in the loud silence of someone staring into space in the final weeks of his life—and bring a different energy in. Not the white-knuckled grip on the steering wheel of a car that's careering over a cliff, but a different kind of ease. A lightness. I hope he could feel it. I hope it made his leaving easier for him too.

Think of a hillside covered in snow. Over time, sleds and walkers form well-worn tracks crossing through the snow. Because these fresh pathways are visible, they encourage other sledders or walkers to travel on those specific lines down the mountain. A suggestion becomes a pattern. The tracks dig deeper. The same thing is true with our thoughts. We can easily fall into grooves of thought patterns and behaviors, much like a sled running on a defined track.

"Shaking the snow globe" is an analogy that neuroscientist Dr. Robin

Carhart-Harris uses to describe what psychedelics do to the brain.[26] Psychedelics shake up the snow globe in such a way that when the snow resettles, it covers up the old tracks. Our sleds don't immediately default to old patterns of traveling. Suddenly, we have the space to create new ways of moving, new ways of thinking about things and relating to people.

That's what I experienced in that yoga studio all those years ago, a nudge to a new track. And the growing body of research on grief and psychedelics supports how useful the experience can be.[27] Researcher Dr. Joshua Woolley at the UCSF Weill Institute for Neurosciences conducted a study with eighteen older long-term AIDS survivors to see if a combination of psilocybin and group therapy could impact their feelings of demoralization.[28] A heartbreaking chapter of American history, the AIDS epidemic ravaged the LGBTQ+ community, a medical epidemic overlaid with severe cultural prejudice that added heavily to the death toll and overall despair.

In his study of AIDS survivors processing the grief of having lost friends to AIDS, Woolley found that nearly 90 percent of participants experienced a lessening in how demoralized they felt after taking psilocybin. The substance, the researchers found, had acted as "a catalyst for reconstructing their identities from rigidly centered on their past traumas to more flexible and growth-oriented life narratives." The combination of mushrooms and community gave them the space to explore alternate relationships to the grief in the present tense.

In a separate study of grievers in Spain who took ayahuasca, participants reported a decrease in the intensity of their feelings of grief, which continued to last at a check-in point a year later.[29] And it wasn't that the experiences were an escape from grief, rather that they included deep work of "emotional confrontations with the reality of the death, the reviewing of biographical memories, and a reencounter with the deceased."

Psychedelics aren't for everyone. In many cases, the right mind-altering substances aren't psychedelic but pharmaceutical. A study led by Columbia researcher George Bonanno found that people who struggled with anxiety and depression before a loss experience, likely continued to experience their anxiety and depression afterward.[30] Of the 6 percent to 25 percent of individuals who experienced the loss of a loved one and ended up with something doctors would consider prolonged grief disorder—where grief is relentless and getting in the way of caring for oneself months after the death—antidepressants or other pharmaceutical interventions can be a godsend, either as a bridge or a longer-term support. So it's up to us, in this spirit of responsible experimentation, to find the right combination of tools that work for us, and the peer and professional support who can be present with us, as we're present with our grief.

The last time I did ayahuasca was in some mega-mansion in the hills of Ojai with a bunch of people I didn't know, who all wore white and who I think were also selling some sort of wellness subscription plan. The message I got this time was clear: *You know where to find us.* I've come to understand that sentiment as a confidence builder in my ability to access this kind of spiritual perspective without having to ingest a plant grown in the Amazon, shipped through customs to a city where I'd never been, into a room full of people doling out uncomfortably long hugs. There was a feeling of assumed intimacy, a lack of boundaries, that pushed me away. For a long while, I'd likened the experience of psychedelics to the elevator in Willy Wonka's Chocolate Factory, in how fast it moved to make me feel connected to the universe and the spirit of my dad. But that day helped me realize it was time for me to learn how to take the stairs to get that same feeling of connection. So I turned to the tools I had in my own body: meditation and breath.

To mark the ten-year anniversary of my dad's death, which fell on the first day of a new decade, my siblings and I spent one evening in the weeks prior at the base of Coit Tower, but for the week of, I checked my-self into a meditation center in the Sierra Nevada foothills. Over the past years, I had grown to love meditation, but I had only ever meditated for minutes at a time. This would be ten days of no talking, no eye contact, no reading, no writing, no alcohol, marijuana, or sex. If I felt great sad-ness on the day of the anniversary, there would be no getting in the car for a drive, no rolling down the windows to let the breeze in, no trying to shake off a feeling of despair with a self-serve frozen yogurt topping bar. There would also be no waking up hungover on New Year's Day, his death anniversary, with a delightfully muted nervous system after a night of rabble-rousing with friends. Most horrifically, there would be no caffeine.

The last few days of the year, and the first few of the next, were dappled with golden light. In the cold mornings, mist rose from fields of grass. Clouds passed through the blue skies of the afternoon like the countless thoughts through my mind. There we were, a hundred people coexisting in silence, doing lots of little things. Sitting, adjust-ing. Walking slowly. Gathering around a table, eating meals without exchanging a word, a glance. We were cutting off the things that nor-mally gave us a surge of endorphins. The red alerts on our phones, the ordering of dessert, the smiling at a stranger. I'd spent my twen-ties reaching outward—building community and staying busy. During these ten days I committed to being fully present with myself, free from distractions, especially during a significant grief milestone when the urge to escape into busyness would be strongest.

One important thing I learned is that there's nothing that makes me want to misbehave more than an earnest spiritual retreat center. I wanted to break the rules by reading one of the books I had smuggled in or striking up a conversation with a groundskeeper. I didn't want to mindfully eat popcorn on New Year's Eve, slowly lifting each kernel to my mouth as if in slow motion, taking tiny sips of the sparkling apple juice in my paper cup. So in the final hours before the New Year's bell rang and it officially became ten long years since I sat at the bedside of my dying dad, I regretted the decision to attend the retreat.

I wished that the retreat had been on a beach somewhere, with dancehall music and festival-grade speakers. Instead of tiny cups of Martinelli's, I wanted shots of mezcal; and rather than sitting on a zafu all day, I wished we were learning to surf. I didn't want to be sleeping alone in a twin bed two feet from a woman whose name I would never know, but rather in a warm tangle of limbs with my husband, who was also at the retreat center but, as a veteran meditator, refused to sneak me a cheeky wink. As the milestone approached, I found myself reaching for the sensual places I usually go to outrun an incoming wave of grief. I made it through New Year's Eve, and the ones after, and then finally, after a week of silently complaining yet consistently returning to my breath, it all landed.

There was a New Year's Day concert happening at the retreat center. Those of us on the silent retreat weren't invited, but I listened eagerly from outside, standing by a cracked window, jonesing for the novelty of the sound of music. A woman was there, playing the cello, and after settling into her seat and lifting her bow to the mahogany instrument, she let it absolutely rip. She was playing Bach's Cello Suite, the anthem of bitter-sweetness. Hot tears poured down my face as I stood with my back to the wall and an ear to the window. I saw that in the moments of quiet during the preceding days, when I wasn't running from something, busying my-self, my senses had alerted. I was present, and tender and alive. Some of the callousness had sloughed off, the burn-out in my brain, mended.

I cried for the anniversary, remembering the look of bliss on my dad's face when he turned to his favorite form of meditation—playing the piano. I cried for the miracle of the last decade, and how one song, like one human body, could hold beauty and sorrow all in one. I cried in appreciation for the overwhelming blessings of my life, particularly those that had shown up in the aftermath of his departure, mostly in the form of friends.

What I was experiencing was that there are other ways to shake the snow globe of our minds, beyond just psychedelics—and that in bone-sober, slow-motion meditation, we can close our eyes and let snow fall, covering the well-worn tracks that might be icy or grinding. It's what I turn to now when I feel my thoughts sticking in patterns that feel a little off; when I feel a narrative about my relationship to grief settling into a story that feels heavy or queasy or otherwise worthy of investigation. Whether it's on a cushion in my bedroom, or on a solo walk through nature, or with my grandmother's rosary cupped in my hand, I use meditation to take a look down the hillside in front of me and see where my sled wants to travel, not because it's been there before, but because I'd like to choose that particular ride.

As you explore your own ways of meditating, the practices that help you clear your mind, allowing you to notice thoughts passing through but not being ruled by them, keep these universal truths at heart: treat your practice like an experiment, not a competition; find friends who get it and teachers whom you admire. And believe me when I say, even if you feel incredibly lost in your grief, you know where to find yourself, and your preferred form of meditation might be the tool that uncovers the way.

# RESTING

I HAVE A GRIEF FANTASY that, when the next inevitable disaster of a loss happens in my life, I'll check myself into some kind of seaside sanitarium. I'll stare into the oceanic abyss with a wool blanket over my legs, drinking tea and listening to sad songs while I watch whales breach until I'm good and ready to get up. For a worst-case scenario, it sounds absolutely ideal.

But knowing what I know and seeing what I've seen, what I'll more likely be doing is paperwork. And memorial planning. And staring down a tsunami of to-do items, like "mail death certificate to [x]" and "babysit for [y]" and "cook meals for a, b, and c."

And then when those to-dos are done, there's the next set of tasks we might assign ourselves as we attempt to orient ourselves in life after. Pick up that pencil, buy that journal. Have that hard conversation with the family member who surely didn't mean it but hurt your feelings when they said that thing. Decide what we're going to do with the storage unit, with our life, with the tax returns, with the memories. Try to remember the last conversation we had. Try to date. Try to eat better, sleep more, work harder, stress less. In the world of getting through a loss experience, we can drown in the sea of "shoulds" that come lapping at us from all directions. We can fall victim to the feeling that we're not doing grief right, that we should be approaching it differently and doing it better.

For the record, I've come to greatly admire the part of our humanness that has the capacity to get shit done when we're thrust into the business of life after a loss. Onlookers might think we're in shock, or denial, that our ability to be anything but a slobbery mess means we're repressing, or not letting ourselves "go there." The fact that we can write a eulogy, navigate the bureaucracy of insurance claims and obituary publishing is a feat of human strength. Sometimes the show must go on, and there are times in our grief where we surprise ourselves with our ability to keep up the act.

It ends up, we can often handle harder things than we imagined we could, even when our circumstances match our cringiest nightmare. Lennon's mom died just days before Lennon's stage debut in a college rendition of *A Midsummer Night's Dream*, and she swept the audience away as Puck. Mary's mom died of a terminal illness the week before her wedding, and she still walked down the aisle. Shay, who you'll meet here, went to school the day after her mom died, and kept going to school every day thereafter.

According to NYU-based researcher Katharina Schultebraucks and partners, many people get to the grieving part and find it's easier than they thought it would be. Two-thirds of people fall under a trajectory the research labels as "resilient, showing little to no signs of depression before or after a traumatic event."[31] They were back to work sooner than they had imagined. It hurt, but they could put one foot in front of the other. We may be more ready than we give ourselves credit for.

All the same, even beyond the initial years of acute grief, so many of us wonder what's driving a feeling that something's just not right. Like the world around us is a little off-kilter. We pick at all the other things in our lives that aren't going as we hoped. So often, if we could follow the thread of the discomfort to its source, we'd find that it's rooted in our grief. While we were busy, we didn't have to face it. But what if our relief was going to come from doing just that, putting down the distractions and doing absolutely nothing at all?

In the findings from researcher Laura Brady's surveying of our community, we found that 73 percent of survey respondents reported one of the most helpful care practices was not producing, processing, creating, or closing out—but giving themselves permission to do nothing. To just be flattened by their grief and not feel wrong about it. Even this—especially this—is renegade.

We live in a world where the art of doing nothing requires a real resistance to the cultural currents we swim in. Over a third of Americans see leisure as wasteful—not even "nice to have," just purely a bad use of time.[32] We're productivity-mad, too, often equating our self-worth with our output. More than 134 countries have a limit to how much we can ask people to work in a week, but the U.S. isn't one of them.[33]

The problem is that grief doesn't particularly care about how important your job is, nor is it time bound to the hours outside our work shifts, classes, or client appointments. It wants you to stare out the window, to be slow in getting out of bed, to spend time rendering to the world without your person, which might not be something you can do while multitasking.

There are, after all, robust cultural traditions around this idea. In Judaism, sitting shiva encourages bereaved families to just be still for seven whole days after the death of a family member. It's not a time to do your makeup or shave your beard, let alone look in the mirror. Guests aren't allowed to greet you with the empty phrases that can be impossible to answer after a loss, like, "How are you?" In shiva, there's a structure in place that allows people to take a break, a protocol that protects a griever's need for space, food, and quiet. These principles are present in many Latin American countries, in the practice of a novenario, or nine days of reflection, prayer, and coming together. Even the Victorian-era practice of wearing black to symbolize mourning—while reserved for elite circles and spurred by the emergence of ready-to-wear clothing—shows the world that perhaps you're not available for standard season bullshit.[34]

But not all of us have that kind of cultural protocol in place, or the ability to slow down. When I asked a friend who is Jewish whether her family sat shiva, she laughed. She was too busy making sense of the high-pressure family business she had inherited overnight, after both of her parents died.

So how do we balance handling our business when that's what's required, as well as having compassion for the part of our grieving selves that needs rest? In Renegade Grief, we're resisting the valedictorian vigor of making our loss something else we need to "ace"—and instead, realizing that taking care of our grief in the most direct way might on certain days look like doing absolutely nothing at all.

In the years after her mom died, Shay Bell, a community manager with The Dinner Party, was not well known as someone who took it easy. In fact, she was featured in a video released by the City of New York profiling women who had worked hard to succeed in the face of adversity. Each woman represented a word, and the one chosen to represent Shay was "perseverance." The video, with upbeat music emblematic of mid-1990s propaganda, starts with Shay explaining why she has such tenacity. "Perseverance is important because I don't have any other options. I don't have any choice but to keep going."

Watching this video now, it smells of early girl boss culture. It lauds Shay for being an accomplished musician, for writing a book of poetry, for being at the top of her high school class. She went on to graduate on the dean's list of Rensselaer Polytechnic Institute, a top engineering school in her home state of New York. The video celebrates her mother, Marilyn, for being a positive influence. Marilyn earned a scholarship to attend MIT at just sixteen years old, and then went on to become a computer scientist who worked with major corporations like IBM and American Express, from her office high up in the World Trade Center. Thanks to Shay losing her bus pass, Marilyn was late to work one September morning and lived to tell the tale.

But the video also digs into Shay's complex family history. How her dad left the family when Shay was young. How her mom eventually got caught in the web of an exploding crack epidemic in New York City and was inevitably killed by her addiction. Shay found her mom's body the week before her high school graduation. She had been working on her valedictory speech just moments before the traumatic discovery.

The video in its upbeat closing speaks of how Shay "overcame her chaotic home life," just like that. How "she never let her issues get in the way of her success," and how the adults around her were "surprised by how strong she was," as she stayed late in after-school programs to avoid going back to the instability of her home life, or as she walked across the stage at graduation without her mother in the audience. "She was under a lot of pressure. But pressure makes diamonds," shares one of her mentors in the video. But what if Shay didn't want to be a diamond? What if she didn't want to succumb to the "strong black woman" trope, a racist archetype that pressured her to be fine, strong, and productive even during devastating heartbreak. For Shay, like for many other women of color, being renegade in grief meant resisting the pressure to prove their resilience, choosing instead to rest and to feel.

For many of us grievers, the survival mode we can click into is celebrated by the world around us. We are mature; we are together. We are strong. But how do we make room for the parts of us that felt pressure to succeed as if our very lives depended on it? And what happens if, after years and years of churning forward, being "amazing," some inner motor finally gives out and we realize we are exhausted, and our inner resources tapped? For many of us, it isn't until we've gotten ourselves somewhere safe that we finally get to fall apart.

In photos that Shay shared with me that did not make the cut of the New York City video, I see a different version of her story. Not just an overachiever, but a deeply feeling person. And of her mom: not just a woman caught between the rat race of single motherhood and her addiction, but a stylish, exuberant woman with a warm smile. Marilyn, in a leather jacket with puffed sleeves, gold jewelry, a glowing smile, iconic '90s sophisticated fashion. Shay and Marilyn making faces at the camera. And Shay in her teenage years, with locks of hair cascading over her eyes, a T-shirt that reads "I Hate You," commando boots, studded biker gloves, and face paint. Not just a good girl, but a goth, fresh out of Hot Topic, grappling with themes of darkness even before she buried her mom.

When Shay joined The Dinner Party as a community member, she was drawn to a Table exclusively for women of color. She was longing for a space that felt like home, where she could rest with people who shared her context and experiences, with whom she didn't need to translate or defend. "I could ask and explore questions without feeling bad for 'making everything about race.' What was it like, specifically, for a Black daughter to lose her mother? What was it like, specifically, for a little Black girl to grow up without the safety and protection of a father figure in the household? What was it like for people of color to lose someone—and for a death certificate to not mention the impacts of generations of oppression?"

Through her work now with The Dinner Party, Shay helps people find companions in their loss experience. She's since swapped high-pressure, diamond-making conditions for a life that prioritizes peace. For her, rest has become critical. For Shay, rest isn't just about tuning out and escaping, although she finds value in those aspects of it as well. On the phone with me, she describes how taking the time to be still and quiet allows her to tune in. As she explains, "For me, grief is about space. It's about the space that person occupied in your life, that is now a different kind of space, an emptiness. Grieving requires us to take space to actually feel into who we are. It requires us to tune out from the outside world and turn into the infinite space within ourselves."

But Shay emphasizes that it doesn't have to happen in some luxurious fashion. It's not about flying an ocean away for a grief quest or falling into the consumeristic trap of self-care products (although she has turned me on to a particularly perfect scented candle). For her, it's about knowing how to comfort and soothe herself within the confines of her own apartment, and reminding herself that in the moments of burnout, she always has the agency to choose. "Even if it's as simple as, what kind of tea do I want to make myself? What show do I want to watch? Which chair do I want to sit in to take this call? Which candle do I want to light?" She uses small moments in her day to tap into her desire, to calibrate what feels right for her in that moment. For her, real rest can only come when she's developed a deep self-knowing. "If I'm not taking time to know myself, then how am I going to know my grief?"

Who has easeful access to time and space to take a breath, and who does not? Being a renegade griever is resisting the hustle culture that keeps us on the hamster wheel of life; but it also means we must recognize the systems of oppression that prohibit some of us from getting off. With no federally mandated bereavement leave days, fewer and fewer of us can afford the space that grief often demands. The stress of losing someone while lacking financial stability can gravely compound a person's worry and precarity as they navigate loss. In a recent study led by Joanne Cacciatore, Zen priest and professor at Arizona State University, poverty was the strongest predictor of psychological distress for bereaved mothers.[35] Bereaved parents living in poverty are also less likely to reach out for support. Access isn't just about whether resources are available, it's about whether people have the privilege of time and space to turn to them.

If we're working multiple jobs, if we're raising multiple kids, if we're caring for ailing family members, or just trying to keep up with a rising cost of living, taking time to rest might feel like a far-off possibility. This isn't the kind of thing that an hour in a tub with spa music playing is going to solve for us. We need systemic ways of addressing the broader fatigue of trying to care for ourselves and our people in a culture that relates to care as a nicety instead of the societal pillar that it is.

For Shay, the work of Tricia Hersey of the Nap Ministry has been a guiding light. Hersey has heralded the burnout we're facing as an issue of social and racial justice. The Nap Ministry was founded by Hersey after her deep recognition that grind culture isn't getting us anywhere other than burnt out. Going to seminary, raising a son, commuting to school via bus because she sold her car to afford tuition, left her, as the *New York Times* wrote, "bone tired."[36] But by giving herself a few minutes to rest on her couch, book on her chest, she felt renewed. Hersey began inviting people to nap collectively—first through a performance piece she called "Transfiguration," and then as the Nap Bishop. The project became a growing community of people who have found nondenominational spiritual support in Hersey's work.

Hersey talks openly about how resisting rest means we're also resisting our grief. "We are grieving and may not even want to recognize it or hold space for it because of our socialization to 'Keep Going!' This denial of the process of grieving creates more trauma and disrupts our healing in the long run." She has pushed my thinking as someone biased toward action, that oftentimes nonaction is the most radical way of tending to our grief. "Everything in culture is working in collaboration for us not to rest," Hersey told an interviewer. "We've been trained from the beginning to ignore our bodies." But as Hersey points out, the experience of grief can be a powerful doorway through which we learn to pay attention. Her book, *Rest Is Resistance*, reminds us that "grieving is a sacred act and one of the ways we can begin to reconnect with our bodies, as we craft a rest practice."[37] If we can learn how to rest in our grief, we can build a new pathway for ourselves that we can come back to even when our grief isn't acute.

What happens when the ways we've coped with loss, the places we've found that ease our hearts, the routines that let us fully exhale, start to feel more like they're rooting in us than we're rooting in them? How do we know when, after a month of reading romance novels in bed, it's time to put on jeans and call a friend; or when the joint we roll to make us feel better on a bad day starts making us feel worse; or when our self-soothing stop at the ice cream store feels more like a compulsion? How do we keep an eye on the things we do to release the valve and make sure they're still doing their job and not turning around and adding a layer of shame, regret, or denial into our already heavy hearts? When do we know it's time to change it up?

For Shay, it's a constant part of her calibration, knowing what types of rest will really be rejuvenating for her, versus just checking out. And as someone who's taken a vow of silence for as long as thirteen days before, Shay has a deep relationship with quietude. "Sometimes, you think you're resting by watching Netflix, but your mind is still in overdrive, and you don't realize that you're still overstimulated," she says. "We're bombarded every day with ads, other people's thoughts and opinions about what we should and should not be doing. My relationship with solitude and quiet affords me these deeper realizations. . . . My mom's life would have been so different if she'd had the opportunity to rest and grieve. So I do it all for her too."

For Shay, and for other renegade grievers, there's a real call to arms in opting out. "I am going hard," Shay told me while we curled up on our respective couches on the phone, "by going soft."

# DREAMING, NIGHT OR DAY

AND THEN THERE'S THE DEEPER version of doing nothing—not just staring into space, but fully clocking out. Sleep is never more important than in times of grief, and paradoxically, it's also the hardest time to get it. You might find yourself in a Goldilocks predicament of insomnia, or inescapable fatigue, never able to fully rest. Sleep and grief act bidirectionally—our lack of sleep can intensify the experience of grief, and grieving can make it challenging to fall asleep.[38]

According to research cited by the Sleep Foundation, 91 percent[39] of people with complicated grief report they have trouble sleeping, and almost half say that struggle occurs three times a week. For bereaved people, something called "middle insomnia" is extremely common, meaning we wake up in the middle of the night and have a hard time getting back to sleep, our heads spinning with our loss. I've heard people describe falling asleep after a loss like trying to land a seaplane on open water; every time you're close to hitting the water, aiming to dive deep into some dreamy realm, the plane lifts off again, with some new thought as cargo.

On the other end of the spectrum, we can do nothing *but* sleep, and still, no matter how hard we rest, the tiredness never quits. What we used to be able to accomplish in a day takes five because we can't find the magic number of hours to wake up feeling rested, and the kind of tired we feel is a weariness beyond REM. There's the moment of waking up, and as the world we're returning to renders, we remember it wasn't all a bad dream.

But when we do get to sleep, good work is getting done. When our minds finally get out of the way, our good sleep gets our cells to regenerate faster, our wounds heal cleaner, our immune system can fight viruses way better.[40] One research study even equates sleep as a time when we do some forgetting, "as if one of the essential functions of sleep is to take out the garbage, as it were, erasing and 'forgetting' information built up throughout the day that would clutter the synaptic network that defines us."[41] I think of this like the crew that comes in to clean an airplane between flights, refilling the tank, collecting the trash, before we can get back in the captain's seat and fly the next leg.

Dinner Partiers experiment with all kinds of ways of getting the sleep they need, as elusive as it might be. From rules like no devices in the bedroom, to white-noise machines cranking; from earplugs and eye masks to soothing audio books babbling through the night. I've heard of grievers asking friends to spend the night for platonic cuddles, wanting a warm body in the bed, or getting a pile of satisfyingly heavy blankets to stack on top of themselves. I've heard of people moving the furniture around in their room to reorient their space, of safely lighting a tea candle that can stand vigil during the night, of CBD tinctures, of tried-and-true-and-doctor-approved sleeping pills. If Renegade Grief requires us to experiment and find the thing that works for us on this particular day in this particular place, we can apply that same spirit of experimentation to getting our rest.

At Dinner Party gatherings, there's one conversation that comes up and draws everyone in a little closer. Eventually, we tune in to the late-night love-jam radio station about "grief dreams"—dreams that include appearances from the person who passed away or involve themes that feel related to our own reckoning with loss—and stay there for a while.

Whether the people around a Table understand certain grief dreams as the firing of scientifically measurable synapses or as a visitation from some different dimension, they're often sheepishly mentioned but quickly dogpiled on. More than 86 percent of people who have lost a spouse or a partner report having had at least one dream of the deceased,[42] and 55 percent of kids at a bereavement camp reported having at least one dream of their deceased parents.[43] We don't have to be sitting on the chaise lounge of a Jungian therapist to interpret our dreams. They're powerful tools, and it's up to us to make sense of the symbols, feelings, and messages we're receiving there.

As a person who gets a lot of satisfaction out of steamrolling grief taboos, I've heard plenty of stories of grief dreams that take my breath away, the reality of our lives once again proving more poetic than fiction. There are the dreams in which someone appears no longer as the cancer patient, the hollowed-out addict, or the identified body, but as their healthiest, most vibrant self. Often, there are conversations, simple words exchanged, hands held, smiles flashed. In our dreams of our people, we often experience them as uncannily alive, and for many people, we wake up a little easier. Dr. Joshua Black, a Canadian grief and bereavement researcher who has done significant research around grief dreams, has developed a theory that one function of these dreams is a way of continuing bonds. The name of the grief game isn't forgetting or moving on; instead, it's about figuring out how to maintain an ongoing connection without getting stuck in sorrow. Black maintains that the connections we find in these dreams, with their scenes of reconciliation, can provide healing equivalent to years of talk therapy.

Dr. Black's inspiration? He's in the club himself. A dream about his dead father, with whom he had a complicated relationship, left him feeling surprisingly resolved at not just the death, but with the hardships of the relationship. He was left wanting to know what this phenomenon of grief dreams is, and he was surprised to see that it wasn't being studied.

When I asked Shay if any of her resting had resulted in grief dreams, she shrugged off the question before describing a series of dreams she had of her mom, a poetic way of describing her shifting relationship to her grief. "In the past, I have often had a recurring dream (nightmare-adjacent) of me waiting around somewhere for my mom to pick me up, and she never comes. Eventually, the trope of this dream started to transform into one where, instead of waiting around, I began to find my own way back home. Over time, the dream completely transformed to a landscape in which my mom would find me and come pick me up, wherever I was waiting, and we'd ride in a car together."

When we look outside of modern Western contexts, the role that dreams can play in times of loss becomes kaleidoscopically more interesting. Across precolonial cultures, grounded in places like the Australian Outback or the Great Plains or the southern tip of Africa, people have viewed dreams as a way of communicating with ancestors and connecting to a collective mainframe of spiritual reality, greater than the conscious mind. Carl Jung, a kingpin of modern psychoanalysis, popularized dreams as a way for our subconscious to communicate back to us. Indigenous cultures worldwide and across time see dream-time as highly powerful pathways to connect to the memory of our ancestors, and to get a different take on how to perceive a situation in waking life. Grief dreams are more common than we all let on, so why not normalize them?

Dr. Black told me that many of the subjects he interviews are sharing their dreams aloud for the very first time because they hadn't felt safe enough to confide in others before. His podcast, *Grief Dreams*, has now shared hundreds of these stories.[44] For those who have shared their dreams, some report making whoever they were telling uncomfortable, or they received back uneducated advice that minimized or challenged their understanding of the dream. We're met again with the lack of grief fluency getting in the way of moments of connection and support. He's also heard stories of people not sharing their grief dreams, not wanting to make other family members jealous. Yet in these instances, we're skipping over the chance to ask ourselves, or the people we care about, what we make of these dreams: *How did that dream make me feel? Is there a useful insight or image that can help me in whatever season of grief I might find myself in, be it five days or five years or five decades out?*

Through grief dreams, even people who have had a very complicated relationship with their person are sometimes able to change the
narrative. Moments of mercy and compassion blossom in the dream of
an abusive father, asking for forgiveness in a dream. For Shay, she's come
to understand her dreams about her mom not picking her up as her
subconscious processing the feelings of abandonment she experienced,
at first in childhood and then even more profoundly after her mom's
death. That the dream's narrative has now changed to her and her mom
cruising off together, shows her how those feelings have started to subside with time and healing.

In this way, charting how someone is portrayed in dreams might
help you reflect on where you're at in your own healing. Let the dream
world be an ally, providing you with a peephole into the below-the-
surface tending that our subconscious mind is doing. Let's pay attention.

Inevitably, someone around the Table will pause, and ask: "But do
you actually think it's a visitation from them?" That is, are such dreams
just some amazing holographic image that our subconscious has figured
out how to re-create to help us make sense of the loss, or is this a visitation? Is it evidence that there's life after death? The answer? It really
doesn't matter where you land. Trust that whether the intelligence is
otherworldly, or the brilliance of your own subconscious mind, these
dreams are yet another tool to understand how you're *really* doing, not
just how the external world says you *should* be.

And what about those of us who've had no comforting dreams
of the deceased at all, and find this whole theme annoying and un-
relatable? If you're in the dreamless camp, there are ways to increase
your dream retention upon waking, by writing them down and talking
about them more. Dr. Black is confident that you're probably dreaming of the deceased more often than you're remembering, as he has
found that the more you remember your dreams in general, the more
you remember dreams of the deceased. Think about all the dreams we
lose when we roll over and go back to sleep, or in the quick-draw of

picking up our cell phone upon waking. The satisfaction we might be longing for is lingering in the air, so choose how to spend those precious moments of transition, and I challenge you to spend more time there to catch it.

For a while, I didn't dream about my dad, even though I would hear about dreams of him from family members, as well as his coworkers and random family friends. It seemed like he was being generous with his dream cameos, with everyone except for me; or more likely, there was something about dreams of him my waking self wasn't ready to remember. One of his mentees even downloaded a twenty-three point business strategy from him in a dream the year after he died, one final pep talk on where her career was heading, and how to steer the ship he was leaving behind. She was a little embarrassed to share it, uncertain if it might confuse or upset me. I'm glad she emailed it to me, as weirdly envious as it made me feel. I've scoured through it, wondering if there was something in her recap that stood out to me, an Easter egg he meant for me to find. Nothing applies. Whenever I read through it, it mostly just feels like flipping through someone else's mail.

Yet over time, my dad did start showing up occasionally in my dreams. They aren't show-stopping. I don't wake up with a gasp. But I've gone from dreaming about him as a cancer patient with a tumor-induced limp to dreaming about him as the way I hope to remember him most, in a Sunday kind of T-shirt with a stretched-out collar from a marathon he'd run or a band he loved. A big, toothy grin, and a particular eye twinkle that, the older I get, the more I understand was the reflection of my own eye in his.

Most recently I've had dreams where I learn that he never fully left—that instead of dying, he decided to abandon the American experiment and secretly move to Europe, unattached. I had a different dream where I found out that, all this time he'd been cruising around the vastness of the ocean in a personal-sized submarine, on some kind of secret mission.

These dreams were both comforting and unsettling that, somehow, he was here all along but yet still felt impossibly far away; I felt happy to think of him on the map, on some next grand adventure in Europe or under the sea, but it stung that there was anywhere other than his old life that he would rather be. They showed me the push and pull of longing and letting go still happening within me; still quietly asking for my tending.

In the first dream, where I found out he lived in Europe, I frantically rushed to the airport to board a plane to find him, waking up before it landed. I wonder if there will ever be a night when I dream that way again. If I do, I wonder if, instead of rushing to see, whether my dream self might find some way of reaching out while staying firmly rooted inside my own life. I hope to write him a postcard, to pick up the phone and call, or simply wave to him from across the sea.

For those of us who aren't dreaming about our people, Dr. Black encourages people to daydream, to spend time envisioning the dreams you *wish* you had—the apology, the "I love you," the reassurance that your person is fine, and so are you. It's less about implanting ideas that we hope come up in dreams, and more about being honest about the kind of resolution we're craving. Dr. Black guides people to take the time to wonder what dream it is that you wish you could have. What would your person say, what would they be wearing, where would you be? And how can we, even by imagining it, re-create any sliver of its revelation?

Dr. Black's prompt reminds me of Christina Tran, an artist and early Dinner Partier, who shared a ritual writing practice called *Dear Daughter* she took on in the years after her mother's death.[45] The project is a series of messages that she wants to share with her hypothetical, future daughter, layered over photos of her late mother. In the ritual practice of writing these messages, something powerful shifted for Christina. "Through the alchemy of art, who can say whether I am sending messages into the future for my children, or whether they are messages sent backward in time to a younger version of my mom when she was a daughter herself, or whether these are channeled through my maternal ancestors so that they can send me the messages which I yearn to hear in my present-day life." The power of imagining the types of conversations we would like to have or the messages we would like to hear, with the ritualistic intention of invoking their memory, in a subtle way can bend time itself; what's below the surface can come to mind; the answer to the question *Where am I at with my grief at this exact moment in my life?* may be answered in a way that might surprise even you.

# FORMING INTERSPECIES FRIENDSHIPS

SOMETIMES THE MOST DIRECT PATH to being present to our grief is to sidestep the human condition and spend some time relating to the natural world, to see what the nonhuman realm, which has gotten quite good at its own cycles of life and death, has to say about it all.

In a civilization that's increasingly disconnected from the natural world—an era where children can name more Pokémon characters than wildlife species[46]—it's renegade to relate to nature not as a backdrop to our grief, but as its master class. Nature is chock-full of grief wisdom, protocols, and offers of support. For some, their deepest companion and counselor in grief is the ocean or bodies of water; for others, time alone in the woods; but in this chapter, I'll be focusing on another branch of the earth's rich taxonomy here—mammals, both domesticated and wild as can be.

In addition to the lightbulb epiphanies of psychedelics, the ever tender companionship of my rescue terrier, Biscotti, with her quiet demeanor and bad breath, has been wildly supportive when it comes to being present with my grief. A good deed of fostering a rescue dog, found prowling around Dodger Stadium on the edge of giving birth to a litter of puppies, turned into a foster-fail, meaning she became my partner in crime a few years after my dad died, and I've never looked back.

Being in relationship with animals makes us more human. Biscotti gave me a reason to get out of bed, interrupting my late-night, mindless scrolling so I could take her for a stroll to the grassy corner of our block, where I could take in the stars and she could let out a pee. Biscotti is the reason I met my neighbors and got to know the contours of my block much better than when I didn't have a reason to stop and smell the roses while she stopped to sniff the fire hydrants. Watching her follow the sunspots across our apartment so that she could find the perfect nap spot gave me a reason to notice the way the sun traveled across a day and throughout the year. The unexpected joy I get from the sound of her lapping water from the other room. The way she'll audibly sigh in the middle of a nap in a way that coregulates my own nervous system with her breathing. Or the way she'll shake off a scary noise, releasing the fear from her body. Whenever I hear it, something releases in me too.

While the world of emotional support animals might seem like a carnival at times—people bringing peacocks and rabbits and miniature horses on planes—there's real proof that being with animals gives us the kind of companionship and loyalty that many of us need to get out of the swirl of negative thoughts and harmful behaviors so we can be in the present moment.[47] A study done in Boulder, Colorado, found that pet parents experiencing homelessness credited their animals for saving or changing their lives.[48] A woman told researchers how getting a dog, a German Shepherd who was close to being euthanized in a shelter, gave her the purpose she needed to quit hard drugs, leave an abusive relationship, and care for her HIV diagnosis. Another subject reported that his dog helped him fight the debilitating depression that led him to life on the streets in the first place. Another woman referred to her cat as her "suicide barrier"—the reason she kept going, despite her extremely challenging circumstances.

✶ ✶ ✶

One of my early supporters of getting a dog of my own was Lindsay, who brought us the question "*Where are you at with your loss right now?*"

Lindsay's mom died when she was eight years old, a loss that was compounded when her dad partnered up with a woman who, let's just say, reinforced the whole evil stepmother stereotype. "When my mom was alive, my life was fine. After my mom died, I could never do anything right. Love in our household became very conditional. I would meet the condition, and the goal post would move." Her stepmother, who had a daughter a few years older than Lindsay, would insist that grieving nine-year-old Lindsay was a bad kid, disruptive to the family, and she eventually advocated for Lindsay to be sent to boarding school. During holidays, she would demand that Lindsay spend time with her grandmother while the rest of the family went on vacations. Not only did Lindsay lose her mother, but she also lost a home environment in which she could feel safe and nurtured. Instead of developing support and trust in humans, especially from her caretakers, she was forced to survive the loss of her mother on her own.

Lindsay, understandably, grew up with some big defenses, which meant that when her dad died when she was twenty-one, she had gotten good at callousing over emotion. Of being strong, but really, being hyper-independent and emotionally numb.

It wasn't until Lindsay met Shorty, a black lab who had the pedigree of a major show dog but the disposition of a high-school dropout, that she decided it was time to bring an animal into her own life. When Lindsay met Shorty through her aunt, she wasn't in the acute "take the day hour by hour" stage of her grief, but she was still struggling with ongoing depression, anxiety, and general mistrust of relationships that were a result of her cascade of losses. She had a feeling that a good place to start repairing that trust was with a four-legged creature.

With Shorty, Lindsay had that irrefutable reason to get out of bed in the morning. "I'm not going to *not* walk my dog. My responsibility to her kept me present. I couldn't just sleep through the day, be sad, or numb-out on TV or food or sleeping—I couldn't do that anymore." But maybe even more powerfully, Shorty gave her a new imprint of what unconditional love feels like, something she hadn't experienced since her mom's death. Thanks to Shorty, Lindsay is in a place where she can "love and trust humans again, because I can love and trust this animal. I can be responsible for other people and relationships, because I can be responsible for her. I don't have to be perfect, but maybe if I can care for Shorty, I can care for friends, I can re-engage in love."

Shorty was nine years old when she and Lindsay met, which meant that in dog years, she was well on her way to seniordom. When Lindsay adopted Shorty, it was clear that in the nearish future, she was going to have to say goodbye, yet again. Lindsay went into her relationship with Shorty with her eyes wide open. "Getting a pet is signing a pact that you will face death in your life. In getting Shorty, I stood tall in the fact that I am strong enough to love and lose. That felt empowering." They got five glorious years together. Lindsay also decided to get another dog, a lab named Huckleberry, to overlap with Shorty. There was something about her dogs having a shared context, a lineage, that made it easier when it was time to say the inevitable goodbye to Shorty.

Knowing that the animals we're bringing into our lives are going to die in our lifetime makes being a pet owner a renegade act. To be a griever, to know how hard it can be to lose, and to nonetheless open our hearts to care for an animal, is a leap of faith. *I'll lose this one. It'll be hard, but the grief will be worthy of the love.*

It's not just comfort and cuddles that can come from spending time with the natural and animal worlds during times of grief. There are times when, going through the most human thing there is, can make us feel estranged from the human culture around us. And yet, we can look to nature and find the normalization we're looking for. Nature doesn't shy away from or avoid death, and can become the grief instruction manual we've been waiting for.

What might we come to understand about our own grief process, by seeing how the natural world makes sense of its ongoing loop of death and rebirth? With deep respect for the billions of years that earth has been iterating, what truths about ourselves might we find there, from members of that complex natural world, if we just lift our gaze up and away from our own navels to look out across the land, the sea, and the skies?

One initial insight you'll find is that everything is in a constant state of dying. The fall leaves become the fertile forest floor. Predators take down prey. The decay of certain objects becomes the food for others. The circle of life involves a whole lot of death. We can look to nature to understand that all things come to an end, that energy is never destroyed, just reformatted. Although grief can feel isolating, there is a comfort in knowing that humans are not the only species reckoning with endings and beginnings; in fact, we're not the only species who grieve.

* * *

In her study of grief, Dr. Barbara J. King, an anthropologist and professor emerita at William & Mary, has documented reports of keening and angry outbursts.[49] She's written about grieving companions who try to revive the bodies of their lost loved ones, and who lean on one another for physical support to stand. There are burials and graveside visits as well as haunting the site where someone was last seen. She's heard of death-by-suicide in situations of deep pain or anguish, and staring longingly into photographs of late partners. Sometimes there's a family member who expresses deep emotion while the rest continue as if nothing's happened. An individual might sink into months of lethargy, cutting social ties, and then, over time, begin the process of reaching out once again for more social connection. Except, her subjects haven't been humans mourning the loss of someone close to them; they've been housecats, apes, elephants, and other four-leggeds. Studying animal grief across species lines, King has found that loss in the animal kingdom doesn't look all that different from human loss.

Dr. King will be the first to tell you that not all animals grieve, as far as we know. And yet, we discussed that when people assume that describing an animal as grieving is anthropomorphizing—or projecting human characteristics inaccurately on another species—they're off base. "Attributing grief to other animals, if done carefully, based on their visible behavior, is by definition not anthropomorphic because grief is not only a human emotion; it doesn't belong only to us." We can't just say we know grief when we see it; simply because an animal appears to our human eye to be impacted by a loss doesn't guarantee that that's what's going on inside their animal mind. And yet, the research of King and others has proven out: we're not the only grievers on Planet Earth.

To me, understanding the way that animals grieve shows us that the things we're feeling aren't just some weakness of constitution, some bad mood we should be able to shoo away, some longing for modes of healing that are off base. "We grieve with human words but animal bodies and animal gestures and animal movements," says King. What might we do with those same animal bodies if we allowed them more latitude to inform our grief?

Shorty was the gateway dog for Lindsay's love. After bringing Shorty into her life, and then Huck, Lindsay eventually met someone who she was excited by the possibility of spending her life with. I went to the sweetest backyard wedding in Berkeley for Lindsay and Nik, with their camper van turned into a photo booth, and a raucous round of trivia instead of toasts. Despite the losses that made her close herself off, she remains resolutely hopeful about creating love and connection amid the chaos of life and loss.

In the years after moving to Portland, Lindsay got pregnant with a boy they named Ever. It's a good name that doesn't get said nearly enough. Ever died during labor, before he had a chance to leave the warm confines of his mother's body. That year, Lindsay was one of almost two million mothers who lost a baby to stillbirth labor—and yet, the experience was deeply isolating.[50]

In the wake of Ever's death, Lindsay felt like the people who cared for her were so eager for her to be okay. She felt pressured to put on a happy face, when what she wanted to do was show her son to her friends and family. To carry him with her a little longer. To not have had this being inside of her for nine months and then have him vanish before her brain and body could catch up to the fact that before he fully arrived, he was gone.

But there was one mother who Lindsay felt deeply understood by. Tahlequah, also known as J35 in scientific circles, was an orca whale who lived in a pod not far from Lindsay in the waters off the coast of the Pacific Northwest. Tahlequah's pregnancy—which lasts seventeen months for orcas—overlapped with the time Lindsay was pregnant with Ever.[51] The orca's daughter was a highly anticipated arrival. Due to the diminishing supplies of salmon in the Salish Sea, the bioaccumulation of toxins in the water, as well as orcas captured and taken into captivity for places like SeaWorld and Marine Land, the orcas of Washington's waters had their breeding population cut in half, and they've struggled to recover ever since. The orcas in the Salish Sea are an endangered species relying on an overfished species to nourish them and their young. This would be the first calf in three years for this particular pod. With the pod getting older, the species was arriving at a tipping point, and conservationists were holding their breath as Tahlequah approached her due date.

The baby, Tali, was born—and then, after about thirty minutes of life, she died. What was astounding was that, instead of letting her daughter's body slip into the waters of the Salish Sea, Tahlequah kept her child afloat, carrying Tali with the soft slope of her nose as her pod swam.

Lindsay followed the story of Tahlequah and wept with her as she carried the body of her young daughter for seventeen days, one day for each of the months it took to gestate her. At last, Tahlequah relinquished her daughter to the sea. Lindsay described it to me, saying, "It was such a beautiful thing. I don't know what they were thinking, but I feel like animals grieve in the present in a way that we don't. We want it to be gone. People want to see us happy as soon as possible. I think humans are so uncomfortable with grief." Lindsay was moved by how Tahlequah's pod appeared to mourn with her. "It was like they loved that child still. It felt really powerful."

It's a behavior that's been witnessed with other whales and dolphins. Chimps too. Mothers seemingly say, *I'm not ready to let go.* When Lindsay heard the story, she finally felt understood, mirrored, kindred to someone, even though that someone was a whale. She resonated with this urge to carry her son around. "When Ever died, I remember thinking of these weird Victorian novels of the woman who carries around her dead baby. If I could have people look at my kid, to show them that he existed, I would do it."

There's evidence that some animals don't just carry their dead with them, but that they have what looks to researchers like a vigil, standing around the body of dead relatives. A female giraffe at a Kenyan Conservancy stood around the body of her dead calf for four days, and was joined by other family members, wrapping necks around one another in a sort of hug. Dogs will stand on the graves of their owners, or where other animal companions are buried. In Tahlequah's case, scientists even observed the moment when her pod began circling together at moonrise, in what the onlooker described as something that felt ceremonial, like a family gathering together to mourn.

Lindsay was not the only human watching. Global discussion erupted around whether or not animals grieve, a world surprised and moved by the unmistakable sign of a mother who doesn't want to let go. For the Lummi Nation, a tribal community indigenous to Washington State, orcas are related to as family members, and called *qwe 'lhol mechen,* which translates to "relatives that live under the waves." "Anyone else out there who's a father or a mother, I think we have to attempt to empathize with her," said Jay Julius, chair of the Lummi Nation.[52] For Lindsay and others, empathizing went one step further, to reflecting on the cause, not just whether they grieved, but who caused this grief in the first place. The threat and near collapse of the orca's food source—salmon—from human intervention was suddenly shed in another light, as a family bereaved. Our impact on nature, not just captured in a report but in the image of a mother, longing for her lost babe.

Then came Beatrix. Three years later, Ever's sister was born. Lindsay's not a big fan of the "rainbow child" phrase—commonly used to describe a baby who comes after a miscarriage or stillbirth. "It implies that Ever is somehow the darkness, or bad, and that Beatrix is the light." While she gets the connotation, it overshadows the part of her son who wasn't a negative thing at all, but her baby for whom she still grieves, even as her hands and heart are full with this new toddler.

Three months after Beatrix was born, Lindsay heard great news from the Portland sound. Tahlequah had another baby, this time a boy, and healthy. He's named Phoenix, and he's thriving. Lindsay remembers the deep relief of knowing that this mother also got the joy of seeing her child in the world. There was something about these parallel storylines between her and Tahlequah that moved her beyond words.

Picture a whale body drifting slowly to the bottom of a calm, fathomless stretch of water. Imagine the quiet, the beams of light slowly fading, the ombré of darkness that it moves through. Know that, when it lands, a new life cycle begins.

This is called a whale fall, the resting grounds of whale carcasses, and has been found in the last few decades to be some of the most nutrient-dense, biodiverse pockets on the seafloor. For the next century, a whole chorus of different species will live off and evolve within the flesh and bones of this decomposing whale. Tali likely died too close to shore to become a part of this cycle, but for whales that perish on their migration path out in the deep sea, their descent to the bottom kicks off a whole new era of life.

Octopi, mussels, lobster, some species of which have been discovered for the very first time in the container of a whale fall, thrive in these settings.[53] It's also thought that the whaling industry, in taking some of the biggest animals out of the sea and depriving the sea floor of its whale fall nutrients, have changed how the ocean floor has evolved. Whale falls sequester the same amount of carbon as thousands of trees.[54] Death in the wild provides the foundation for massive amounts of life. When we sanitize and sweep away, interrupt and remove, the natural cycle suffers.

I am continually moved by the way that the colossal losses in our own lives, even if small in stature, can shift over time. How the heartbreak of a loss on the surface can become a source of strength and nutrients deep within the dark, quiet oceans of our inner worlds. Of how renegade the act can be to not look away. It's not tying a pretty bow around a life cut short. It's about feeling the ongoing ripples of a person's presence, which last far beyond their years at sea level.

Being present with your grief is about finding ways of letting the bigness of this experience wash over you, and to settle within you, and to let our body do the digesting that it knows how to do. It can be intimidating, but intimacy with our grief is intimacy with the most fertile floor of life.

Within Lindsay is the whale fall of Ever. Within Shay, her mother, Marilyn. For Sol, his father, and his other father, and his mother next. At each Dinner Party Table, new friendships form, families finding one another in the wake of hardship. Each loss feeding us in some way, even if it's hard to picture it from a boat getting rocked by waves far above.

*  *  *

For these big losses of our lives, our grief never fully goes away, just as our memory of them never leaves us either. For many of us, we would have it no other way. In fact, the more time we spend on earth, the more loves we have and friendships we form. As long as the people around us, ourselves included, gradually, consistently get older, the more loss is a muscle that we'll have to employ; a verb that we must continue acting on. We may only have a few great death losses in our lifetime—if we're lucky—but regardless, once we've been initiated into this club of ours, there's no forgetting it.

That's why, in this section, we've explored ways to be present with it. Instead of spending our time and energy avoiding or worrying or reducing or ignoring, these care practices we've moved through are a handful of ways that you might come into presence with your grief, unplug your ears, and see what it has to say. These are some of the practices people I know have found helpful to tend to their grief; ways to download its hard-earned wisdom. And within each of them, there's a pathway to finding the people with whom to be in the thick of it, as you explore how that wisdom might inform the way you move into your future.

# ACT 3

# CREATING
# YOUR FUTURE

IT WAS WINTER IN LOS Angeles, and Lennon and I were sitting on the front porch of the house we moved into a few months after meeting. By then, we had hosted our first half a dozen or so dinners, long enough to realize that we were onto something. We had a fresh piece of oversized paper covering the patio table in front of us, and were staring at ideas and numbers, words and images, of the thing we were starting to build.

As the sun set against downtown LA's sparkling skyline, we mapped out what this organization might want to become, as if we were laying tracks for a train that wanted to arrive in the world, figuring out the direction in which the idea wanted to head. It was our own form of future casting. The scent of markers and their high squeak carried through the air as we scribbled ideas, asked ourselves questions, and dreamed of the possibilities.

We filled and refilled glasses of wine and broke out a fresh bar of chocolate. We said things aloud that I'm sure were naive and ungrounded, unaware of the amount of work and resources required to turn any big idea into a reality. Still, giddy as we were, we understood that creating a new paradigm around grief and loss required us to zoom out from how things currently were and focus on the hazy horizon line of how they might be. I remain so grateful we let ourselves dream big. The creation of The Dinner Party required some imagination.

In the years since that night, I've learned so much from the people who look at social change work as a visionary practice, who engage with the parts of it that are, at the core, acts of sheer make-believe.

Author and emergent strategist Adrienne Maree Brown speaks of how "I often feel I am trapped inside someone else's imagination, and I must engage my own imagination in order to break free."[1]

Much of the default world we live in is the result of power dynamics and cultural forces; biases and unspoken agreements made by humans, for humans. If we can't imagine a different world, there's no way out from the current one. It applies to organizations and movements, but it also applies to the small details of our own lives as we integrate a loss. We can use our imaginations to step out of the default reality, and in return help usher the world—in a macro sense, or in a small and quiet personal sense—toward that alternate future vision. This isn't about hacking our way out of grief itself—and I am skeptical of anyone who promises you such a reprieve. But maybe there are some changes we can make to how our culture responds to our grief that will make the whole experience a little more focused on what does matter, instead of cultural noise.

I remember talking to friends and family about The Dinner Party early on, and I was often met with a "That's nice," or "Are you sure you still want to think about/work in/deal with this grief stuff?" But the possibility of it was so much more than that. It was a connection to a future that seemed bigger and more meaningful, one built around bucking the norms around how our society treats loss and death. I was lucky to find in Lennon a partner who wanted to hang out in the possibilities of that world too. A partner who took the helm as our executive director and has captained the ship through many a storm. Someone who also hoped that, for the next generation of grievers, the world might be a little more of a hospitable place, the process a little less ragged, a seat at the table ready. Maybe that next generation is you.

I've long since lost that piece of paper, but one piece of it I remember keenly: the corner, where with a big circle around it we'd written "10,000." Lennon and I had asked ourselves when we'd know that this project of ours was complete—and we decided it was when ten thousand people had joined us around the proverbial table, finding friendships in their grief experiences. It seemed huge then, almost unfathomable. When we soared past that number a few years ago, Lennon and I looked at each other with a shared knowing, both excited and exhausted. That train we were laying tracks for was much longer than we had foreseen that first night, markers in hand. It ends up, years after that, the train is still moving.

In no way am I suggesting you must spend the next ten years building a grief-related community, although if that calls to you, let's talk. What I am suggesting is that you spend some time reflecting on how the grief you're grappling with might be used to inform your future. To be clear, this isn't about forcing some silver lining in the smoke cloud of a garbage fire. But, in our avoidance of spending time reflecting on loss personally and collectively, we often miss the chance to really distill down the learnings, not just from someone's death, but from their life; and to honor the person, or people, who were here before and who mattered. And it's that bit of processing I'm inviting you to take time with.

You might ask yourself: All right, this fucked-up thing happened, but *how am I different? How am I seeing the world in a deeper way? In what ways does this make me want to change or course correct how I'm showing up?* Or simply, *How has my grief completely erased my tolerance for bullshit of any kind?*

The medicine in grief might be straightforward, or it might be a complicated cocktail. You might realize you want to spend more time with family, or less time worrying about a mean boss who is probably just their own kind of miserable. It might be the learning that, wow, the pharmaceutical pain management industry is corrupt as hell and needs to be dismantled. Or that because you had a parent who was boundaryless right up until the day they died, you want to consciously nurture a different relationship style in your life. Even in these insights, there's material for our own evolution, for our uncovering of what matters most to us.

It might make you realize that as you move into your future, tending to your grief is not going to look like bubble baths and yoga classes, or at least not that alone. Instead, you might commit to being an active part of rebooting the cultural systems that prevent all people from caring for their mental health. You might decide to fight the injustices that leave families unnecessarily grieving in the first place, a too-common story that might be yours too. Your grief might be the jet fuel that makes you an activist, a leader, or the friend you wish you had in the early days of your loss.

I've talked to other grievers who are afraid that their loss experience will harden them, calcify them into some new dysfunctional shape; that it will make them hard to connect with, held back, less open to connection or kindness or kismet. And there are times when we're in the thick of it, where that may be the type of posture we need to hold to keep ourselves upright. No shame in self-protection. There are seasons of grief when sticking the turtle head into the shell and hanging out until the waves settle is undeniably the right move.

But then there are the times when we're ready to poke our heads back out. And that can be a moment to ask how we might nurture the kind of world that makes us feel most alive, a feeling we can grok even more intimately once we've said a real goodbye.

# MAKING YOUR HOME

THICK CIRCLES OF JADE AND peat-colored glass filter beams of light onto the earthen floor. It's a place that's been at rest, with cobwebs accumulating in corners and serrated oak leaves sweeping across the floor. Misty's bottle house has sat uninhabited in the shade of a shrubby mountain for a few years now, but it still carries the landmark air of a place that has mattered.

Misty, a woman in her thirties wearing high-waisted jeans and a white tank, stoops to walk through the doorway. Once inside, she surveys the state of her handiwork, all created by her during the summer she turned eighteen. As she turns in a circle, taking it all in, I sense the memories coming back to her. The table for two, covered in a dusty cloth. The small cot, where she warns me scorpions now sleep. A cabinet filled with the bobs and bits of a sewing hobby that became a passion during the time she lived here. We went from acquaintances to friends around the inaugural table of The Dinner Party, and I am thrilled to see the bottle house in person that she told us about during those first nights together—the care practice that helped her the most in the aftermath of her mother's death.

Misty was a freshman in college when she got a call telling her that her parents had been in a terrible car accident. Her father was likely going to make it, but her mother, Betty, was in grave condition. Misty reached home just in time to say goodbye. Her dad, shaken by the loss of his wife and traumatized from the accident, leaned into his drinking habit. In hindsight, Misty can see how he was suffering, but at the time it felt like abandonment. When he was drinking, it was claustrophobic to be in the house with him, and she didn't have anywhere else to go. She felt barely functional—not ready to go back to school or strike out on her own. The longing and grief for her mother would hit her in waves, and she was afraid that if she didn't find an outlet, they would overtake her. She longed for a place where she could be alone, or with friends, and a setup where she could make something with the sea of feelings inside her.

Researching what other people did to create alternative places to live, she came across the work of Grandma Prisbrey,[2] a folk artist from a nearby town in Southern California, a quirky lady who sifted through local dumps to find the building material for her art. Over time, Prisbrey constructed something bizarre and beautiful—an entire village of buildings and fountains around a plaza, all built with discarded glass bottles and cement. Having barely survived a major earthquake, Prisbrey's Bottle Village has an end-times beauty that spoke to Misty. Maybe she could create something from the mess of her and her dad's lives with the glass bottles that were abundantly available in the recycling bin at their curb.

So she took a shopping cart through the aisles of her local hardware store, attracting some side-eyes from the contractors as she heaved wood planks and bags of cement into her sedan. She learned how to mix cement from internet tutorials, and after sketching up a simple four-walled structure, started erecting a home of her own in her dad's backyard. Row by row, stack by stack, six-pack after case of wine after handle of liquor, Misty built her new home. Her dad, supportive of the project, fixed a corrugated metal roof over the walls and added an old window. He seemed happy for her to have taken on a creative project, despite his own struggles. Sometimes our most complicated relationships aren't with those who died, but with those doing their best to keep on living.

While the bottle house was a helpful retreat, Misty remembers the making of it as being the most therapeutic part. We can find sanctuaries not just in physical buildings, but in patterns of motion, not just in places but also states of mind.

Misty needed somewhere she could funnel her energy, and the rhythmic motion of washing labels off beer bottles, blending water and cement mix, setting bottles before the sealer dried, and slowly and methodically turning a jumble of trash into a neatly organized wall was the medicine she found her way to. When we're busying our hands, we're distracted from our ruminations, the old circuits of our brooding. The active task of building kept Misty's mind occupied, which paradoxically allowed her to be present with the grief moving through her.

How do we ever feel like we're at ease in the world when the person who was our home is no longer physically present? One of the things many of us are left to grapple with after a major loss is creating the kind of sanctuary for ourselves that someone else once provided.

There are cultural suggestions galore for how to spend time at home immediately after someone's passing—like building private altars, hosting a wake, or sitting shiva. But once we've made it through the social infrastructure those first few months provide, it's up to us to navigate the next big set of home-related questions that come up, and which are unique to our own story. Whether we're adjusting to sleeping in a bed without them or are longing for a sense of comfort that they never provided to us in the first place; at some point or another, a part of renegade grieving is reckoning with our relationship to home.

There's the undeniable, practical, Maslow's hierarchy of needs questions about grief and housing. Times of death and loss can be some of the most financially unstable for families. We learned that rent can be deferred when there's a pandemic impacting the planet, but what about a death impacting an individual family, a crisis of one household?[3] Organizations like the Economic Security Project and the Tenant Union Federation[4] are working diligently to build social protections for families as a way of building economic resilience, both in times of crisis and in everyday life. Modern social protections like guaranteed income, rental assistance, affordable housing, debt-free college and more are being piloted across America—and it's up to us to apply pressure to our local policymakers to make these protections a reality.[5]

To make it specific, here's a heartbreaking story.[6] A baby tragically fell out of a broken window in a Kansas City apartment building—a window that the parents had been trying to get a negligent landlord to repair to no avail. The parents, while grieving the loss of their child, are now in a legal battle with their landlord and the city over whose fault it is. The Tenant Union stepped in with mutual aid support for the family, and advocacy for their case, raising awareness of the dangerous conditions of their housing complex—to hold the landlord accountable for any future injury or death, any future unnecessary grief.

But even having a roof over our heads doesn't always mean that we have a place where our nervous system can settle. Where we can exhale and surrender to wherever our grief might be on that very day. Where we can start to create the kind of day-to-day for ourselves that might not include them, but that honors them, and where we can imagine creating a future, albeit one different from what we may have hoped.

Misty sent for her boxes from school, officially dropping out. She unpacked blankets, books, and clothes, turning her bottle house into a place where she could get cozy. Her mom had rearranged her bedroom after Misty left for school, setting their family's old sewing machine on a table, waiting for her to return. Almost like she knew. Misty lugged the machine into her new space, ran an extension cord from the main house, and set up her own glass bottle atelier. She started by taking her mom's clothing, tearing apart garments, and rebuilding them into new clothing pieces to wear, or sculptures made of fabrics. From inside her bottle house, she found she could start breaking down and rebuilding, using the materials around her to move the feelings inside her.

The word "sanctuary" means holy place; a place where we're protected. In the bottle house, Misty was erecting her own version of such a place. Little did Misty know that the whir of the sewing machine would be a soundtrack to the next decade of her life, as she started her own clothing company, one that would be featured on the pages of some of the world's most glamorous magazines. The move into the backyard, only a few hundred feet from her childhood home, initially a way to cope with the present, became a pathway into her future.

As with all these care practices, there are countless variations on the theme, each of us facing our own unique take on how to, in this case, create a sense of home. For some of us, the work becomes saying goodbye to a center of gravity and setting out on a search for another. Lennon had to sell the house where she grew up, and where her mom ultimately died. I remember her flying back to North Carolina from the group home we moved into together the year we started sitting down to dinner. She got everything out of the house, but for her, it was leaving something behind that felt like the creative act she needed to close that chapter on her own terms. Maybe someday, whoever lives there now, or the people who call it home after that, will find the letter under the attic floorboards that she slipped through the cracks before walking across the threshold for the last time. It was time for her to move out, but not without a record of the lives that had unfolded there, a retelling of the memories within those walls. Since then, her exploration of home has been creating a sense of it with found family, in the group house where she lived for the next decade.

For others, we realize that we've outgrown the kind of home we chose in the initial aftermath of our loss. For Sundari, her reckoning with the idea of home in the wake of her mother's death started with a chance visit to a retrofitted school bus festival, and the epiphany that she didn't want a traditional living situation at all. From the outside looking in, she had it all figured out at the time: living in an ocean-front condo in Miami, with a thriving business as a doula. But something wasn't sitting right. Part of her healing, catalyzed by her grief, was to "step outside of what life should *look* like and [make] an intentional decision to lean into what life should *feel* like. I wanted out of the rat race."

Once the dust of her mom's death settled, Sundari was ready to release herself from the life she thought she needed, for the life she really wanted. Inspired by her stop at the festival, she bought an old school bus, fixed it up immaculately into a home on four wheels, and drove across the country, visiting friends, and staying in campgrounds, a stretch of desert, or vineyard parking lots that called to her. And then, as goes with the ever-evolving nature of grief, she shifted once she realized even that had run its course. On the other side of van life, she's now more interested in having a home with a larder, where she can stock a spacious pantry, reclaim ancestral traditions, and in her words, "[explore] my grief and [expand] my life in much slower and softer spaces as time goes on."

For others, the renegade act might be in owning that we're more comfortable in the in-betweens, rather than a single place. I remember meeting Kalayaan, a Dinner Partier in Los Angeles, and was immediately struck by her warmth and kindness. I learned that she had struggled with housing instability her whole life, which was exacerbated when her mother's struggles with schizophrenia led to their estrangement, her brother was incarcerated, and her father—who had moved back to their native lands of the Philippines—passed away during COVID. Because of travel restrictions, Kalayaan didn't get the chance to say goodbye.

For Kalayaan, it was a single word, a new idea, that helped her find a sense of home even while living in a transitional housing program and coping with this series of seismic losses in her family. The word "nepantlera," popularized by Chicana feminist scholar Gloria E. Anzaldúa, is a Nahuatl word that means "in between."[7] According to Anzaldúa, it's a "word for the space between two bodies of water, the space between two worlds. It is a liminal space, a space where you are not this or that but where you are changing."

For Kalayaan, coming across this word while studying Chicana/o Studies at UCLA, was like finding solid ground inside herself. It helped her contextualize her own identity as a Filipina/Pinay woman living with family across continents; of being someone who had a family with relationships that were mixed with conditional care and PTSD; of being someone who was more comfortable having a bag packed and ready to go than a closet neatly hung.

Over time, the word stayed with her as she navigated through a period of shoring up her own foundation. It stayed with her as she worked two jobs and saved up to get an apartment of her own. It stayed with her during conversations with friends, encouraging her to unpack the bag she was used to keeping by the door and settle into the new place, even if it wasn't her forever home. She thought of it when she was flipping through a colorful interior design book she found at the library, which gave her some ideas for making her four walls into a place that reflected how she was starting to feel on the inside: inspired and safe, vibrant and warm.

When I interviewed her on the phone, she was sitting on the couch she had just gotten for her apartment. She was feeling a little less like a person caught in between two bodies of water and more and more like someone on her own slice of land, with tapestries on the walls, a candle lit, a clean kitchen. She was in a place where memories of an unstable childhood and the years of prolonged grief could be logged as that, memories, and she could look toward her future with a strong sense that there was somewhere she belonged.

✳  ✳  ✳

Misty's bottle house story has always stuck with me, because it feels so outside of the normal repertoire of grief stories, the quiet grin-and-bear-it-attitude that is the cultural expectation after a major loss. Her story is about the construction of a literal clubhouse, a hideout where she didn't have to hide. Visiting the bottle house with her that day, I felt closer to her, and inspired by the young woman who followed her creative senses to create a sanctuary with actual trash.

Lennon, Sundari, and Kalayaan's stories hold the same spirit. In the midst of a transition, saying goodbye to the person or place that felt like home and feeling our way into the formation of a new version is an act that takes courage and creativity. There are no steps to follow, because everyone's relationship to home is unique. But there are some questions that we can ask.

How has your loss impacted how "at home" you feel in the world, or in the place where you live? Are there rituals or other practices that might help you feel like you, too, have a clubhouse? It might not involve cement mixing and bottle collecting, retrofitting a school bus or hiding a letter under floorboards, or finding a home with friends. It might come from building a relationship with a hike in your neighborhood, where the familiar contours of a trail start to feel predictable in a way you really need; or rearranging furniture in your bedroom; or getting a library card and finding a table with natural light where you can sit and stay awhile. We might not be handed a place that feels like sanctuary to us, but with creativity and curiosity, we might be able to find one, and invite people to join us there who are starting to feel like our home too.

# CARING THROUGH ACTION

WE OFTEN HEAR THAT PEOPLE who are grieving feel like they put on a disguise to conceal what's just below the surface. Be it in the grocery checkout line, on a first date, or a run-in with an old acquaintance, we learn when it's comfortable to lead with our story of loss, and when it's best to tuck it away below a different forward-facing story—oftentimes for our own well-being.

In the year after my dad died, while I was finding people with whom I could share my grief, I was also getting practiced at wearing that disguise. Of being the hard-working employee or the seemingly carefree person at the party, while never revealing the suite of feelings that would knock a casual conversation into a very weird gear. Memories of seizures. The tension that comes with watching tumors grow. Existential curiosities that a year sitting with someone dying will inevitably leave you with aren't, I learned, everybody's version of cocktail banter, although most of the friendships I have cultivated since then would strongly disagree.

That's why I started going to the desert. Driving the two hours outside Los Angeles to camp overnight in Joshua Tree National Park gave me the peace of mind and space to take off the mask I had been wearing and assess how I was really feeling inside.

I had never been somewhere that felt so otherworldly, and I immediately fell in love. It was the opposite of the misty oceanside where my dad was buried. I could exhale with the newness, the lack of baggage, the ability that anonymity gifted me to be nothing other than where I was in that moment. Taking a hike. Ordering Indian food alone in a tiny restaurant. Watching the sun set from the plastic chair outside my motel room door and writing a poem no one would ever read. As much as I was a raving fan of peer support, I was also learning about the power of solitude.

I was floored by the desert's palette; the way my eyes adjusted to the vastness of the expanse. How at first glance a place that read beige would accordion over a few days into a wild range of subtle hues. I loved the carving caress of the wind, the shapes of boulders and the faces within them. I loved the cries of coyotes at night, and the white flash of a cottontail darting under creosote bushes fleeing their pursuit. The way the moon rose, and the sun set, and how every night I could take in the exquisite display of stars and Milky Way dust, the very best show on earth.

There was unspoken information about my grief in the desert. About how life can survive with less water than you think. That there were places I could go that didn't remind me of my dad at all, but where, oddly, I could connect to him, on my own terms. That sometimes a landscape that looks barren and dead by day will begin teeming with life as the sun sets.

I eventually moved there and joked to friends that it was only a matter of time before I went full desert rat and started building sculptures from scrap metal and howling at the moon. Deserts encourage solitude, and through our solitude, we discover new parts of ourselves that were quietly there all along. The word *hermit*[8] originated in ancient Greece as a word for a "desert-dweller"; it's a place to which humans have turned for the solitude to reflect, repent, reorient, or pray. I went there to have a place to live with my grief that didn't pretend to be anything other than what it was, where I felt like I could do the same.

Later, I'd learn about the life of a woman named Minerva Hoyt, and this love affair made more sense, as things often do when reflected in our rearview mirror.

\* \* \*

If we think of the personalities behind our national parks, it's generally bearded outdoorsmen, walking sticks in hand, with a rugged esteem—a Teddy Roosevelt or a John Muir. But Minerva Hoyt, the woman responsible for the creation of Joshua Tree National Park, was more the type for pearls, lace, and a heeled boot. Minerva was born a Mississippi socialite on a plantation in 1866, a complex place of origin that she left at age thirty-one, when she moved with her surgeon husband Albert to New York City, and later to South Pasadena. The daughter of a state senator, and the graduate of finishing schools, her world was far from the wild west of rattlesnakes and cacti. Yet, starting with the view out of the train window as she made her way to California beside her husband, she started falling in love with the desert, a "world of strange and inexpressible beauty, of mystery and singular aloofness, which is yet so filled with peace."

Minerva dove into the upper-crust social circles of Los Angeles, hosting teas and garden parties that got written up in newspaper society pages. Her five-acre garden was considered one of the finest in the country, and she played a pivotal role in establishing and leading important cultural institutions in Los Angeles in the 1920s, like the Boys and Girls Club and the LA Symphony Orchestra.[9]

Minerva was inclined toward civic engagement, but her magnum opus wouldn't come until a time in her life thrumming with grief. After the death of an infant son, and her husband, Minerva sought the quiet of the desert to soothe her soul: "During nights in the open, lying in a snug sleeping bag, I soon learned the charm of a Joshua Forest. . . . Above, the bright desert constellations wheeled majestically toward the west, a timepiece for the wakeful." She, too, in the contemplative nights following a major loss, found solace in staring into the clear sky of the Mojave Desert, the hundred-year gap between us suddenly not such a big difference under the timelessness of stars.

But when Minerva returned many months later, she found the landscape much altered. Cacti had been dug out, trees removed—likely by commercial landscapers who then ferried the plants back to Los Angeles, where desert gardens were trending. The rise of automobile traffic meant that previously inaccessible stretches of wilderness were now open for off-roading. "A barren acreage with scarcely a Joshua tree left standing, and the whole face of the landscape a desolate waste, denuded of its growth for commercialism."[10] Minerva was mad. Here was a place that had held her in grief—that had protected her—and which in turn needed her protection. So she took it on. All the way on.

Now, we're not all socialites with spare time, political ties, and ample resources likely from slave-owning grandparents, and thank all the gods for that. However, Minerva could have just continued hosting teas and putzing around her Pasadena estate. She could have complained to friends at her gardening club about the destruction she witnessed in the Joshua Tree forest, and then changed the subject to the season's latest fashions or idle gossip. But seeing the destruction in the desert flipped some switch in her. She would not quit until the place that gave her solace in grief was protected, and at the highest degree.

Over the course of the next three decades, she executed a wildly successful organizing campaign that convinced decision-makers in Washington, DC, to protect a place they'd never seen, a landscape that many of them could hardly fathom, or might even consider barren and ugly at first glance. To help the world get a sense of the desert's beauty, she turned a train car into a living diorama, a miniature embodiment of the Mojave Desert. If they wouldn't come West, she would roll the West to them. She loaded airplanes with cacti flowers, flying the Mojave Desert to London—not just for show, but to educate the world of horticulturists that desert plants need conserving too. She founded the International Desert Conservation League, and after twists and turns, and stick-with-it-ness galore, President Franklin Roosevelt designated the area as a national monument in 1936. It was later turned into a national park, decades after her death.

Fast-forward to today, and nearly eight hundred thousand acres of desert habitat (an area larger than the state of Rhode Island) is now protected thanks to Hoyt and the fruits of her organizing, political savviness, funding, and unbridled passion.[11] It was the work of decades, but it paid off. And her legacy continues in the form of an award given annually in her name to an individual or organization who's made a significant accomplishment in the protection of California's desert lands, through actions like activism, education, or scientific study.

For me, moving to the desert was a lesson in solitude, but also a lesson in reciprocity. That when we've been cared for, or moved, or have fallen in love with an aspect of the world, it's up to us to listen to what it needs and courageously protect it. Studying Hoyt's life taught me that, in times of grief, we may feel the pull to withdraw and walk alone, despite the ever-chirping devices we carry and never-ceasing roles we play. Sometimes it's time in the deserts of our lives that help us get clear on the question of what it is that we're living for.

You may not be in the season of grief where fighting for a national park or changing policy seems appealing, or doable. Your grand effort of the day might be getting your kids out the door with edible food in lunch boxes. Or you might find meaning in quieter and more personal ways, like genuinely caring about your cashier's response to the question "How's your day?" or maintaining a friendship with a person who mattered to the human that is gone.

But if you are feeling fired up about something related to your grief, you're tapping into a powerful force. Trace the nerves that drive someone to make a change, and it's not rare to find a story of loss rooted in its origin. Grief, my cofounder and friend Lennon Flowers has written, can be "a seismic force for change."[12] David Kessler, a grief therapist who studied with Elisabeth Kübler-Ross, even amended her five stages of grief to add a sixth one: "make meaning."[13] Because for Lennon, like others, "those five stages make no mention of grief's power to motivate, not just out of anger, but out of a quest for meaning, purpose, and agency."

And what better way to make meaning than by taking the kind of action that can bring about equality and justice, in slight or significant ways. To change the conditions that caused your person's life to end unjustly, or to protect the things that made their life worth living. To reject the platitude of "thoughts and prayers," and to demand harmful laws change.

Evidence abounds that grief can be our jet fuel. You can look to Mothers Against Drunk Driving (MADD), which has mobilized a nationwide conversation around the dangers of drunk driving, all because one mother funneled her grief into action. Or you can look to the survivors of the Marjory Stoneman Douglas school shooting, who exhibited "courageous grief" as they led the March for Our Lives and pushed through Florida's Marjory Stoneman Douglas High School Public Safety Act. The legislation raised the minimum age for buying firearms to twenty-one and established waiting periods and background checks for gun purchasers. The state's governor commented, "To the students of Marjory Stoneman Douglas High School, you made your voices heard. You didn't let up, and you fought until there was change."[14]

Our grief can drive us to powerful places and shift the world for the better, if we let it. And some of us are driven to protect the space for people to grieve in the first place.

Artists Arianne Edmonds and April Banks, for example, hosted a Sunrise Mourning Meditation on Juneteenth during the summer following the murder of George Floyd. "2020 has been a brutal year from deaths due to the pandemic to police brutality to economic hardship.

We wanted to mourn together, to bear witness to our community's pain, to provide a moment of levity, and to do it in the presence of nature,"[15] Banks shared in an interview. Their ritual began with a meditation at sunrise and was an invitation to offer flowers to the ocean, in the spirit of Afro-Caribbean traditions like Santería or Candomblé and MAAFA,[16] a racial healing commemoration of ancestors from the transatlantic and domestic slave trades. The event created a reflective chance to grieve together, before heading into the citywide protests later that day. They intentionally chose a stretch of beach in Santa Monica known as the Inkwell, a historic haven for African American communities during the Jim Crow era. Beautifully articulated by April Banks, "Grievance and grieving go hand in hand. Organizing, protesting and fighting for racial justice is never-ending hard work. We recognize our collective need to recharge and be silent for a moment."

Joyal Mulheron is another advocate working to provide space for others to grieve. In the years following the death of her infant daughter, Mulheron decided to go all in on policy reform for bereaved families with her organization, Evermore.[17] Appalled by the lack of federally mandated bereavement leave, or corrupt business practices within the funeral industry, or ways in which there's no representation for bereaved families on Capitol Hill, she got to work. With a background in lobbying, formerly with Michelle Obama's Let's Move! initiative, Joyal knew that these kinds of reforms don't just happen on their own. Joyal and her team have worked to build bereavement leave into Biden's Build Back Better plan, among a litany of other interventions. If Renegade Grief is swimming against the current of a grief-denying culture, Joyal's work is setting out to change the tides.

There's a way of looking outward into the world, to advocate for something that feels important to you, that makes caring for others a care practice for yourself too. So what will it be? Where is your compassion calling you? Or your joy, or your rage? Will you join the folks who've come before you, moved by their grief and motivated to switch career paths into a caring profession? How might there be an opening for you to take care of the parts of the world you hold dear, that feel even more precious or prescient now that you know loss? There's a future that you can be a part of creating, by letting your grief be your guide.

＊　＊　＊

Joshua Tree protector Minerva Hoyt made a major difference, but the ongoing act of tending to a place requires attention far beyond one person's lifespan. There are big threats to her beloved desert, from the impacts of annual wildfires and a warming planet to the encroachments of developers reacting to an increased demand for housing. Spending time there, I can't help but ask, what would Minerva do?

Across any area where we aim to show care comes complexities. Yes, Evermore founder Joyal Mulheron is working diligently to protect the rights of the bereaved, but she describes the work as overwhelming, like the impossible task of cleaning up a teenager's room: "Where do you start? The rotting trash in the corner? The heap of dirty laundry under the bed?" Her push for President Biden (a person no stranger to grief) to include mandated bereavement leave in his planning didn't make the cut.

And yes, the Parkland students started a movement, but their actions didn't halt the rise of school shootings. As they've grown from high school students into young adults, many of them are looking forward to forging identities beyond the shooting at their school, as empowering as their response has been.[18] At a certain point our desires change. Tending to our grief might look like spending less time fighting, and more time figuring out who we are outside of our activism. For the volunteer hosts who lead Tables within The Dinner Party, many find that, after a few years of hosting, their needs change, and they pass on hosting duties to another attendee, or the Table comes to a natural ending. In many cases, the host has made the friendships they came looking for and is ready to move into a chapter that is informed by their grief, but not where it's foregrounded.

One of the big polarities of Renegade Grief is holding hope with despair; standing strong in our confidence in ourselves as agents of change, and our humility to know that we can't figure it all out on our own. We care for what we love, and we find people who care right along with us, people who can be in it with us for the long haul, as we change the world, and the world changes us right back.

✳ ✳ ✳

There's a canyon behind my house that's a small and exquisite stretch of land. I didn't know it was there when I moved to the neighborhood, but I soon realized that whatever instinct had dropped me in the middle of the desert also placed me within walking distance of a trail that ends at a natural spring. Water, as you can imagine, is an intensely precious resource in one of the driest places on earth. Taking my regular walk down to the spring, putting my hand on a boulder that's stained ochre from the spring's trickle, noticing the bees that gather there, and the plants that I rarely see in other places sprouting from the cracks of rocks reminds me just how precious a place it is.

Over time, I've learned more about its significance as a sacred site for local tribes. The ownership of this canyon was recently transferred back to an intertribal agency focused on native-led conservation efforts and off-reservation sacred site protection, still actively practicing their customs at this and other spots in the area. While Minerva Hoyt was busy fighting to protect the lands, what was lacking was a recognition of the communities that had lived there before prospectors and cowboys pushed native people out; communities that knew conservation practices tested by thousands of years of habitation; who had a relationship to the land deeper than a Southern belle socialite, no matter her good intentions and impactful efforts, ever could.

The barren desert that Minerva wrote about had been inhabited for centuries before the early automobiles allowed weekenders like herself to explore its beauty, and those communities should have had a say in the evolution of the place. The more time we spend diving into the issues we care about, driven by the renegade instinct to be an agent of change, the more complex those questions become. The more time we listen and learn, the more they expand, and the more nuance we can see. The horizon line continues receding.

Over time, I've come to learn that there are petroglyphs etched into the stone walls of the canyon. At first, my naive eye saw squiggly-looking lines and stick figures. But, spending time with volunteers of the inter-tribal agency, as we pick up the trash that inevitably gets washed down into the canyon during rains, I've learned to see these markings differently. Most of them carry messages that are in effect: "Water, this way." I think of the relief of someone passing by under the blazing sun and seeing that symbol; to know that another person familiar with that kind of thirst had placed a signpost, encouraging a left, instead of a right; I think of the power of paying-it-forward, and how impactful making the path a little clearer for the next person can be. It's the difference between suffering in the sun and finding shade and a life-giving drink.

As you reflect on the way your grief calls you to care for others, I wonder in what direction you'll be called into action, what signpost you'll leave behind; what thirst you'll help quench in the desert of some-one's life, as they look up into the same night sky.

# BECOMING A GRIEF ALLY

GETTING COFFEE WITH HANNAH, the nutritionist from the chapter on feasting, I asked them what support they received, if any, in the years after their dad died, that really felt good. That worked. That got through the tough outer layer of armor they'd been forming and reached the tenderness of their heart. Their answer shocked me with its simplicity. It's zero cost. It's neutral inquisitiveness.

Hannah told me about a time, many months after their father's death, while sitting shotgun on their way to see a movie with a friend, that the friend just flat-out asked, "So, your dad died. How's that all going?"

It wasn't cloaked in sympathy but grounded in curiosity. It gave Hannah an opening to just speak about what it really was like, instead of having to go through the social choreography of accepting condolences. They could just talk about the question we are all asking: *How is it going?*

Fifteen minutes later, Hannah and their friend were settling into their seats with popcorn. The lights in the theater dimmed, but something had lit up inside Hannah—the feeling that their story didn't have to be kept under lock and key. That this friend, sitting in the red velvet seat to their left, was someone safe to share their experience with. That this friend cared, was able to get around the self-consciousness of bringing up a sensitive topic and was able to pose the question in a way that wasn't at all leading, allowing Hannah to respond in a way that was honest and real. Checking in on their grief experience didn't have to be a big deal—which was, paradoxically, a really big deal.

I will always remember this anecdote, because oftentimes around The Dinner Party community, the topic of "ways that the living disappointed me after my loss" comes up to collective exhales and nods. I've heard stories of friends and family members missing the mark after a death experience that are caricatures of the theme: friends who flat-out stop calling, brisk encouragement to just "get over it," questioning when the griever will be getting back on their meds as if they ever stopped; distancing from the bereaved because they're momentarily no longer the life of the party.

It's not surprising that many of us freeze when someone is grieving, that we don't have the cool ease of Hannah's friend asking the big question. It's not easy sitting with uncomfortable feelings that have no quick fix. Grief literacy is not something we learn in school.

Besides, for those of us who are grieving, no one has a magic wand that's going to abracadabra it away, and there isn't a thing someone can say or do that will resolve complex emotions about a loss. In some ways, it's renegade to show compassion back to the people in our lives who, for whatever reason, aren't able to show up in the way we wish they would; to not make a character judgment because of a lack of availability; to communicate explicitly about what it is that we're needing, as best we can, and if they can't meet us in that, to not make them wrong for it. There are some skills to be learned on the job, in asking for the help we need, but also in remaining unattached to the outcomes. That living with grief requires the cultivation of grace.

But I wonder, what would it take for everyone to feel a little more comfortable finding a moment of quiet attention, like the last leg of a drive to the movies, to ask their grieving friend, "How's it all going?" and see where the conversation leads? Becoming a grief ally can begin not with a solution or a care package or a cure, but with a simple, open-ended question, and an equally open ear.

\* \* \*

As we explore the idea of being a grief ally, I'm reminded that there are inexplicable realities about some life experiences that only people who've lived it can truly know. What it feels like to give birth, to be a twin, to have seen Prince or Beyoncé live.

The same, in some ways, is true for grief. At dinner recently with a beloved friend who was a caretaker for a niece who died at nine of pediatric cancer, she shared with me that it wasn't until this first major loss experience that she understood just how intense this whole grief thing could be—saying goodbye to a child includes the particular misery of an out-of-order loss, combined with the inevitable family dynamics that complicate what is already a brutal season. We talked about how, once you've lived it, there's no way you can unsee it. And how this experience will change how she shows up for other people living through a loss, because she can grok it now, in her own way.

My conversation with her reflected the kind of conversions I've seen happen over this last decade; people who've been through their own grief experiences become the grief allies they wish they'd had.

We can start modeling what it looks like to show up for people who are going through it, because we know just how impactful gestures of support of any size can be. Who better to change the cultural patterns that leave us with that feeling of vague disappointment than us grievers? We can lead by example. We can, relationship by relationship, reboot the insecurity around what to say that leaves us a text away from a person we love who is hurting.

Here are some ways to start being a grief ally. Take some time to reflect on the comments or actions that made you feel supported in your loss, whether minuscule or bigger, and consider how they might apply to someone in your life going through it. Put the death anniversary in your calendar so you never forget. Take ten minutes to write the postcard, so they know you're thinking of them. You might be resentful of the lack of support you received, but to be the type of grief ally we each wish we had, we have to spread the love that helped us or that we wish we had received.

And it's never too late to start. Just because you didn't have it together to show up in the weeks after the accident doesn't mean you can't merge into a care team down the line. I get texts regularly from friends who are trying to figure out what to do for someone who's experienced a loss. While it's nice to show up in the immediate after, there's a long tail to grief, and you can be the person who steps in when the dust has settled, the celebration of life is long over, and the care packages have stopped arriving. Grief expert and friend Hope Edelman wrote a beautiful book called *The AfterGrief* where she describes a "phase we enter after the most acute elements of grief—shock, numbness, helplessness, sorrow, despair—start to subside. It's where we reenter the larger flow of humanity, where we discover all the ways we're still ourselves and also all the ways we've been fundamentally changed."[19] It's helpful to show up for our people when they're in this part of their loss experience, too.

We can get into hot water when we assume that what we would have wanted is the right solution for someone else, without taking the time to reflect on their relationship to the deceased and their preferences generally, or taking the time to ask them if what we have in mind sounds right.

Let me be a shining example of overeagerness without thoughtfulness. When a man who I worked with shared that his dad had died, I rolled out a multilevel support plan to cover for him. All the time off he needed, a care package from the team delivered to wherever the funeral was going to be, his email paused so that he could totally check out from work and not feel pressured to check in. In the end, he didn't want to take time off. His relationship with his dad sort of sucked. He was, in fact, kind of cool with him being dead. And he was in the middle of a project that he took a lot of pride in and didn't want to take his eye off that ball. He had a wife and a daughter, and continuing to build a career that would allow him to support his family was the medicine he needed. I backed away, apologetically, realizing the plan I had fought for was just reflective of what *I* had wanted, when I slipped out the back door of an internship the week my dad died and just never went back.

I know I had good intentions, but if I were to do that all over again, I would have shared some options with my colleague, and then asked him what sounded right for him at that moment. Then I would have assured him that if he woke up tomorrow morning and changed his mind, we could roll with that too. In other words, instead of launching an operation with NASA-level precision to make sure he was well taken care of according to my definition, I would have had a *conversation*. Because it ends up, instead of having some kind of cure-all, the thing that makes us a good grief ally is our ability to listen.

Since that incident, The Dinner Party has trained people from dozens of workplaces on how to be grief-ready; making sure that managers and other leaders on teams have the comfort and skills to have conversations with people experiencing grief on staff, so that appropriate and equitable plans can be made. It ends up that by acknowledging, normalizing, and planning for how grief is impacting your workplace, organizations can model their own version of Renegade Grief and reduce the churn that inevitably results in denying or ignoring grief's presence. And in studies of workplaces, particularly pioneering research that took place at Google, it's been found that teams with the greatest psychological safety are also the highest-performing. It ends up that creating a culture where people feel safe taking interpersonal risks, and aren't expending energy hiding or avoiding, means they can be more candid, invested, and, inevitably, work at a higher level of excellence.[20]

I am now thirty-five. It's the age that the grown-ups in my life were when I was a child. The people who were in charge when I was young, who seemed, from my perspective, established and done in their maturation. Now when I think of thirty-five as some pinnacle of "maturity," I laugh. These days, I am shaken thinking about the fact that people my age are allowed to operate roller coasters. Are sent home from hospitals holding

babies without operating manuals. That they build skyscrapers; launch fellow thirty-five-year-olds into space; operate on an open heart.

We like to think that the more times we've been around the sun, the more equipped we are to handle life's hard things. Because, yes, maturing is a thing. Yes, wisdom from lived experience shouldn't be diminished. And yet, sometimes, even now, after more than a decade in deep conversation about life after loss, I will get tongue-tied when learning that the person I'm talking to recently had someone die. I, too, put my foot in my mouth when finding ways to show up for people who are grieving. In some ways, I think it's because learning how to "hold complex and hard" only gets harder with time, because the older we get, the more complexity we can truly see.

As I've grown to recognize that getting older doesn't mean we have the answers, I've shifted from judgment to curiosity about our cultural limitations around how we support the bereaved. What is it like to live for more time on earth carrying the weight of our own mortality? If, by thirty-five, I still don't always get it right, what makes me think that by fifty I will? And what does it mean anyway, getting grief right? It's not a competition, and there isn't a prize.

I'm learning that we don't necessarily get the answers as we get older. It's not about slipping into a therapist-voice when asking how they're feeling or avoiding the topic because we're not sure we have the perfect thing to say, but just being yourself as truly as you can.

And sometimes you are anxious. Sometimes you are worried about your friend, and sometimes you also may have known the person and you're grieving, too, albeit in a lower-key way. You might find yourself slipping into the socially approved phrases like, "I'm sorry for your loss . . . They're in a better place . . . I can't imagine what you're going through." But instead, there's power in taking a beat, a breath, and asking if there's another way to express your care and concern that's less Hallmark embossed and more true to you. Try these on for size, and be gentle with yourself if it comes out a little clunky. We're all learning.

*I'm so sorry this happened. It's hard for me to fathom, but I just want you to know I'm not going anywhere.*

*I can't actually think of the right thing to say, because I have a feeling there are no words that would make this better.*

Or to echo back to Hannah's friend: *So, your dad died. How's that all going?*

✳   ✳   ✳

While saying something is better than saying nothing at all, there's one phrase that I'm trying to expunge from my vocabulary. It still slips into conversation more often than I like to admit. I would like to propose that the phrase "let me know if I can do anything to help" be retired from the rotation.

It's a loophole phrase that intends a kindness, but one that the receiver will have a hard time accessing. It's like giving someone a present that's too hard to unwrap so they just give up, and the offer ends up collecting dust.

I remember people asking if there was anything I needed, and a dozen years later, I finally have some ideas. At the time, I was in shock. I was overwhelmed. I wasn't in a place to delegate or break things into small tasks. But now, here you go.

*Sure, you can wire me money or find me a lover who doesn't mind I've been in sweats for two weeks. You can rent me a private plane to a remote island where I can lay in the sand like a salamander. Or if you can swing it, you can find some magic box with a letter from my dad explaining how this is all a big hoax and I just have to go to a certain coordinate under a certain full moon and meditate a certain way and I will then find the portal that brings me to him.*

*But in the meantime, you can take some work off my plate, be around in a way that's not thirsty or weird, help my family figure out the dynamics of death, give me a platonic back rub, or hire someone to do it better than you would. You can draw me a bath. You can make me a meal. You can leave me alone and not get mad if I forget to initiate. You can make me laugh but be okay if that laughter slips into a sob.*

That's mine—what is yours?

After being on the receiving end of "let me know if there's anything I can do to help," I like to get specific with what I'm offering as help. Of course, still in ways that allow the person to exercise some agency over the situation. Us grievers don't need to be dictated to. Well, maybe sometimes a good sleeper choke hold would do our bodies good, and that said, an unprompted delivery of something wonderful is never going to hurt. But normally, it feels good to be able to exercise some control and choice, with the option to opt out entirely left on the table. Here are some ways to get specific.

*I'm getting you a delivery this week. What night would be good?*

*We are free this weekend—when was the last time you repotted your house plants? Can we come over and play plant doctor?*

*I know the anniversary of your mom's death is coming up. Do you have plans that night? Can I make a tentative reservation somewhere in case you are in the mood to toast her that day? Or do you suspect you'll want to get out of the house and talk about anything else?*

In the moments where we wonder what we can do—send flowers, again? a text message, even though we never really text anymore?—take some time to make a list of the weird and simple, basic and cheerful and comforting things you know they love, be it a freshly washed car, a new sheet mask to try, or good bagels that they can toast and butter. Then let them choose their own adventure.

Whatever you do, something is better than nothing. And practice making your offer without any attachment to some kind of gesture of gratitude in return. As you do, know that you're a part of a broader swell of people changing the culture around grief and loss one considerate act at a time.

✶  ✶  ✶

Another straightforward way we can be a good grief ally is to get ready for our own deaths. We know how helpful it can be for someone to be clear about their wishes, taking a little bit of time out of their busy lives to consider, *How might I take care of my people not just when I'm alive, but also when I'm on the other side? What messes might I be leaving, and are there a few things I can do to turn that mess into a moment that's going to mean a lot when I'm no longer here?*

Because we know how confusing and hard it can be when the opposite is true. My dad died without clear wishes expressed about his funeral arrangements, and while we could intuit some of what he would have wanted, it also created some tension between family members in a moment where we mostly needed to be united, guards down. When Amelia's dad died with storage units full of stuff, it became her problem and consumed the years after his death. For many grievers, the grief itself has to wait until the person's affairs are in some form of order, which can be brutal, to say the least.

One thing we can do to help the next generation of grieving people, particularly the ones we care about the most, is to bust through the barriers in our culture that make us think that planning for our death is squeamish or macabre. Author and activist Chanel Reynolds refers to it as "getting your shit together." Emergency contact lists, cell phone passcodes, wills and files of important documents—there are tons of very practical things that we all would be better getting clear about. As Chanel puts it, "In a world where so much is out of control, let's take care of the stuff we can change. Present Day Self can make sure Future Self isn't screwed over by getting started."[21]

In the years since The Dinner Party began, there's been a parallel proliferation of tools to make this less hard. For example, a whole suite of board games, like *When My Time Comes*, now exist, designed for the express purpose of easing conversations about end-of-life planning within the comforting family tradition of circling up for game night. Margareta Magnusson's book, *The Gentle Art of Swedish Death Cleaning*,[22] written when the author was "aged between 80 and 100," gives excellent brisk, European-accented advice on readying your home so it's not a nightmare for those left to deal with it. There's a ripe, emerging movement of death doulas, people like Going with Grace's Alua Arthur, who are reimagining how families can approach the final chapter of someone's life. Alua trains death doulas in the art of providing council and support for the dying, but also for relatives grappling with the reality of someone's passing. One of the many reasons I admire Alua is that she's bucking the stereotype of who you might expect to find hanging with the dying. Less goth Morticia Adams, Alua is vibrant, hysterical, down-to-earth, perennially dressed in bright colors and spilling over with life. She reminds me that death and beauty are not mutually exclusive, but two sides of the same coin.

A friend once told me that knowing The Dinner Party exists helps her exhale into the reality that someday her two parents will also die, and that there will be a community available to her with people who get it. There's something about knowing your options on the other side of a major loss that allows you to show up more lucidly, more openheartedly, when it's someone's time to go.

There are more things to consider now than ever before, with our own end-of-life plans a creative act in and of itself. Not just which blouse you want to be buried in or which plot in the only graveyard in town to reserve. Options have expanded in recent years, letting you choose whether you'd prefer that your body get eaten by a bunch of friendly mushrooms, or burned on a Viking-esque funeral pyre (but only if you are one of about 150 people who live in Crestone, Colorado). Or do you want to be turned into a big fat diamond through a company like Eterneva—or have your ashes shot into space? Closer to earth, do you want your entire Facebook snail trail to be deleted? Or do you want to nominate a Legacy Contact, a person who can be responsible for your online presence?

In engaging in questions around our end of life, we are turning our attention to our final adventure. If we can shift out of the shadow of cultural denial around death, we can shift planning for our end of life into its own renegade act—countercultural, creative, and liberated. Chances are, getting clear about the way we want our death to go—or the parts of it that we have any say in, at least—we'll get clearer about how it is we want to spend our time while we're alive. In that way, reflecting on death can not only be a way of walking the talk of being a grief ally, but becomes a cheat code to a more fulfilled life.

# CENTERING YOUR SACRED

WHEN I INVOKE THE WORD "spirituality," everyone reading this text will likely have unique images come to mind. For you, the word "spirituality" might remind you of the religious community in which you were brought up, whether the association is warm or wary. The word might make you picture me in yoga pants with big-believer eyes; you might worry I'm about to pitch you on an essential oil MLM, or ask if you believe in signs, which, on most days, I admittedly do. Or perhaps, finally mentioning the S-word might feel like a big exhale, because we are at last addressing what it is we are talking about when we talk about grief.

To clarify, what I mean by "spirituality" can stretch across multiple understandings of the word. I use it to express the ways in which we explore the possibility that we are more than just meat suits with computer brains who will fall into total blackout when we die. To me, exploring spirituality is a look at our internal knowing that there are parts of life that are sacred, not because someone told us they are, but because those parts make us feel alive, connected, and at home in the chaos of the world; that within us lives some kind of energy that, according to laws of physics, is never created or destroyed, but just changes form.[23]

I'm not interested in influencing what you believe when it comes to your spirit, or in helping you decide what you hold sacred. I am here to normalize that in the wake of a loss, we're often left contemplating big questions about the spiritual side of life and death;

our curiosity about the afterlife often feels a little less abstract and more—*where the hell did they just go?* And that part of being renegade in your grief is taking the time to come into closer intimacy with what we do believe, or the questions we do want to be exploring, in a time where our relationship to the great beyond just got a whole lot more personal.

Grief from a significant death is one of the deepest rites of passage we'll experience, with the potential to soften us, awaken us, and force us to grow up. So the question becomes, how in the challenge of this time can you develop the practices that help you stay in touch with your own spirit and find the community, faith-based or otherwise, that can meet you there?

Whether we like them or not, know them personally or not, have experience inside them or feel flat-out allergic to them, religious communities have historically been the place where grief is held. Have a problem with your sewer system? Call public utilities. Concerned about smoke coming out of a neighboring house? Call the fire department. Wondering about matters of the soul, with what to do about a death now that the funeral home is finished with their part of the gig? Go to the meeting, or to church, temple, or mosque. Religions have been, until recently, our shared headquarters for holding grief.

At their best, faith-based communities are extraordinary when it comes to caring for the bereaved. They can be the places where the status of someone's health is being named every week, keeping the person's struggle front of mind; they are the places where meal trains can be organized, where childcare is provided while the adults get a chance to sit and breathe. For many of us it's the one place where we can see people regularly with whom we have something in common beyond a job. The rhythm of it can be wonderful; you spend time pondering parables with big lessons, and then socialize with neighbors afterward—a perfect one-two, if you ask me.

At its best, our religious traditions can give us the framework with which to make sense of our grief, a rope to follow through the fog. A hypothesis around what the person who died might be experiencing, and a tested set of motions to go through when you can't think straight. And they provide us with containers to hold that which is far beyond our individual selves.

While neuroscientist Mary-Frances O'Connor doesn't fully buy into the metaphysical beliefs of her family's Catholic faith, she told me that she's found immense comfort in the church's traditions. The rituals of Catholicism, she said, remind her that "someone else has stood in this place and felt what you are feeling, and survived. You can borrow their optimism." For O'Connor, traditions from the church help her connect to the universality of grief, without having to erase any of the particulars of her experience.

A. Helwa, a wonderful writer and thinker on Islam's relationship to spiritual development, taught me about some of the customs that mean the most to her from her faith tradition. There are tools for forgiveness, such as the Islamic Janāzah prayer, which is recited at every funeral and asks for the souls of the dead—and also for those of the living—to be pardoned. This last part especially struck me as wise. Rarely do families moving through a loss experience have zero complaints about one another. They almost always have relational nicks or wounds. This tradition allows the imperfections of us humans to be named, and gives us a way to release our resentments, toward ourselves and others; to let them go as best we can.

At birth, the *adhān*, or call to prayer, is whispered in a baby's ear, which is normally a call-and-response, but in this unique case no prayer is performed. Then fast-forward to when a Muslim dies, a communal prayer is performed at the cemetery with *adhān* recited. The wisdom behind this act is to symbolically remind Muslims that life is so short that the *adhān* of your birth is for the prayer of your death. It's traditions like these that can make poetry of the moments that can be so hard to make sense of when we're in their midst. A quiet gesture that in some way contains the broad, sweeping elegance of a life.

A. Helwa also shared how Islamic tradition gives an incredible role model in grief through the story of the Prophet Muhammad, who wept for years after his wife Khadijah passed away. "In the Islamic tradition, we were all created from a single soul, so the spirits continue their connection beyond the grave, because the body dies, not the spirit. His humanity continued to grieve for the absence of her presence, while his heart was content with God's decree. He modeled for many Muslims that you can grieve and be faithful. In fact, to be human is an act of faith. To feel the fullness of our grief, and to see in our emotions messages from God, is an act of faith." Helwa's teachings have helped me realize that, even in the existential chaos of deep grief, we can also find a pathway to deepened faith, wherever it is we end up landing as a spiritual home.

But not all of us come into the world with the promise of a religious community realized, and for many of us who did, that relationship might feel hostile or rote. We're in a time in history when having a relationship to religion can be a bit of a crapshoot. Less than half of us belong to any kind of faith institution, a slippage from the 70 percent that held steady throughout most of the twentieth century.[24] Actual physical churches are closing at a rapid rate.[25] Many of us are left on the hunt for answers.

For Tommy, the faith community that he leaned on when his dad was sick started to feel a little wobbly after he died. There was a sense he picked up from others that, if he really trusted in God's plan, he wouldn't be so distressed about his dad dying. If Pops was in a better place, why fret? It was challenging enough for Tommy to lose his dad, but to then have his faith questioned when grief emerged in the year following?

Over time, the level of alienation he felt from his beloved church made him realize he was going to have to separate from that community.

Since then, Tommy's faith has deepened into new ways of expression that feel sacred to him. As a result, he obtained a degree in social work, which has allowed him to grow more skilled in supporting people who are struggling. He made a move to New York City, and took on a role with The Dinner Party, where he connects people in secular spaces for some of the most sacred conversations. For him, reading texts from leaders like Franciscan priest Richard Rohr and other books that preach a gospel of unity and belonging rather than exclusion or division has allowed him to explore his relationship to Christianity on his own terms.

For me, it was *The Tibetan Book of Living and Dying* that I tore through when my dad was dying. My dad was a Catholic-turned-atheist, who experienced cruel behavior growing up in Brooklyn's brutal Catholic school system during the 1960s. The idea of joining a congregation, *any* congregation, was a no-fly zone in our household. But I found *The Tibetan Book of Living and Dying*, written by Sogyal Rinpoche and published in the U.S. in 1992, in an old bookstore in San Francisco as I was searching for any wisdom I could find on how to deal. At twenty years old, I had zero cultural connection to Tibetan Buddhism, and I found the text to be pretty out there in a thrilling way, describing in detail how souls move through these different liminal states between death and reincarnation called "the bardos." I remember feeling weirdly freed up that the heaven-or-hell paradigm that I had come to distrust in the Western world as overly simplistic had some solid alternatives when you broadened your geocultural lens.

The book had beautiful insights on how to be with someone who is dying, which felt radical at a time in my life when admitting what was happening seemed to shut down any conversation I had, rather than open it up. It gave me some crucial scaffolding that I needed to embrace the human rite unfolding in front of my eyes. It helped me realize I had, to some degree, a choice in front of me. I could stay present through his death, as uncomfortable as it was. It made me realize I didn't want to miss it.

In the foreword to the book, the Dalai Lama says about death, "Knowing that I cannot escape it, I see no point in worrying."[26] He turned death from something that was purely fearful into a grand adventure. And encouraged meditation as a practical tool to manage the emotions behind it all. I wasn't a Buddhist after reading it, but the book left me thinking deeply and feeling like I had more room to breathe. I had more room to breathe, even as my father's breaths were shortening. This, at the time where panicking was a highly tempting state of being, felt nothing short of a miracle.

In many ways, that time was my conversion to becoming a "none"—officially, unashamedly, enthusiastically yet non-evangelizing, "spiritual but not religious." It's the box that 22 percent of Americans check on forms if we respond to the question at all.[27] Or in shorthand, "nones."

What I didn't realize then was that the process of exploring spiritual possibilities around grief was its own grief care practice. Research has shown that people who claim to have a strong spiritual belief system have an easier go at a major loss, resolving their feelings of grief more quickly than those with no spiritual framework.[28] But books alone weren't going to scratch the itch. I needed community too.

Right around the time The Dinner Party was taking off, Casper ter Kuile and Angie Thurston at the Harvard Divinity School released a field-building report called *How We Gather*,[29] which examined the ways in which the rise of spiritual-but-not-religious millennials were finding the kinds of social value that one could get from churches, outside of explicitly religious spaces. Millennials, the authors noted, were "flocking to a host of new organizations that deepen community in ways that are powerful, surprising, and perhaps even religious." These spaces of communion and connection ran the gamut from CrossFit gyms to Camp Grounded, an adult digital-detox summer camp. The Dinner Party was named as a case study too.

This cross section of organizations might seem like they have nothing in common, but they're quenching a similar thirst. *How We Gather* shares that "the lack of deep community is indeed keenly felt. Suicide is the third-leading cause of death among youth. Rates of isolation, loneliness, and depression continue to rise. As traditional religion struggles to attract young people, millennials are looking else-where with increasing urgency. And in some cases, they are creating what they don't find."

What Casper and Angie's report offered was a new way of think-ing about the community we were building. There could be a space that was secular—we didn't often discuss religion or dogma around The Dinner Party table—but it could still be seeped in sacredness. And that maybe the feeling that brought us together—our own little congregation—was scratching an itch that had more to do than just companionship around our loss. Grief was, in the end, the entry point, but once the conversation was moving, no topic was off-limits. We had created what we couldn't find, a place that held sacred the stories of our lives, no matter how macabre or mundane. Those early-day dinners were magic, and made me a believer.

Since the days when I was whipping through *The Tibetan Book of Living and Dying*, I've continued to try to explore this beyond-my-meat-suit side of life. After seeing mediums and past-life readers, taking varying combinations of vision-inducing drugs, studying with a Native Amer-ican elder in the mountains of the Southwest; after silent retreats and hot yoga and Burning Man and attending business accelerators with a spiritual bent, it's been funny to find myself leaning into the same Catholic religious practices that my dad couldn't talk about without get-ting red in the face.

I didn't just jump in, though. I had to find my own entry point. The way in was the rosary, the prayer beads my grandmother used to keep in her purse alongside her crumpled-up old-lady tissues and her cigarettes. I love how analog the rosary is: no blue-light glow, no ads in an app. I love the tactile, visceral experience of feeling beads, repeating a prayer that I've adjusted from the original Hail Mary recitation so that it resonates with me, less focused on sin. Chanting and mantras are a tool across so many wisdom traditions. They give the mind a bone to chew on, so the other parts of ourselves get a break from the incessant chatter. The heart can soften, and aspects other than our busy minds can come to the foreground. Leaning into the version of prayer beads native to my people gives me a connection point to religious traditions older and deeper than Vatican prejudice. I feel closer to my grandmother, for sure, and I'm surprised that I can access my dad's voice there too.

I've turned to some of the writings, too, approaching them with the same reverence with which I read the myths of Greece or other fables; stories with lessons, kept alive through retelling. My current favorite character in the Catholic liturgy is Saint Mary Magdalene, as I'm drawn to the women of the Bible who have roles in addition to "mother" or "wife." She was part of Jesus's crew, there with him through the brutal, bitter end, crucifixion and all. Visiting his tomb after he was buried— her own form of grief care practice, we can assume—she is believed to have received the visitation from him, with his assurance that death was not an ending but a chance for redemption. That even though the worst-case scenario had happened, it wasn't the end of the story.

While awareness of Mary Magdalene has been gaining in recent years, finally declared the Apostle of the Apostles by Pope Francis just in 2016,[30] I had to discover her through my own investigation rather than in Sunday School growing up. Over time, I've grown to see her role as side character rather than heroine as part of the source code that explains why we're so out of alignment with grief in Western contexts.

Christians have spent the last two thousand years so devoutly oriented around the story of Jesus and his crucifixion. But what about the people—really, the women—who didn't just get miraculously airlifted out of a sealed chamber into heaven, but who were left on earth to continue the work? A person who oiled a man's feet knowing full well he would be gone the next day? A hard-core mystic who received a download on the story of transcendence and reported it back to the rest of the disciples, who then mocked her for being a girl, because why would Jesus go to her over any of his bros? She's the one who lived out her life on earth, feet on the ground, heartbreak in her chest.[31] I'm drawn to her story because, in the way I understand it, it's another myth in the canon that points us toward Renegade Grief.

I wonder at how much of the modern Western world and its obsession with resurrection and emphasis on love and light and positivity has become a way to avert our gaze from the awful beauty and messiness of death—and really, life—itself. And I wonder what lessons we've lost by keeping our gaze so focused on the person who ascended that we lose the part of the story concerning the people who loved and grieved them; the caretakers, who rode on the hard road of life and figured out a way to make it work, even in the absence of a person who mattered a lot.

Even as I've deepened through exploring my family's ancestral religion, and while I love to light candles in a church, I remain more drawn to places where the feeling of worship is less about duty and requirement, and more about inspiring awe and feelings of love. Lounging around a fire with my girlfriends, unfurling what's been going on in our internal worlds. Waking up in a sunbeam-streaked bed with my husband and our dog. My church, an old library with that book smell, where every spine is an open door into someone else's world. Standing in a grove of redwood trees, or diving into the belly of a cresting wave. The moment sitting around The Dinner Party Table, when everyone takes a beat to refill glasses and let it all soak in; when we've explored the depths of our experience and come back to the surface. We bring with it a pearlescent glow that comes not from avoiding our grief, but from revering the realness of it, holy and imperfect, wildly unique and somehow also the same.

There's no single answer for how to approach the sacred of your life as you live through grief with a renegade's lens, but here are some considerations. Be wary of anyone who claims to have the answer; lean toward the voices who will help you sit more deeply in your own knowing; take the time to consider what is sacred for *you*, the thing that helps *you* feel connected to a greater sense of possibility, protection, or faith. It could be like one Dinner Partier who makes an annual trip to her nearest body of water to toss a message in a bottle into the river or the waves, written to her late dad; or for another, an annual backpacking trip with friends that keeps her sane for the other fifty-one weeks of the year. Whatever it is, however strange or unique or silly or earnest it might sound, go for it. Fan the flames of it. Commit to caring for the sacred in your life; the thing that, even in the disorientation of grief, helps you remember that there's always ground beneath your feet; and in the times when even gravity escapes you, the beliefs and the people that can become your tether.

# PROCEEDING WITH CAUTION

US HUMANS ARE TOOL-MAKING FIENDS: fire starters, socks, vibrators, Snuggies. We're geniuses at finding solutions to nagging problems that get us what we want, faster and with more ease. And of course, we've applied that process of innovation to our grief. Indeed, many of the care practices described in this book can be understood as using tools, such as altar-building and letter writing, analog technologies to help you move through times of loss in a more intentional way.

But even in the years since I joined the club, the tools and options available for coping with grief have proliferated and taken on a decidedly more cyborg edge. Did you know that dead people can crash your birthday party in a lifelike hologram, and give you a pep talk on a big screen as if they know the ins and outs of your present-tense life? Or that on reality TV one night, Korean television broadcast a mother emotionally reuniting with her seven-year-old daughter, three years after her daughter died, via an augmented reality simulation? At some point in the last decade, the future became the present, and the present became an even weirder time to grieve.

Whether you're in the hopeful camp that the emergence of the internet and artificial intelligence is "the greatest redistribution of power in history,"[32] or fall more on the dystopian side, curious if this is the beginning of our collective end, we can likely all agree that the information age we're living in is changing how we live, die, and grieve.

The future we've entered is giving the dying more avenues to pop up in our lives after their passing. Sometimes these come to us through the thoughtful intention from someone before their death, like the highly organized people who preprogram messages to their family on specific milestones which are sent posthoumously via online services like The Postage. A message from Grandma on your wedding day, or an annual card for every birthday for the next thirty years? All things that can now be outsourced and arranged.

On the other side are the technology touches that remind us of our person, but lack grief sensitivity, like the relentless sales emails from companies reminding us to buy Mom a present, even though she's no longer alive; or the push notification that "on this day last year," we were all together in the flesh. We have to learn, how to manage these technological drop-ins, and the ways in which they can both console us and collapse us in on ourselves, depending on the day.

While some of these developments may be dubious, it's also true that technology has made it easier to find the people who are moving through the same grief world we are. Across the internet you'll find support groups for parents of children with rare diseases, where people exchange doctor recommendations and offers to host one another when traveling for care. There's Nora McInerny's Hot Young Widows Club, and Jessica Zucker's I Had a Miscarriage movement. There's Modern Loss, a platform all about candid conversations about grief, and Alica Forneret's organization Pause, dedicated to supporting people of color through grief and end of life with safe, culturally sensitive, and expert-informed resources. All communities that have come together online, changing harmful narratives and stitching together impactful friendships. Bless the internet's big, bottomless heart for that.

For a long time, though, I remained a little leery about online communities. I wasn't certain that commonalities discovered online, no matter how profound, could necessarily translate into lasting connections and relationships. The original Tables of The Dinner Party were filled through friends and friends of friends, which seemed more authentic than connections made online. Sure, the internet was great for finding people to normalize your experience to comment, like, and share, but what about the creation of a real social safety net? I liked how the internet could help us see that our grief was normal, but I wasn't sure it could actually help us feel less lonely in it. But I was wrong. With the rise in our nation's crisis of isolation, we'll take the connections in whatever form we find them, meeting us where we're at—and if not for the courage of people connecting with their Table over the internet, our community would have stayed within the same small circles.

Over time, we learned that in-person connections aren't the only worthwhile ones. Bonds formed online can be powerful balms. During the first year of COVID, the rise of online memorials, while not ideal, proved that within constraints comes great adaptation and creativity. During this same time, The Dinner Party Tables we were worried would falter moved to meeting online without a hitch. That's when the organization launched what's referred to as our Buddy System, bringing individuals together one-on-one, who were fine with the fact they would likely never meet in person, and sometimes never even speak on the phone, preferring the convenience of asynchronous conversations via text. We are reminded again that giving people agency and choice, while not the norm in times of loss, is deeply needed. Having someone who has shared an experience, even if confined to the squares of a Zoom, was better than no one at all, and sometimes even better, if it meant you didn't have to find a babysitter, or sit in traffic, or the other sources of friction in our lives that stop us from finding time to connect.

Meanwhile, a 2022 visit with artist Rafael Lozano-Hemmer's piece at the Brooklyn Museum, *A Crack in the Hourglass, An Ongoing COVID-19 Memorial,*[33] reminded me how technology is allowing artists to create reflections on grief and loss not possible in purely analog mediums. The exhibit was an active one, in flux as you viewed it. In it, photos submitted of people who died during the pandemic were drawn in sand art with the help of a robot, a line of sand flowing like ink from an hourglass. Upon completion of each portrait, the canvas would tilt and release the sand back into a bucket. These beautiful portraits, which look like they were taken with an old tin-type camera, not sketched by a sand-spewing robot, were stunning to behold. It moved me for days after seeing it, a testament to its potency. It reminded me that if there's a craving you're having related to your grief, we can look to art and technology as tools to satiate it, projects we can create that externalize what what we're feeling, no matter how amateur or professional we may be.

We have some video recordings of my dad talking, giving a speech at a conference, and home videos from growing up. My brother has turned to them for comfort over the years. For him, hearing our dad's voice is always helpful, a refresher on the parts of a person that can lose their viscosity in memory alone. The intonation of a voice. The specific gesticulation of a body. The shape of a grin preceding a certain laugh.

I haven't touched them. I wonder if there will be some kind of death anniversary of his I'll pass, after which point, I'll be ready. Almost like I'm saving them for a rainy day, knowing that there's a good chance they could be washed away in the deluge of old email threads and expiring Dropbox links between now and when I'm ready. I like knowing they're there and being able to abstain. I'm fearful that watching those videos, that form of remembering, would blow the seams off wounds that have mostly healed, and the scars that have formed around them; it might pinch back off a person who I've spent a decade incorporating into the fabric of who I am. I fear that would feel like another kind of loss. They're still in my inbox, I just checked. In the meantime, it's nice to know he's in there, chatting and laughing and smiling, and that I could drop back in on those moments, should I ever long to, and visit him in some other kind of cloud.

So how do we proceed with caution? It's important to tease apart which are the tools that really provide deeper connections, and which are, basically, pay-to-play models that insert someone else's authority between yourself and your relationship to that person's memory.

I get a little sweaty thinking about what capitalism might do with #grieftech, the greedy bitch that she is. Given any technology is a tool that can be used for harm or good, there's some quivering anxiety underneath how venture-capital funding could take some of these ideas and determine their fate, not based on a moral code but on profit. The dystopian possibilities abound. Might AI companies one day charge you for messages from your deceased person? Or could someone's likeness be used to manipulate or harm, especially in the tender times after a loss? Are the ways in which deepfake technology is inciting violence in the world sending more people unnecessarily into the grief club? Scenarios like these make the case for ethical governance of the internet, universalizing some kind of Hippocratic Oath for developers and other AI professionals working in tech related to grief, but also everything.

And yet, in the same way that two people can be grieving the same loss and reach for opposite care practices, by whose preferences should those decisions be made? Who gets to decide how technology might become a tool that assists us in our grief? Maybe the idea of a VR rendering of a dead person, based on a composite of their videos and emails, is the future's superpower approach for continuing bonds. Or maybe it can make our grief more complicated, more costly, even more confusing for those of us navigating the hall of mirrors as it is.

As we learn how to grieve, we're learning how to surf waves of unimaginable change. Whether we're game or not, it's a useful muscle to strengthen as we navigate the changes ahead, and decide how we want to use the tools that are available to us, without getting used by them.

# CELEBRATING

IN THE HARDEST DAYS OF grief we may feel as if we've fallen out of love with the world. Permanently, and for good. Especially when the person who is gone is the one we loved most of all. Sometimes the best thing, and I know this might seem impossible, is to make space for celebration. Hearing that, you might very well ask, *What is there to celebrate?* To which I'd answer that you're celebrating the person who was here, as well as the person *you* are becoming in this wild time. Someone who will always be a member of this club, but also a person with so many other interests, facets, and stories to tell. A person who, like Walt Whitman wrote, contains multitudes. A person who is learning to make fire, even in the dark, even with wood wet with tears.

I learned about celebration as a renegade act from my brother José, who stood on the other side of our dad's bed slugging tequila with me. I'm still so impressed by the ways that two people who share blood and the same loss experience can walk away from the wreckage with such different strides, heading to very different places to find their way to healing. While I zigged after death into meditation and psychedelics, hosting dinners and starting a nonprofit, Jose zagged to music festivals and bacchanalian rabble-rousing. I'm pretty sure his "grief journey," as it's so often called, was way more fun.

While I worked to fix, to understand, to try to solve, my brother led with celebration. If life was short, he wanted to spend the time he had with his friends, dancing late into the night, falling asleep in a tent in a field of other partiers, and waking up to do it again. With the phrase "Mirth is King" tattooed in an Old English font over his right shin, it's not surprising that in the months after our dad died, José hit the dance floor with a devoted mantra of not sweating the small stuff. Unless something was life or death, he wasn't going to let it get in the way of enjoying his time on earth. He was tapping into the truth that, alongside the heartache and somber tones of the grief world, we've also got to prioritize appreciation for this crazy, beautiful, wrecked life we've been gifted.

Collective celebration has been a part of human culture for as long as we can remember. In her book *Dancing in the Streets*, the writer and activist Barbara Ehrenreich[34] charts the way that festivals have been a way we tilt ourselves in a new direction—whether to shake off the stiffness of winter or mark a war's ending—for as long back as we have history. But over time, figures of authority in the church and landholding elites made it harder for citizens to lose their minds on the dance floor, seeing that level of revelry as a threat to security and civic control. As she writes, "Not only has the possibility of collective joy been largely marginalized to the storefront churches of the poor and the darkened clubs frequented by the young, but the very source of this joy—other people, including strangers—no longer holds much appeal."

It's not surprising that cultural narratives around grief are focused on what to do with the parts of it that feel bad, as opposed to the parts of it that can wake us up to the preciousness of our lives. Ehrenreich observes that "to this day, and no doubt for good reasons, suffering remains the almost exclusive preoccupation of professional psychology." Forty-five-thousand articles have been published in the last thirty years on depression, yet only four hundred articles have been released that explore joy. While the noise is louder around the suffering, let us not miss the quiet calling of its opposite.[35]

And not to be a cynic, but so many of our reasons for collective effervescence are littered with commercial breaks. Nowadays, it's more about the industry turn of seasons—the Super Bowl, the Oscars, the holiday shopping sprees. So how do we reclaim celebration, not as a time to consume culture, but as a chance to create it with the people we love?

That's why it's renegade to connect with the cultural rituals, be they ones that already exist or those of our own creation, that put celebration at the center of a community's response to loss. New Orleans' culture of jazz funerals, colorful and loud celebrations, are so packed with wisdom and catharsis that I wish they could be the norm for funeral culture, not the exception. My friend Alua Arthur hopes that when she dies, her family members clap for her, a round of applause to celebrate the completion of her life. While we joke that the reason we named our organization The Dinner Party was that the website domain was available, it actually felt really important to claim that we could talk about death in an atmosphere that felt festive and alive; that we didn't have to dissociate conversations about grief from the pleasure of a party.

However, while my brother's festivals happen in groups, in crowds of strangers, celebration can happen in tiny, quiet moments too. Getting into clean sheets, spotting a sweet exchange between strangers, or the day's first cup of coffee are all microcelebrations worthy of their own squeals of delight.

But there is power in the collective. And while we can have dance parties of one, there's something profound about inviting others to celebrate with us. The question then to ask in Renegade Grief is how do we get clear on that type of celebration that we're longing for, and bravely invite other people to join us?

I learned an important lesson about this from a Dinner Partier named Lisa on the final night of Camp TDP, a retreat at an old family summer camp in Wisconsin that we hosted a few years back. Dinner Partiers flew in from twenty-six states for a long weekend in the woods. Between classic camp activities like kickball matches, s'mores by the fire, and craft stations, there were also less-typical camp conversations; breakout groups about mourning someone who died from addiction; a meetup for people of color to talk about the intersection of race and grief; a self-care station where campers could lie in a ball pit while a sheet mask was draped over their face.

By the end of day one, campers were already heralding the weekend #Crychella, and asking which weekend they should block off next year. There was even an enthusiastic camper who arrived with a freshly inked tattoo of the words "Camp TDP" on her ankle, a tribute to her dad and a celebration of the fact that she was ready to be in community around her grief.

The final night's "No Talent" Talent Show was the weekend's big finale. As the MC for the night—nominated by our team, either as an honor, a metaphorical short straw, or both—I swallowed the dread that our important closing night could be a total flop. What if no one signed up? What if the no-talent part of the talent show went off the rails? How would we make sure no one left feeling even more isolated than when they arrived?

But an hour in, my nerves were kneaded out. The first few acts were powerful and silly, heartfelt and honest. There was a dance choreographed to a Top 40 song by a woman with long black hair that whipped around as she danced. She got the whole room on their feet. She was followed by a quiet man who, towering a foot taller than everyone else in the room, rattled off every president of the United States in a rhythmic cadence, an epic party trick that left the room howling. Someone had read aloud an essay that braided their mother's love of Rihanna with the story of her death, performed with a "This American Life" persuasiveness. By the end, everyone was belting out "Shine bright like a diamond," and there wasn't a dry eye in the house.

As I watched all of this from the side of the stage, I was reminded over and over again that we are so much more than just people in grief. We are people with interests and vices and hobbies and yes, talents. And yet, on this night, our ability to relate to each other through the lens of loss meant the slight crack in a performer's voice was audible to everyone around the room, a grief dog whistle that pulls everyone present a little bit closer. The past thirty-six hours had rolled together pain and joy, absurdity and somberness. If we were strangers before, by now we'd become kindred.

I still remember looking down at the sign-up sheet I was holding and announcing, "Next up, we have Lisa, who will be singing us a song." The room erupted into supportive cheers and clapping that accompanied Lisa to the front of the room. I handed over the mic, and Lisa motioned to the person manning the "DJ Booth"—an iPhone trailing an auxiliary cord—to not turn on their song quite yet.

Lisa spoke into the microphone, and said, "I want to invite you all to my wedding." The room looked back at Lisa, wondering where they were going. In an interview years later, Lisa shared that they were "hoping for chuckles or laughs but the room was silent, maybe a little nervous for me. I needed to reassure the crowd to release tension, so I explained myself a bit."

Lisa spoke into the microphone and told us about their dad, who died of a stroke five years earlier. "It was sudden and unexpected. As a nonbinary person who doesn't necessarily ever see themselves getting married, I still have a pang in my heart every time I see father/daughter dances. Working on a catering staff, I watch a lot of them. I also grew up in a big extended family with lots of weddings. I had a difficult relationship with my father, but we always bonded by singing and dancing together. We would have had the most beautiful and tearful father/daughter dance. Tonight, I would like to ask each of you, whoever wants to come up, to be my plural multi-gendered father and come up and dance with me."

Grief is often felt most overwhelmingly in the smallest details—the empty chair, the unread books, the handwriting on a discarded grocery list. In Lisa's case, it lay in thinking about the dance they'll never get at their wedding that leaves them breathless. So tonight, Lisa's request was that we re-create the moment, together.

Lisa signaled to our DJ, who hit play on their requested Van Morrison track. Between the irresistible guitar riff, the tambourine slap, and the scratchy vocals, by the time we heard the lyrics to "Brown Eyed Girl," all hundred campers were on their feet, circling around Lisa, taking turns spinning them around, a mosh-pit embrace that sent everyone's spirits soaring. Lisa's dad might not have been around for this dance, but we would gladly stand in for him, encircling them in shared recognition and joy. We can't ever replace someone who's gone, but we can find ways to flow into their absence, with an arm around a shoulder, a knowing glance, a check-in call. Or, as we were doing that night, we can dance.

At one point, the room erupted into the chorus: "Do you remember when we used to sing," and the shimmying and spinning of a sea of bodies lifted their hands up into the sky. I looked past the swaying shoulders that surrounded Lisa, to see their eyes closed and head grooving, tears rolling down their cheeks, a big smile on their face. The song ended, and the room collapsed into a spontaneous group hug, the first of its kind I'd ever witnessed without someone having to suggest and cajole it into happening. We became Lisa's best men, women—humans—and while we'll never replace "that dance with their dad," we were there and ready to make the most of their next best plan.

And this is where I'll leave you, sweaty on the dance floor. In this last section, we've reflected on how to take the lessons from grief to create a future that's true to us, woven with the wisdom that grief gives—in navigating our way to a place that feels like home, fighting for the world we want to live in, and rebooting cultural norms around loss by being the courageous grief allies we know are possible.

Grief isn't linear, so we'll continue to find ways to honor the memory of your person through the building of altars or the making of meals; by spending time with their objects or telling their story; and continue coming into presence, to not ignore the range of emotions related to your grief, but to get curious about what lessons it has to offer; the importance and privilege of resting, of listening to your dreams, of looking to nature, and finding the people who can be present with you too.

Arriving here at the end, I hope you have new ways of looking at old things; some inspiration for creative angles on how you can tend to your own story of grief; and (what I wish most) a confidence that comes with knowing you are far from alone, as lonely as it might feel at times. Whether these are the care practices that help you find restoration within your grief, or you find in this book the beginning of a breadcrumb trail to the places, rituals, practices, or people that help you breathe a little easier—I salute you.

I realize that the other renegade in the room is grief itself—an experience that's always bucking norms, defying containment, leaving us on our toes. Unexpected, ever shifting, kaleidoscoping. In the end, walking the path of Renegade Grief is about staying awake at the wheel, as much as the culture we live in would have us close our eyes to grief's complexities.

True, the sadness and the hardship are real. But by staying awake, you start to see that this path is about much more than just our grief, than just the impact one person's departure has on our lives, as intense as it may have been. The longer I spend on this path, the more I realize that what we're all learning through grief is how to live with impermanence—how to keep our grip on the handlebars of this cosmic motorcycle club we're now in, not too loosely, not too tight. Because while someone dying might be the experience that forces grief onto your personal radar, it won't be the last. In a moment marked by wars and climate change, pandemics and civil divide, it's never been a more important time to build your familiarity with grief; to get practiced at not turning away but welcoming this long-evolved metabolic process; to let it help us find the balance between letting go of that which we can't change, and finding the courage to face the rest. The care practices I've detailed here are ways of focusing our energy as we learn to find that balance within ourselves. But the practice is yours to take from here.

At some point, the longer you learn how to ride, the more you learn how to fold the experience of your loss into your heart, and the process stops being simply about grief. Over time it metamorphosizes into depth. It becomes, if you stay awake to it, an orientation toward a soulful life.

# EPILOGUE:
# ASKING A GRANDMA

SOMETIMES I CATCH MYSELF SOAPBOXING about the ways in which the culture we live in denies us space for our grief, and I wonder to what degree I sound like a conspiracy theorist. Is it really so bad? The world can't come screeching to a halt every time someone dies. Was there ever even some kind of "golden age of grief" where it was done "right"? Haven't there been leaps and bounds of cultural improvements even in the last decade around tending to death?

But then I inevitably experience a way in which I see a person's grief so mishandled—pushed to the side or met with queasy discomfort—or learn about a grief ritual that is so exquisite but was minimalized or criminalized or otherwise written off, and am reminded that this work is far from done.

It's up to all of us to continue reprogramming the small and big ways that grief as a rite of passage isn't given the respect it deserves. We do that reprogramming every time we ask their name instead of changing the subject; every time we consider how a death experience might be impacting someone, and offer concrete ways to lighten their load, remaining unattached to their response. We do it every time we take political action to protect the social and economic safety nets, particularly for communities that hold more than their fair share of grief.

Here was one of those reminders, for me. I would be curious to hear yours too.

* * *

A dear friend experienced a series of major losses that knocked the wind from her chest. As an active supporter of Black Hills Landback work—a movement to return property in the hills of South Dakota to the Lakota people who were guaranteed them in the Fort Laramie Treaty of 1868— she was invited by an elder to participate in something called a Wiping of the Tears, one of the Lakota's seven sacred ceremonies. The Wiping of the Tears was a grief ritual I'd heard about over the years, and one that stood out because of the focus not just on the dead or dying, but on those who remained living, often occurring a year after a major loss, to welcome someone back into the circle after a time spent apart in mourning. I was to be her guest.

The ceremony was cohosted by a woman with quiet fortitude named Loretta Afraid of Bear Cook, a descendant of generations of ritual leaders, who has dedicated her almost eighty years on earth to reintroducing Lakota ceremony to her family and the world. Over the course of the ceremony week, I would take in Loretta's warmth and generosity, and how she seemed to be running the show from her folding chair on the sidelines.

The Wiping of the Tears was to be part of a concluding component of an annual Sun Dance, a Lakota ritual to honor life on earth. This, and all Lakota religious ceremonies, had been prohibited by law from the late eighteen hundreds until the American Indian Religious Freedom Act was passed in 1978.[1] Loretta's ancestors were some of the first to document their ceremonial history, before the ceremonies went underground to avoid legal persecution—and she took on the assignment to dust them off, revive them, and through the ceremonies, bring reconnection and healing to her community. But one of the biggest lessons in healing occurred for us before we even arrived.

Leading up to the ceremony, my friend and I decided we'd fly in and stay in Rapid City, which had the closest major airport. I was in charge of making our hotel reservations. Wading through a list of new-construction chain hotels skirting the airport, I figured there must be a place with a little more character, some semblance of history. The search led me to the oldest hotel in town, named after Alex Johnson, the hotel's original owner and an early twentieth-century railroad tycoon. *This'll do*, I remember thinking.

As I confirmed our dates and went through the other steps of reserving a room through the hotel's website, I scrolled past the expected add-ons, a "Pampered Pooch Package" or a chocolates-and-champagne basket for celebrating lovers, when my cursor stopped at an unusual option. A K2 electromagnetic sensor could be waiting in the room for us upon check-in, for an extra fee.

Digging deeper, I discovered this hotel was not only known for, but flaunted its reputation as, haunted. It had been on one of those ghost hunters shows that use dramatic music and night vision filters to turn groaning pipes into high-suspense television. A page on the hotel's website described how specific specters made repeat appearances on certain floors: the woman who killed herself on her wedding night on the eighth floor; some lady in white; Alex Johnson, the hotel owner, himself. "Think you're brave enough to stay in one of our reportedly haunted rooms?"[2] the website asked. After conferring with my friend, we decided we would not be purchasing a ghostbuster package or paying a premium for a haunted room, but we also weren't going to change plans and head to the Holiday Inn. The purpose of our visit was to enter a mourning ritual, native to those hills, that tends to grief and the lives of the departed. In such a context, the hotel felt like it had the trappings of an opening act, rather than a sterile layover.

A few weeks later, we were checking in. At the front desk I craned my neck to look around me. The lobby was looked over by bison heads and war spears. We rode an old rickety elevator that had moderately reliable buttons up to our floor and walked down a carpeted hallway that evoked *The Shining*, before collapsing onto our beds after a long day of travel.

Yet far more haunting than the hotel's aesthetics was the realization that Alex Johnson's investment in this Rapid City hotel was related to the gold rush in the Black Hills. Construction on the hotel began in 1927, just one day before work began on another nearby attraction, Mount Rushmore. Now, you might have a warm association with Mount Rushmore as a place of American kitsch—think family road trips and vintage souvenirs. But it's a complex and heavy place, rife with injustice and unnecessary grief. Originally a sacred site for the Plains Indians, a mountain known as Tȟuŋkášila Šákpe, or Six Grandfathers, the land was granted to the local tribes in perpetuity, until gold was discovered there. In 1870, the treaty was illegally rescinded, and in came the prospectors.[3]

Fifty years later, using dynamite and chisels, the descendants of those prospectors forever defaced a holy mountain, an aggressive and crude intimidation tactic, with faces of their Gods, American presidents, claiming it to be a shrine to democracy. They might as well have lifted a leg and pissed. It would have been less permanent. Environmental activist Krystal Two Bulls calls it "a shrine to white supremacy."[4]

So here we were, at the home base of the oppressor, getting ready for bed. Never an easy sleeper, even before her season of grief, my friend had been struggling with insomnia, so we went double duty on ensuring the room was dark—with blackout shades and a towel over the blaring neon green of the alarm clock, and settled in.

That's when it started.

Around midnight, I woke to a sound that sent chills up my spine. I listened in the dark. It could have been a cat in heat in the alley outside our window, or a late-night horror film from an adjacent room. But after a few minutes, and a steady escalation in volume and emotionality, it could be only one thing. A woman in deep distress, crying, without any other voices on her side of the wall responding to her pain.

Given our blackout precautions, I could hardly see my hand in front of my face, so I stared into the inky darkness of our room. *Are you fucking kidding me?* I thought as I considered that this ghost-hotel scam might actually be real. Was there some gauzy, weepy woman hovering above my headboard that I couldn't see? Eventually, the cries grew loud enough to wake my friend through her earplugs, and in a middle of the night haze, we tried to make sense of what was going on.

We agreed that it sounded like the crying was coming through the wall that our beds were up against. As we listened, the woman's misery escalated. "I hate my life, I hate my life, I hate my life," she cried over and over. We lay there trying to guess what would have to happen to someone to lead them to check into a hotel, by themselves, and moan with such anguish? Who had she killed or cheated on or been betrayed by to lead to this level of pain? As the cries continued, another terrifying possibility emerged: Was she going to hurt herself?

The cries were interrupted by her screaming the word "fuck" on repeat, which snapped us out of the possibility that this was some kind of haunting. Did gold rush–era ghosts, in ruffled skirts and lace nighties, drop f-bombs? We didn't think so. This was simply a person, seriously hurting.

What do you do when you hear someone in a state of deep pain through the paper-thin walls of a hotel, in a town where you know not a soul, as someone just passing through? I called the front desk, asking if they could send someone up to do a wellness check on the woman in the room adjacent to ours. When I heard the elevator doors open, I stepped out into the carpeted hallway in pajamas to see what was happening, relieved that help had arrived in the form of a kind security guard who I had also seen working valet. The cries suddenly stopped; the security guard politely excused himself, unable to identify which room the sounds had been coming from. As the elevator doors closed behind him, she started again.

Upon returning, he called the front desk to confirm there was indeed a female guest registered in that room, putting his own fear of hauntings to bed. He listened with his ear against the beige door, then backed away slowly, shaking his head. "Well, I'm not knocking. Last time I checked in on someone like this, they pulled a gun on me. All I've got is pepper spray."

I was astonished, but probably naively so. The person in charge of maintaining the safety of the hotel was clear that confronting a grieving client was out of his purview; this wasn't his first rodeo, and he didn't feel safe stepping in. There was only one thing he felt like he could do.

So he called the cops. A few minutes later, back in bed with the lights on, I heard the sound of a police officer knocking on the woman's door through our wall. Eventually she answered, her response too muffled to hear. Within a minute, the door was shut and the officer gone. She cried out a few more times that night, but then fell into silence. Checking out the next morning, we saw the cleaning staff push their cart toward her door. We wondered what they might find inside. We wondered if she was already gone.

To me, the real horror story isn't about the specter sometimes seen walking the halls all in transparent white. To me, the horror story is that there's more protocol and clarity around what to do when you see a ghost in distress—EMF monitor on!—than what to do when you see a living person in their own moment of horror. It continues to confound me that the chain of command we have in place as a society is to dispatch the person trained to de-escalate a bank robbery or win a high-speed car chase when someone is in a moment of acute emotional distress; and that instead of sitting down and being a companion, it's a knock on the door, a command to quiet down, and a brisk walk back to the elevator.

We rent an electromagnetic sensor to try to communicate with spirits of the past. But do we talk to the spirits still here with us who are struggling? Do we prevent the creation of ghosts, and ensure that people who are suffering have the resources and relationships they need to not leave unfinished business? To be cared for? To be seen and heard? As my friend and I had sat and listened, it felt scarily familiar—the feeling of being within our own four walls, hearing someone in the adjacent room in a state of distress and not knowing what to do. It's a similar feeling of seeing photos of orphaned children in Gaza on a social media feed or speaking with a friend whose nine-year-old niece has incurable cancer, and being stumped on how to react. The discomfort of grief ripples in its ache, from the people living it, to those looking on; it is renegade to build the compassion and strength to not let those ripples drift us apart.

As we walked to our rental car under the bright blue sky and started our drive to the Sun Dance, I felt disappointed in how the situation was handled—my own role included. And disappointed in my inability to think of an alternative way to console the inconsolable. It was, in some ways, the perfect, if most uncomfortable, opening for the Wiping of the Tears ceremony. Before tears can be cleared off the cheek, they need to be shed.

On the surface, the ceremony itself appears simple, much of the action privately spoken between the medicine man administering it and those being honored. It moved me to experience a grief ritual that has resisted attempts at extinction. The ceremony honors grief and pain in the context of a full community, in a shared circle, a stark distinction from the television-lit cells of a hotel room. What I saw during the ceremony was a place where the dead aren't ignored, but instead become venerated ancestors; where our grief is not something to be denied or erased, but to be acknowledged. And in the paradox of that acknowledgment, our grief shifts from something trapped inside and festering into something that can see the light of day and move through us, as we're welcomed back into the community, both changed and the same.

In the weeks after this trip, I was haunted by my own response to the crying woman. Not that calling the front desk was wrong, but I wondered if it was right. I sat with the question for six months after the ceremony, as the apex of summer became the dark depths of winter. As I thought about the woman in the hotel, I found myself wondering what Loretta would have done, seasoned ritualist and strong-footed walker in some of life's most challenging terrains. I asked if she would talk with me, and she invited me to breakfast at her home in Akwesasne, along the border between New York and Canada.

I picked up Loretta on a clear and cold day, and we drove down the road to her sister-in-law Katsi Cook's house. Katsi, a midwife and environmentalist, greeted us warmly in a hoodie, her gray hair piled on top of her head. Taking a seat at the kitchen table, we drank coffee and ate baked apples while the low light of a winter morning streamed through the windows. Being privy to a cozy midmorning conversation between sisters—sharing reflections on the big questions in life, laughing and crying together, caffeinating and eating sweets—I thought that heaven, if such a place exists, might be like this.

Loretta and Katsi were generous with their time and stories. They shared the Lakota word "Wablenica"—a word for orphan that expresses how losing both of your parents is like getting cut off from a spring of life—but that "Wablenica" are also a society of people that has a duty to look out for one another. It reminded me of The Dinner Party, and the way that members of our community have filled in some of the spaces where family once stood, never replacing, but creating new bonds. I heard how Katsi, a Wablenica herself since the age of twelve, has maintained a relationship with the memory of her parents, and participates in a ceremony in Mohawk territory every spring and fall, to feed the spirits of the dead and acknowledge their presence—a practice that she admits is hard to do in modern-day society. For Katsi, these traditions and conversations go beyond remembering her parents, but help her really connect with the universal life force. "In practicing these ways, you're not lonesome. You understand that you, too, are going that direction." In honoring the dead, she is honoring the ephemerality, and the specialness, of her own life.

Sitting in this morning sunlight, I was reminded that us grievers are certainly not starting from scratch, although it can feel like we're thrust into the void when someone major in our life dies. Instead, there are people who've gone before us, who we can learn from and lean on; traditions that have made sense of the senselessness of death, that have been impervious to the threat of capitalism and modern greed, and still exist today if you take the time to find them; and wise ones whose kitchens we can visit, whether they are our grandmas by blood or by feeling.

As our time together came to a close, I found an opening to tell them about our night in the "haunted" hotel, and ask them what they would, as wise grandma types, have done? Without missing a beat, Loretta proclaimed she would have packed up at midnight and gotten the hell out of there, half-joking, half-not; admitting that the reputation of that particular hotel is creepy, and that she wouldn't have stayed there in the first place.

I laughed at the straightforward practicality of a grandma—no hand-wringing or wondering how to handle a situation, just mind your own business and stay away from situations with unnecessary adrenaline; compassionate but not overextending. As we talked about it more, she admits that, jokes aside, she probably would have given a knock on the woman's door. "For me to hear anguish like that is hard. I would have responded by going to her door and saying simply, 'Hey, are you okay?'"

Katsi liked Loretta's answer, but what if she opened the door? "You can confront someone's agony and suffering, but it's theirs, not yours. You can't contain it. But you can hold space for it." In her work as a midwife, Katsi spends a lot of time with people in the gateways of life, both birth and death, and this training gave her another idea. Katsi pictured herself kneeling in bed, hands on the headboard, mouth up to the wall, singing the woman a song. "I would send a message back to her, and I would sing it loudly."

I pictured myself in the wailing woman's shoes, hearing the warm tones of a grandma's voice, comforting me in a moment of despair, curious as to who might be singing back, the way in which that might stop my sorrow in its tracks, to know that I wasn't alone; to know that my cries had been heard and had not incited agitation or a customer service complaint, but a lullaby, sung from someone's mother.

My morning with the grandmas happened to land on the birthday of my mother's biological mother, a woman I met only once. She had put my mother up for adoption at birth, and my mother had tracked her down. She had been open to phone calls over the years, but largely kept our family at a distance. She wasn't a warm relation, but she was blood.

She was, coincidentally, buried in a city graveyard a few hours south of Akwesasne. I told Loretta and Katsi that I was going from one grandma's house to another, and that I'd be visiting her grave later that day and bringing her flowers.

"They like coffee and sweets too," Loretta reminded me on my way out. Quietly, she suggested, "Maybe you coming to see us grandmas is really a way for you to know your own grandma better."

In all the foraging we do, the collecting of wisdom from the wide-open world on how to honor our grief, all the roads lead back to tending to our own ancestors and their stories, which are our stories too.

A few hours later I was staring into the glass display case of an old bakery in the neighborhood where my biological grandmother had lived her whole life. I wondered if she had been here before, if other birthday confections of hers had been unwrapped from these same pink boxes; I wondered what her preference had been for sweets, but ended up going with red velvet, honoring the fact that my red hair had come from her mother, one thing I knew we had in common.

In all of this, I remembered how tempting it is to, in the name of self-protection, assume we're going to have to do this all on our own. I'm reminded that sometimes what we need is a break from remixing and innovating our own DIY grief rituals, insisting that we have to figure it out on our own. Sometimes we need to put down the rebel spirit and pick up the phone to call an elder. Someone who's lived through this passage many more times than us, someone more immune to the shifting sands of culture that the perspective of more years on earth often gives.

The real work of Renegade Grief becomes resisting the taboos that block us from honoring our grief, but going about it in a way that reveres the wisdom of those who've been here before. To remember that, despite grief being a time of loneliness, where we feel the metaphorical hotel walls separating us more than ever, we are certainly never alone. To remember that, in life, there is always unavoidable death, but there is always inevitably life again.

Arriving at the graveyard as the sun was setting, I found my grandmother's grave marker with the help of a map from the chipper woman working the cemetery office. I placed the red velvet cupcake beside her headstone and used the paper bag from the bakery to clean up a pile of dogshit that sat frozen atop her grave. I poured half of a gas-station coffee on the grass around her and helped myself to the rest. I called my mom and listened to her wish her mother happy birthday from across the country on speakerphone. I thanked my grandmother for my life, and for my mother's, before getting back in the car and continuing on this wild ride.

# ACKNOWLEDGMENTS

THIS BOOK IS THE BLOOM of fifteen years of conversations, friendships, and heartfelt collaborations.

**I'd first like to acknowledge the people who have been a part of The Dinner Party in all its evolutions.** To Lennon, thank you for your vision, leadership, fortitude, and friendship. Thanks to our team, many of whom you've met in these pages, including Sofia Bair, K Scarry, Mary Pauline Diaz-Frasene, Aggie Fitch, Sundari Malcolm, Tommy O'Neil, Shay Bell, Rachel Stout, Mary Horn Jones, Becca Bernstein, Justin Thongsavanh, Jules Vivid, Dara Kosberg, and Mandy Owen; members of our board, particularly Reid Williams, Douglas Weiss, Mary Anne Cook, Sarah Perez, Jeanette Bronée, and Karen Erlichman; to Joanne Heyman, for your mentorship; to the thousands of people who've made donations to keep our mighty nonprofit humming over the last decade, with an extra burst of gratitude for Madeleine Deininger and Joel Peterson, the Benjamin Family, Jeannie Blaustein, Aaron Dorfman and the Lippman Kanfer Foundation for Living Torah's support of our work with ritual, and the team at TOMS. Thank you to the community members who have been the net that I've needed: Jess Brownell, Maggie Greene, Michelle Corral, Shaina Walker, Lindsay Blue-Smith, Eva Silverman, Leora Wolf Prusan, and Allison and Andrea Jones.

**Thank you to the team who took a risk on someone who had only written emails, wedding toasts, and social media captions.** Thanks to Jane von Mehren and Maggie Cooper at Aevitas Creative Agency for seeing the potential in this project, and for being so steadfastly in my corner; LaSharah Bunting and Dana Canedy, for your warm welcome into the Simon & Schuster family, and to Maria Mendez for getting this book over the finish line with such care and cheer. To Carrie Frye, for being the person I could share the batter with; Ruthie Ackerman, whose classes and the friendships formed there emboldened me to pursue this project; to Mary Roos, Lois Bridges, and Pam Allyn who helped plant this seed. To Akilah Cadet, K Scarry, Sean Walker, and Karuna Meda, for being in the cockpit with me; Stacey Sakal, for your meticulous edits, Kayley Hoffman for your finishing touches, and Evan Kraus for contracts and laughs. Thanks to James Gregorio, Chonise Bass, Tyanni Niles, Kathleen Carter, Nikki D'Ambrosio, and Lindsay Ratowsky—I'm so blessed to have your support in bringing *Renegade Grief* to the world.

**Thanks to the people who expanded my creative world**: Thanks to Dr. Delphyne Platner for your spiritual direction and mentorship; this book is a continuation of our many-lifetime-long conversations; Barb Groth and Randi Fiat of the Nomadic School of Wonder; creative role models, Andrea Meditch, Ivy Ross, and Kelly Carlin; thanks to the teachers who are part of my love story with books, Cyndi Gates, Rebecca Sherouse, and Ann Hutchinson; to the team at Enso; Cord Jefferson, for modeling the excellence that can be achieved while in repose; to Ann Friedman, for being a support line; and Sarah Jolena Wolcott, for your companionship at just the right time.

**Thanks to everyone who trusted me with their stories and research,** whether you ended up in the final pages or not, and to the folks who dropped breadcrumbs for me to follow Robin Kobaly, Joseph Zarki, and Melanie Spoo for your generosity with the life of Minerva Hoyt; Nicholas Adamski and Ty Crisafulli for your perspectives on whales; and A. J. Cincotta-Eichenfield for your thoughtful take on grief in the internet age.

**I'm deeply grateful for the places that opened up to me for reflection and writing:** Vassar College Library, The Center For Fiction,

The Rose Reading Room at the New York Public Library, the Greenberg's perch in the Berkeley Hills, the Mojave Desert, the bath.

**As an avid believer in the power of peer care, I am once again blown away by what friendship makes possible. Thank you** Tessa Stuart; Eve Bradford; Lucy and Kate Adams; Brittany Berryman; Amelia Rose Barlow; and Isis Krause; my author support group, Alua Arthur, Scott Shigeoka, Arianne Edmonds, and Liz Tran; Rebecca Thom; Mara Abrams; Grace Kim; Bianca Butti; Madeline Gryll, Kelly Erlandson, Kate McLaughlin, Elizabeth Benjamin, Luke-Amaru Chappellet Volpini; Isaac Aptaker; Dev Aujila; Jen Azlant; John McCreery; Chloe and Ace Webb; the Grody Patinkin family, particularly Kathryn for reading, walking, and talking; Isabel Wilder; Jonathan Harris; Tabea Soriano; Kiana Reeves; Conor and Yoshi Powell; Quiet, particularly Sol Guy, Seema Thakker, Kerry Stranman, Mauricio Mota, and A Helwa.

**A few particularly epic people died while this book was in process, and the impact of their departures is deeply present in this text.** My grandmother, Effie Christiansen; Elaine Barlow; Leah Justine Barlow; John Perry Barlow; Gabriela O'Leary; Michael Grody; Ben Hughes; Bobbie Ogletree; Susan Haas; the small but mighty Liv Labow and Theo Benjamin Levit. You are missed, to say the least.

**And to my family. One of the greatest privileges of my life is belonging with all of you.** My incomparable mother, Jan Fernandez; my fairy stepmother, Kathy; my siblings, José and Claire, and their partners, Maria and Eli; my niece, Maya, and nephew, José Fernandez V. My grandfather, José Fernandez II. Elizabeth, aunt extraordinaire; James, ever pushing my thinking; and Tommy; Rick and Rene Christiansen. My amazing in-laws, the extended Cash Shornstein family, whose commitment to creativity and mindfulness have informed me deeply. And to the family members no longer in physical form, but who were certainly present in the process; my grandmothers, Arlene, Effie, and Nancy; my grandfathers, Carl and Dapper; and my father,

José Fernandez III, who was my original imprint of the renegade spirit.

To my best friend, Biscotti; and to my husband and greatest champion, Ivan Cash. May we live for many more years in sweetness, health, and prosperity.

# ENDNOTES

## Introduction

1    California Department of Fair Employment and Housing, "Family Care and Medical Leave Guide," https://calcivilrights.ca.gov/employment/family-care -medical-leave-guide/.

2    Bridget Alex, "When Did Ancient Humans Begin to Understand Death?" *Discover* magazine, February 11, 2020, https://www.discovermagazine.com/planet-earth /when-did-ancient-humans-begin-to-understand-death.

3    Annie Nova, "The U.S. Has No Federal Bereavement Leave. What to Know About Options at Work When Someone You Love Dies," CNBC, January 26, 2024, https://www.cnbc.com/2024/01/26/what-to-know-about-bereavement-leave -at-work-when-someone-you-love-dies.html.

4    U.S. Bureau of Labor Statistics, "Funeral Leave (paid)," Glossary, https://www .bls.gov/bls/glossary.htm.

5    Lorie Konish, "This Is the Real Reason Most Americans File for Bankruptcy," CNBC, February 11, 2019, https://www.cnbc.com/2019/02/11/this-is-the-real -reason-most-americans-file-for-bankruptcy.html.

6    U.S. Department of Health and Human Services, "New Surgeon General Advisory Raises Alarm about the Devastating Impact of the Epidemic of Loneliness and Isolation in the United States," News release, May 3, 2023, https://www.hhs.gov /about/news/2023/05/03/new-surgeon-general-advisory-raises-alarm-about -devastating-impact-epidemic-loneliness-isolation-united-states.html.

7    NASA HubbleSite, "Hubble's Exciting Universe," 2020, https://hubblesite.org/ mission-and-telescope/hubble-30th-anniversary/hubbles-exciting-universe.

8    L. M. Brady, "Data Report: Fall 2022 TDP Community Survey," The Dinner Party, November 10, 2022.

9  Brené Brown, *The Gifts of Imperfection* (Chisago County, MN: Hazelden Publishing, 2010).

10 Michael I. Norton and Francesca Gino, "Rituals Alleviate Grieving for Loved Ones, Lovers, and Lotteries," *Journal of Experimental Psychology: General*, 2014, Vol. 143, No. 1, 266–272, https://www.hbs.edu/ris/Publication%20Files /norton%20gino%202014_e44eb177-f8f4-4f0d-a458-625c1268b391.pdf.

11 Asia Society, "Chuseok: Korean Thanksgiving Day," https://asiasociety.org /korea/chuseok-korean-thanksgiving-day.

12 Katie Thornton, "The Elitist History of Wearing Black to Funerals," *The Atlantic*, September 16, 2022, https://www.theatlantic.com/culture/archive/2022/09 /queen-elizabeth-funeral-black-dark-mourning-color/671558/.

13 Aaron O'Neill, "WWII: Share of Total Population Lost Per Country 1939– 1945," *Statista*, August 9, 2024, https://www.statista.com/statistics/1351638 /second-world-war-share-total-population-loss/.

14 United States Census Bureau, "U.S. and World Population Clock," https://www .census.gov/popclock/.

15 Ashton M. Verdery, Emily Smith-Greenaway, Rachel Margolis, and Jonathan Daw, "Tracking the Reach of COVID-19 Kin Loss with a Bereavement Multiplier Applied to the United States," *Proceedings of the National Academy of Sciences* 117, no. 30 (July 10, 2020): 17695–17701. https://doi.org/10.1073 /pnas.2007476117.

16 Sarah Tarlow, "An Archeology of Remembering: Death, Bereavement and the First World War," *Cambridge Archaeological Journal 7*, no. 1 (1997): 105–121.

17 Bridget E. Keown, "'She Is Lost to Time and Place': Women, War Trauma, and the First World War," PhD diss., Northeastern University, 2019, https://doi.org /10.17760/D20318702.

18 S. Freud, "Mourning and Melancholia," In: J. Strachey, Ed., *The Standard Edition of the Complete Psychological Works of Sigmund Freud*, Vol. 14 (London: Hogarth Press, 1953).

19 Edith Maria Steffen and Dennis Klass, eds., "Culture, Contexts and Connections: A Conversation with Dennis Klass about His Life and Work as a Bereavement Scholar," *Continuing Bonds in Bereavement: New Directions for Research*

*and Practice* (New York: Routledge, 2018), https://pure.roehampton.ac.uk/ws /files/1101939/Culture_contexts_and_connections.pdf.

20 Helen Hewson, Niall Galbraith, Claire Jones et al., "The Impact of Continuing Bonds Following Bereavement: A Systematic Review," *Death Studies* (June 2023): 1–14, https://doi.org/10.1080/07481187.2023.2223593.

21 Sigmund Freud, *Letters of Sigmund Freud* (Mineola, NY: Dover, 1992).

## Act 1: Honoring Your Past

1 Elisabeth Kübler-Ross and David Kessler, *On Grief and Grieving: Finding the Meaning of Grief Through the Five Stages of Loss* (New York: Scribner, 2014).

2 Peter Tyrrell et al., "Kubler-Ross Stages of Dying and Subsequent Models of Grief," modified February 26, 2023, In StatPearls (Treasure Island, FL: StatPearls Publishing, 2024), https://www.ncbi.nlm.nih.gov/books/NBK507885/.

3 Vivek H. Murthy, "Protecting Youth Mental Health: The U.S. Surgeon General's Advisory" (PDF), Washington, D.C.: U.S. Department of Health and Human Services, 2021, accessed August 14, 2024, https://www.hhs.gov/sites/default/ files/surgeon-general-youth-mental-health-advisory.pdf.

4 Alberto E. Pérez, Rodrigo M. Tesmer, Juan F. Reyes Sánchez et al., "A Pre-Hispanic Canoe or Wampo Burial in Northwestern Patagonia, Argentina," *PLOS ONE* 17, no. 8 (2022): e0272833, accessed August 14, 2024, https://doi.org/10.1371 /journal.pone.0272833.

5 "The Slave Memorial at Mount Vernon," George Washington's Mount Vernon, https://www.mountvernon.org/george-washington/slavery/the-slave-memorial- at-mount-vernon.

6 Mary-Frances O'Connor, *The Grieving Brain: The Surprising Science of How We Learn from Love and Loss* (New York: HarperOne, 2022).

7 I recommend exploring this resource, to learn more about Elan's ritual and others: "Making It through Together: Ritual Collection for Life After Loss," The Dinner Party, accessed August 14, 2024, https://www.thedinnerparty.org/rituals.

8 "Statistics," National Funeral Directors Association, last updated October 23, 2023, accessed August 14, 2024, https://nfda.org/news/statistics.

9 G. Brockington, A. P. Gomes Moreira, M. S. Buso, S. Gomes da Silva, E.

Altszyler, R. Fischer, and J. Moll, "Storytelling Increases Oxytocin and Positive Emotions and Decreases Cortisol and Pain in Hospitalized Children," Proceedings of the National Academy of Sciences of the United States of America 118, no. 21 (2021), https://doi.org/10.1073/pnas.2018409118.

10  Wagner et al., "Beautiful Friendship: Social Sharing of Emotions Improves Subjective Feelings and Activates the Neural Reward Circuitry," *Social Cognitive and Affective Neuroscience* 10, no. 6 (2015): 801–808, https://doi.org/10.1093/scan/nsu121.

11  L. G. Roos, S. M. Levens, and J. M. Bennett, "Stressful Life Events, Relationship Stressors, and Cortisol Reactivity: The Moderating Role of Suppression," *Psychoneuroendocrinology* 89 (March 2018): 69–77, published online January 2, 2018, PMID: 29331801; PMCID: PMC5878721, https://doi.org/10.1016/j.psyneuen.2017.12.026.

12  Benjamin P. Chapman, Kevin Fiscella, Ichiro Kawachi et al., "Emotion Suppression and Mortality Risk Over a 12-Year Follow-Up," *Journal of Psychosomatic Research* 75, no. 4 (2013): 381–85, https://doi.org/10.1016/j.jpsychores.2013.07.014.

13  John Koenig, *The Dictionary of Obscure Sorrows* (Simon & Schuster, 2021).

14  Clay S. Jenkinson, "Too Much Stuff: Americans and Their Storage Units," Governing, December 18, 2022, https://www.governing.com/context/too-much-stuff-americans-and-their-storage-units.

15  Richard D. Goldstein, Cynthia R. Petty, Susan E. Morris et al., "Transitional Objects of Grief," *Comprehensive Psychiatry* 98 (January 2020): 152161, https://doi.org/10.1016/j.comppsych.2020.152161. PMID: 31978784; PMCID: PMC735 1592.

16  Jonathan Jennings Harris, *In Fragments* (Films, 2015–2021), High Acres Farm, https://infragments.us/

17  Brandon Beyer, Nicole Linsalata, Chantal Cook, and Tynisa Senior, "Students Return to School in Broward County amid New Safety Measures," WSVN 7News, August 12, 2024, https://wsvn.com/news/local/broward/students-return-to-school-in-broward-county-amid-new-safety-measures/.

18  Sharon Aron Baron, "Marjory Stoneman Douglas Observes 'A Day of Service and Love' on February 14," Parkland Talk, February 5, 2019, https://parklandtalk

.com/marjory-stoneman-douglas-observes-a-day-of-service-and-love-on-february-14-4351.

19  U.S. Department of Labor, "It's Time to Care about Paid Leave," www.dol.gov/agencies/wb/featured-paid-leave.

20  Joseph Campbell, *The Hero with a Thousand Faces* (Novato, CA: New World Library, 2008).

## Act 2: Being With Your Present

1   Margaret Stroebe and Henk Schut, "The Dual Process Model of Coping with Bereavement: Rationale and Description," Death Studies 23, no. 3 (April–May 1999): 197–224, doi: 10.1080/074811899201046.

2   Parker J. Palmer, *A Hidden Wholeness: The Journey Toward an Undivided Life* (New York: Jossey-Bass, 2004).

3   Liam O'Brien, @VoiceOfOBrien, "It was exactly at that moment a snap decision in this little game of ours led the story into a direction heavily layered with death and dying. One that lasted to the end of the campaign. The interacio," X, July 18, 2018, 8:45 p.m., https://x.com/VoiceOfOBrien/status/1019744931672350720.

4   Catriona White, "Dungeons & Dragons Is Now Being Used as Therapy," BBC Three, May 8, 2017, https://www.bbc.co.uk/bbcthree/article/ab3db202-341f-4dd4-a5e7-f455d924ce22.

5   Jo-Anne Rowney, "Real Tragedy and True Story Behind Superman's Origin—How a Man's Death Led to the Man of Steel," *The Mirror*, June 12, 2018, https://www.mirror.co.uk/tv/tv-news/real-tragedy-true-story-behind-12386500.

6   Jill A. Harrington and Robert A. Neimeyer, eds. *Superhero Grief: The Transformative Power of Loss* (New York: Routledge, 2021).

7   David Blaine, "Madonna," *Interview*, November 26, 2014, https://www.interviewmagazine.com/music/madonna-1.

8   Malcolm Gladwell, *David and Goliath: Underdogs, Misfits, and the Art of Battling Giants* (New York: Little, Brown and Company, 2013).

9   Robert Krulwich, "Successful Children Who Lost a Parent—Why Are There So Many of Them?" NPR, October 16, 2013, https://www.npr.org/sections/krulwich.

10  Rose-Lynn Fisher, *The Topography of Tears* (New York: Bellevue Literary Press, 2017).

11 Tom Lutz, Crying: *The Natural and Cultural History of Tears* (New York: W.W. Norton & Company, 1999).

12 Joseph Soltis, "The Signal Functions of Early Infant Crying," *Behavioral and Brain Sciences* 27, no. 4 (Boston: Cambridge University Press, 2004: 443–490).

13 Leo Newhouse, "Is Crying Good for You?," Harvard Health Blog, March 1, 2021, accessed August 6, 2024, https://www.health.harvard.edu/blog/is-crying -good-for-you-2021030122020.

14 Lutz, Crying: *The Natural and Cultural History of Tears*, 33.

15 "Songs for the Dead," Directed by Adrian Dunning, written by Michael R. Smith, *The Documentary*, Season 1, Episode 2 (BBC: January 10, 2009).

16 Michael O'Regan, "Mourning the Loss of the Keening Tradition in Ireland," *Irish Examiner*, October 21, 2016, https://www.irishexaminer.com/lifestyle/arid -20415997.html.

17 Mitchell S. Jackson, "How (Not) to Grieve," *Esquire*, April 11, 2024, accessed August 6, 2024, https://www.esquire.com/lifestyle/health/a60314478/black- grief/.

18 The Holy Bible: King James Version, Jeremiah 9:20.

19 "Mourning My Father," *The Comb*, episode 5 (BBC: March 2022), https://www .bbc.co.uk/programmes/p0bys45b.

20 Lauren Patrick DiMaio and Alexa Economos, "Exploring the Role of Music in Grief," *Cuse Bereavement Care* 36, no. 2 (2017): 65, https://www.bereavement journal.org/index.php/berc/article/download/980/988.

21 Michael V. Thoma et al., "The Effect of Music on the Human Stress Response," *PLoS One* 8, no. 8 (August 5, 2013): e70156. https://doi.org/10.1371/journal .pone.0070156. PMID: 23940541; PMCID: PMC3734071.

22 Anantha Narayanan et al., "The Effect of Background Music on Stress in the Op- erating Surgeon: Scoping Review," *BJS Open* 6, no. 5 (2022): zrac112, https:// doi.org/10.1093/bjsopen/zrac112.

23 Saba Mughal, Yusra Azhar, Margaret M. Mahon, and Waqas J. Siddiqui, "Grief Reaction and Prolonged Grief Disorder," In StatPearls [Internet] (Treasure Island, FL: StatPearls Publishing, 2024), accessed August 7, 2024, https://www.ncbi .nlm.nih.gov/books/NBK507832/.

24  Lisa M. Shulman, *Before and After Loss: A Neurologist's Perspective on Loss, Grief, and Our Brain* (Baltimore: Johns Hopkins University Press, 2018).

25  Robert Schwarz, *Tools for Transforming Trauma* (New York: Brunner-Routledge, 2022).

26  Robin Carhart-Harris, "Psilocybin for Treatment-Resistant Depression: An Interview with Dr. Robin Carhart-Harris," Psychopharmacology Institute, n.d., https://psychopharmacologyinstitute.com/publication/psilocybin-for-treatment-resistant-depression-an-interview-with-dr-robin-carhart-harris-2252.

27  Dana Smith, "How Psychedelics Can Help Us Process Grief," *The New York Times*, January 10, 2023, https://www.nytimes.com/2023/01/10/well/psychedelics-grief-mental-health.html.

28  Brian T. Anderson et al., "Psilocybin-Assisted Group Therapy for Demoralized Older Long-Term AIDS Survivor Men: An Open-Label Safety and Feasibility Pilot Study," *EClinicalMedicine* 27 (September 24, 2020): 100538, https://doi.org/10.1016/j.eclinm.2020.100538. PMCID: PMC7599297. PMID: 33150319.

29  Débora González et al., "Therapeutic Potential of Ayahuasca in Grief: A Prospective, Observational Study," *Psychopharmacology* 237, no. 4 (2020): 1171–1182, https://doi.org/10.1007/s00213-019-05446-2.

30  George A. Bonanno et al., "Resilience to Loss and Chronic Grief: A Prospective Study From Preloss to 18–Months Postloss," *Journal of Personality and Social Psychology* 83, no. 5 (2002): 1150–1164. https://doi.org/10.1037//0022-3514.83.5.1150.

31  Katharina Schultebraucks, Karmel W. Choi, Isaac R. Galatzer-Levy, and George A. Bonanno, "Discriminating Heterogeneous Trajectories of Resilience and Depression After Major Life Stressors Using Polygenic Scores," *JAMA Psychiatry* 78, no. 7 (2021): 744–752, doi:10.1001/jamapsychiatry.2021.0228.

32  Gabriela N. Tonietto, Selin A. Malkoc, Rebecca Walker Reczek, and Michael I. Norton, "Viewing Leisure as Wasteful Undermines Enjoyment," *Journal of Experimental Social Psychology* 97 (2021): 104198. ISSN 0022-1031, https://doi.org/10.1016/j.jesp.2021.104198.

33  Amy-Xiaoshi DePaola, "Beyond the 9-to-5: More Than 134 Countries Have a Limit to How Much We Can Ask People to Work in a Week, but the U.S. Isn't

One of Them," BusinessJournalism.org, February 14, 2020, https://business journalism.org/2020/02/beyond-the-9-to-5/.

34 Onyx Ewa, "A Brief History of Black in Fashion," *The Harvard Crimson*, February 3, 2022, https://www.thecrimson.com/article/2022/2/3/ewa-brief-history-of-black-in-fashion/.

35 Joanne Cacciatore, Megan Killian, and Matthew Harper. "Adverse Outcomes in Bereaved Mothers: The Importance of Household Income and Education." *SSM—Population Health* 2 (2016): 117–122, https://doi.org/10.1016/j.ssmph.2016.02.009.

36 Laura Hershfield, "The Nap Ministry: Bishop Tricia Hersey Wants You to Rest," *The New York Times,* October 13, 2022, https://www.nytimes.com/2022/10/13/well/live/nap-ministry-bishop-tricia-hersey.html.

37 Tricia Hersey, *Rest Is Resistance: Free Yourself from Grind Culture and Reclaim Your Life,* (New York: Little, Brown Spark, 2022).

38 T. Buckley, D. Sunari, A. Marshall, R. Bartrop, S. McKinley, and G. Tofler, "Physiological Correlates of Bereavement and the Impact of Bereavement Interventions," *Dialogues in Clinical Neuroscience* 14, no. 2 (2012), 129–139, https://doi.org/10.31887/DCNS.2012.14.2/tbuckley.

39 Danielle Pacheco, "Grief and Sleep," Sleep Foundation, Updated December 22, 2023, accessed August 7, 2024, https://www.sleepfoundation.org/mental-health/grief-and-sleep.

40 Luciana Besedovsky, T. Lange, and J. Born, "Sleep and Immune Function," *Pflugers Archive: European Journal of Physiology* 463, no. 1 (2012): 121–137, https://doi.org/10.1007/s00424-011-1044-0.

41 G. R. Poe, "Sleep Is for Forgetting," *The Journal of Neuroscience: The Official Journal of the Society for Neuroscience* 37, no. 3 (2017): 464–473, https://doi.org/10.1523/JNEUROSCI.0820-16.2017.

42 Joshua Black, "The Relationship Between Bereavement and Sleep Disturbances in Adults: A Longitudinal Study," PhD diss., Brock University, 2018, https://dr.library.brocku.ca/bitstream/handle/10464/13888/Brock+Black+Joshua+2018.pdf?sequence=1.

43 Isaac Taitz, Wendy Packman, and Erin Soares, "Processing Adolescents' Grief

Dreams: A Camp Study," Paper presented at the 34th Conference of the International Association for the Study of Dreams, Anaheim, CA, June 22–26, 2017.

44 *Grief Dreams* podcast, Podbean, accessed August 7, 2024, https://griefdreams podcast.podbean.com.

45 Christina Tran, "Mom," Dear Daughter, https://sodelightful.com/deardaughter/mom.html.

46 Andrew Balmford, Lizzie Clegg, Tim Coulson, and Jennie Taylor, "Why Conservationists Should Heed Pokémon," Science 295, no. 5564 (2002): 2367, https://doi.org/10.1126/science.295.5564.2367b.

47 Bill Chappell, "No More Emotional Support Peacocks as Feds Crack Down on Service Animals on Planes," NPR, December 8, 2020, https://www.npr.org/2020/12/08/944128033/no-more-emotional-support-peacocks-as-feds-crack-down-on-service-animals-on-plan.

48 Leslie Irvine, "Animals as Lifechangers and Lifesavers: Pets in the Redemption Narratives of Homeless People," *Journal of Contemporary Ethnography* 42, no. 1 (2013): 3–30, https://doi.org/10.1177/0891241612456550.

49 Barbara J. King, *How Animals Grieve* (Chicago: University of Chicago Press, 2013).

50 UNICEF, "Stillbirths," last modified January 2023, accessed August 9, 2024, https://data.unicef.org/topic/child-survival/stillbirths/.

51 National Oceanic and Atmospheric Administration (NOAA), "Killer Whale," National Ocean Service website, last updated April 26, 2024, https://www.fisheries.noaa.gov/species/killer-whale.

52 Bridgette Watson, "Grief or Instinct? Interpreting a Mother Orca's Actions," CBC News, July 20, 2019, https://www.cbc.ca/news/canada/british-columbia/killers-j35-grief-instinct-message-1.5216705.

53 Douglas J. McCauley et al., "Marine Defaunation: Animal Loss in the Global Ocean," *Annual Review of Marine Science* 7 (2015): 1–27, https://www.annualreviews.org/content/journals/10.1146/annurev-marine-010213-135144.

54 Ralph Chami, Thomas Cosimano, Connel Fullenkamp, and Sena Oztosun, "Nature's Solution to Climate Change," *Finance & Development* 56, no. 4 (December 2019), https://www.imf.org/Publications/fandd/issues/2019/12/natures-solution-to-climate-change-chami.

## Act 3: Creating Your Future

1   Adrienne Maree Brown, *Emergent Strategy: Shaping Change, Changing Worlds* (Oakland, CA: AK Press, 2017), 21.

2   *Grandma's Bottle Village: The Art of Tressa Prisbrey*, part of the Visions of Paradise series, Allie Light and Irving Saraf, directors (Light-Saraf Films, 1982), gift of Allie Light to the American Visionary Art Museum.

3   Danya E. Keene, Whitney Denary, Annie Harper et al., "'A Little Bit of a Security Blanket': Renter Experiences with COVID-19-Era Eviction Moratoriums," *Social Service Review* 97, no. 3 (September 2023): 423–455, https://doi.org/10.1086/725320.

4   Learn more and support their work at https://economicsecurityproject.org/ and https://tenantfederation.org/.

5   The fight for this economic floor is laid out in Natalie Foster's book, *The Guarantee: Inside the Fight for America's Next Economy*. Natalie Foster, *The Gurantee* (New York, NY: The New Press, 2023).

6   Robert A. Cronkleton and Ilana Arougheti, "Parents Out on Bond in Child's Fatal Fall, as Tenants Seek to Sue Independence Towers Owner," *The Kansas City Star*, August 7, 2024, https://www.kansascity.com/news/local/crime/article290829964.html#storylink=cpy.

7   Gloria Anzaldúa, *Borderlands/La Frontera* (San Francisco: Aunt Lute Books, 1987).

8   Douglas Harper, "Hermit," Online Etymology Dictionary, accessed August 10, 2024, https://www.etymonline.com/word/hermit.

9   Deborah Netburn, "The Woman Who Saved the Joshua Tree for Posterity, and What We Owe Her Today," *Los Angeles Times*, February 14, 2019, https://www.latimes.com/science/sciencenow/la-sci-col1-joshua-tree-minerva-hoyt-20190214-htmlstory.html.

10  Denise Goolsby, "How Minerva Hamilton Hoyt Saved Joshua Tree National Park," *The Desert Sun*, May 11, 2019, https://www.desertsun.com/story/life/2019/05/11/how-minerva-hamilton-hoyt-saved-joshua-tree-national-park/1179516001/.

11  Rhode Island Government, "History of Rhode Island," accessed August 15, 2024, https://www.ri.gov/facts/history.php.

12  Lennon Flowers, "Grief Is a Seismic Force for Social Change," Fast Company: World Changing Ideas, March 23, 2018, https://www.fastcompany.com/40548372/grief-is-a-seismic-force-for-social-change.

13  David Kessler, *Finding Meaning: The Sixth Stage of Grief* (New York: Scribner, 2020).

14  Holly Yan and Ray Sanchez, "Florida Gov. Rick Scott Signs Gun Bill," CNN, March 9, 2018, https://www.cnn.com/2018/03/09/us/florida-gov-scott-gun-bill/index.html.

15  18th Street Arts Center, "Community x Community," accessed August 13, 2024, https://18thstreet.org/communityxcommunity/.

16  Ashenola, MAAFA, https://www.ashenola.org/maafa.

17  Learn more about Evermore and support their work at https://evermore.org.

18  Frances Robles, "Where are the Parkland activists today?" *The New York Times,* July 18, 2022, https://www.nytimes.com/2022/07/18/us/x-gonzalez-parkland-activists-sam-fuentes.html.

19  Hope Edelman, *The AfterGrief: Finding Your Way Along the Long Arc of Loss* (New York: Ballantine Books, 2020).

20  Charles Duhigg, "What Google Learned From Its Quest to Build the Perfect Team," *The New York Times Magazine*, February 25, 2016, https://www.nytimes.com/2016/02/28/magazine/what-google-learned-from-its-quest-to-build-the-perfect-team.html.

21  Chanel Reynolds, *What Matters Most: The Get Your Shit Together Guide to Wills, Money, Insurance, and Life's "What-ifs"* (New York: Harper, 2018).

22  Margareta Magnusson, *The Gentle Art of Swedish Death Cleaning: How to Free Yourself and Your Family from a Lifetime of Clutter* (New York: Scribner, 2018).

23  U.S. Energy Information Administration, "Laws of Energy," Energy Explained, last modified August 7, 2024, https://www.eia.gov/energyexplained/what-is-energy/laws-of-energy.php.

24  Jeffrey M. Jones, "U.S. Church Membership Falls Below Majority for First Time," Gallup, March 29, 2021, https://news.gallup.com/poll/341963/church-membership-falls-below-majority-first-time.aspx.

25  Scott Neuman, "The Faithful See Both Crisis and Opportunity as Churches

Close across the Country," NPR, May 17, 2023, https://www.npr.org/2023 /05/17/1175452002/church-closings-religious-affiliation.

26  Dalai Lama, "Foreword," *The Tibetan Book of Living and Dying: 30th Anniversary Edition,* by Sogyal Rinpoche, edited by Patrick Gaffney and Andrew Harvey (San Francisco: HarperSanFrancisco, 1994).

27  Pew Study: Pew Research Center, "Who Are 'Spiritual But Not Religious' Americans?" Pew Research Center, December 7, 2023, https://www.pewresearch.org/ religion/2023/12/07/who-are-spiritual-but-not-religious-americans/.

28  Kiri Walsh, Michael King, Louise Jones, Adrian Tookman, and Robert Blizard, "Spiritual Beliefs May Affect Outcome of Bereavement: Prospective Study," *The BMJ* 324, no. 7335 (2002): 1551, accessed August 13, 2024, https://doi .org/10.1136/bmj.324.7353.1551.

29  Casper ter Kuile and Angie Thurston, "How We Gather" (PDF), accessed August 13, 2024, https://caspertk.wordpress.com/wp-content/uploads/2015/04/how-we -gather.pdf.

30  Vatican Press Office, "Communiqué of the Holy See Press Office: Audience with the President of the Republic of Cuba, Raúl Castro Ruz," June 10, 2016, https://press. vatican.va/content/salastampa/en/bollettino/pubblico/2016/06/10/160610c.html.

31  Jean-Yves Leloup, *The Gospel of Mary Magdalene,* trans. Joseph Rowe, foreword by Jacob Needleman (Rochester, VT: Inner Traditions, 2002).

32  Mustafa Suleyman, "The AI Revolution: How Artificial Intelligence Will Reshape the World," *Time,* September 1, 2023, https://time.com/6310115/ai- revolution-reshape-the-world/.

33  Rafael Lozano Hemmer, "A Crack in the Hourglass," 2020, https://www.lozano -hemmer.com/a_crack_in_the_hourglass.php.

34  Barbara Ehrenreich, *Dancing in the Streets: A History of Collective Joy* (New York: Metropolitan Books, 2007), https://us.macmillan.com/books/9780805057249/dancing inthestreets.

35  Barbara Ehrenreich, *Dancing in the Streets,* 13.

## Epilogue: Asking a Grandma

1   National Library of Medicine, "1978: American Indian Freedom of Religion

Legalized," Native Voices: Native Peoples' Concepts of Health and Illness, accessed August 10, 2024, https://www.nlm.nih.gov/nativevoices/timeline/545.html.

2   Alex Johnson, "Alex Johnson Hotel, About," accessed August 10, 2024, https://www.alexjohnson.com/about/.

3   Native Hope, "The Six Grandfathers Before It Was Known as Mount Rushmore," July 4, 2022, accessed August 15, 2024. https://blog.nativehope.org/six-grandfathers-before-it-was-known-as-mount-rushmore.

4   Alaa Elassar, "The Fight for the Sacred Black Hills of South Dakota Takes Center Stage in the Documentary 'Lakota Nation vs. United States,'" CNN, updated July 16, 2023, https://www.cnn.com/style/article/lakota-nation-vs-united-states-streaming-ifc-center/index.html.

# ABOUT THE AUTHOR

CARLA FERNANDEZ's work focuses on how circles come together to foster collective care and change culture when a new status quo is called for. She is a cofounder of The Dinner Party, a national network of peer-support circles for young adult grievers, featured in the *New York Times*, NPR, *O, The Oprah Magazine*, and cited in multiple books. In addition to her work in grief, Carla partners with a range of clients through her community design studio as an impact strategist and facilitator, particularly on initiatives related to climate change, democracy, and the arts. Carla is a senior fellow with USC's Annenberg Innovation Lab and a Catherine B. Reynolds Foundation scholar in social entrepreneurship at NYU. She divides her time between the Hudson Valley and Joshua Tree.